GERMAN
AND
JEW

GERMAN
& Jew

[The life and death of Sigmund Stein]

by John K. Dickinson

with an Introduction by Raul Hilberg

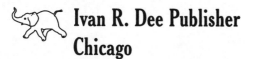 Ivan R. Dee Publisher
Chicago

Published in Association with the
United States Holocaust Memorial Museum

GERMAN AND JEW. Copyright © 1967, 2001 by John K. Dickinson.
Introduction copyright © 2001 by Raul Hilberg. This book was first published
in 1967 and is here reprinted by arrangement with the author. First Ivan R.
Dee paperback edition published 2001. All rights reserved, including the right
to reproduce this book or portions thereof in any form. For information,
address: Ivan R. Dee, Publisher, 1332 North Halsted Street, Chicago 60622.
Manufactured in the United States of America and printed on acid-free paper.

Library of Congress Cataloging-in-Publication Data:
Dickinson, John K.
    German and Jew : the life and death of Sigmund Stein / by John K.
Dickinson ; with an introduction by Raul Hilberg.
        p.   cm.
    Originally published: Chicago : Quadrangle Books, 1967.
    Includes index.
    ISBN 1-56663-404-0 (alk. paper)
    1. Stein, Sigmund.   2. Jewish lawyers—Germany—Biography.
3. Holocaust, Jewish (1939–1945)—Germany.   I. Title.
DS135.G33 D45 2001
940.53'18'092—dc21
[B]   2001028946

To Lenore

[Preface]

From his birth in 1896 to his disappearance in 1945, Sigmund Stein's world was a fusion between Germany and Jewry in which the secret disharmonies of the former revealed themselves as a fatal destiny for the latter.

This book is not Sigmund Stein's biography. It encompasses more, because it is concerned with the configurations of time, space, and material which were reflected in Sigmund Stein's life, and with the consequences of that reflection. It rehearses less than a biography, because it may seem to neglect his status as an autonomous agent. But a careful reading will show that Sigmund Stein was no more or less the master of his fate than Everyman.

Sigmund Stein was on his way to becoming a personage in the central German town of Hochburg when his legal career was destroyed in 1933. Had the Nazis never arisen to interrupt his professional life in this way, his reputation in Hochburg would have increased to an obscure prominence, satisfying him and leaving its mark on the town, but remaining unknown to the world at large.

As a consequence of Nazi ascendance, however, Sigmund Stein's life assumed a form which deserves to be explored for its tragic and sobering meanings, for the way in which it shows how a man can be trapped by his upbringing, his education, and his basic decency into performing a role which other men have condemned out of hand. Finally, Sigmund Stein's life is important for what it says about the men and women who were not saved from the consequences of being German by the peculiarly fateful grace of being Jewish.

The book is not fiction. With no exceptions, all persons who appear in it are real persons. With but few exceptions, the appearance and structure of all events described represent reality as filtered through the process by means of which a book is created. The exceptions do not arise from an effort to dramatize, mythologize, or create an artificial suspense. Instead, certain events have been modified only to temper the complexity that is produced by a twofold commitment: to reality itself and to the nature of the knowledge of that reality.

The names of Sigmund Stein, his wife Esther, his daughter Marion, and of the other men and women with whom the book is directly concerned, however, are not to be found in the archives. Neither are the "Hochburg" and the "Bachdorf" of this book to be found on a map.

The author identifies with the human beings who people these pages: there, but for the vagaries of chance, go I. Even though this attitude has a moral texture, every rendered judgment is, in the end, self-judgment. It would pervert this identification and destroy this texture if the people who have made this book possible and to whom the writer owes an inviolable gratitude were exposed to the effects of the stereotypes that suffering and ignorance have attached to many of the matters dealt with.

This is not a scholarly book, but where it adds to understanding it succeeds. It is not a historical work, but a man at the burning focus of history is its subject. It is not sociology, but it presupposes and has as its goal a rational grasp of society and social process. It is not preoccupied with a selection among the supporting and dissenting views of others, but it is deeply concerned with uncovering those touchstones of plausibility which one portion of the human situation always offers to another.

May this book memorialize only that past out of which it arose.

Writing a book is a joint endeavor, and the writer's gratitude often appears a faded image of real relationships. The obligations I incurred while writing this book were facets of affection, mutual interest, or the graceful performance of accustomed routine. Those whom I mention here, with or without names, rarely seemed aware that they were creating a debt which I am happy to acknowledge.

Foremost among these is the brother of Sigmund Stein. As a man of perspicacity and warmth, David Stein stands out in his own right, but he may also stand for other relatives, as well as for the Jewish friends and associates of Sigmund. I can only marvel at and be grateful for their kindness to me and their courage in turning to look again at past anguish.

It is not very different in regard to the people of Hochburg. Past pain has many shapes, and the readiness of the Hochburgers to let me intrude upon their past deserves the thanks which I am glad to give.

Happily, I am able to name several people. Here, however, it becomes difficult to express an appropriate gratitude without bursting the bounds of acknowledgment. My expedient must be to say that each of these people will know the nature of his gift to me, and none would be concerned to have me embellish it: H. G. Adler, London, England; the late Bruno Blau; Timothy A. Dickinson, Cambridge, Massachusetts; Milton Mayer, Deerfield, Massachusetts; Elisabeth Noelle-Neumann, Allensbach am Bodensee, Germany; the late Fritz Pappenheim; Yvonne Pappenheim, Cambridge, Massachusetts; Barbara Schultz, Darmstadt, Germany; Paul and Vera Williams, Stony Point, New York.

Publishers and editors are facts of life; having happened, they need add no more than details to one's horizon. Thus, appreciation is called for when, as in the present case, the horizon itself is expanded.

I had no hesitation about dedicating this book to my wife. I have every hesitation about trying to explain or celebrate in any sufficient way the nature of my gratitude to her.

[A note on the 2001 edition]

I understand this preface, nearly thirty-five years after writing it, as a perspective on my first foray into the swamp of Nazi anti-Semitism. I sought, and still seek, to understand the grotesque enmeshment of human beings in atrocity, as victims, complicit bystanders, crazy perpetrators, and courageously desperate resisters. I take a melancholy pride in the somber tone I then struck. I am melancholy to find myself and the world still echoing that tone. Yet I also take pride in that, surviving change in myself and the world, my core belief remains: The human imagination that sees my neighbor as myself may still overcome the Original Sin of perverting Reason to Elaboration of Excuse.

My decision to disguise persons and places in this book was a response to the request of Hermann Reis's brother, Julius. Outside of Germany, and as correctly in a few cases as it was cruelly wrong in others, calumny and the slimy epithet of "collaborator" attached itself to Jews in Nazi Germany who saw themselves and were seen by their

neighbors (Jews and non-Jews) as seeking in good faith to mobilize per-
ceived decencies in the name of survival and sanity. Julius Reis's conviction of Hermann's decency and honor was certainly no less than mine.
In the sad images of the immediate postwar period, his request for The
Mask was compelling. My decision to reveal the truth behind the
masks, in this new edition of *German and Jew*, is based on the equally
understandable but joyfully welcome request by living relatives of Julius
and Hermann Reis.

J.D., July 2001

[Introduction]

When John Dickinson's book first appeared in October 1967, it was one of a kind. He had written an account spanning the life of a man who died in the Holocaust. The subject of this biography was neither a hero nor a celebrity but an ordinary victim, one of millions. Dickinson gave him the fictitious name "Sigmund Stein," and he called the city in which "Stein" had spent his adult years "Hochburg." The real "Stein" was Hermann Reis, and the city is Marburg, which is hilly and capped by a medieval *Burg,* or castle.

To unearth the story of this obscure person, Dickinson questioned 172 people, equally unknown, to whom he also gave pseudonyms. The interviews, in the mid-fifties, were conducted on a "shoestring" budget without the intrusion of a tape recorder. Dickinson took notes and wrote them up, whenever possible, within four hours. Phrases from these conversations appear in the book, but long sentences are not quoted, and no words were put into the mouth of anyone. Always probing, and frequently pondering the meaning of answers he was given, Dickinson reveals himself as an acute observer who was mindful of the smallest facts that could shed light on the situation and attitudes not only of "Stein" but of all those who talked about him.

"Stein" was a lawyer in private practice, and Dickinson illuminates the environment in which such a business was conducted. He explains the hierarchy in the German legal profession, what an *Assessor* was, or a *Referendar.* "Stein" was also a family man, and Dickinson offers a wealth of information about ways of life and interactions of the people in Marburg, particularly relations between Christians and Jews. He dwells on a comment by one of his interviewees that the Jews were "practically fellow citizens." The original German word would have been *Mitbürger,* or co-citizens, which is used with reference to Jews even today.

When "Stein" was born on September 16, 1896, the Jews of Marburg were almost completely emancipated, with equal rights under the law but not with unrestricted access to private social organizations, such as the Freemasons, or the fraternities with a Christian membership at the university. The Jews of the area were predominantly Orthodox, and "Stein's" parents were observant. He attended a Jewish primary school and in adolescence dated only Jewish girls, whom he took to dances. By 1915 he was in the army, and went on to serve in the field artillery on the eastern and western fronts. He received an Iron Cross Second Class but did not become an officer. After the war he attended Marburg and Frankfurt universities, obtained a law degree, and married a young Jewish woman from a relatively well-to-do family. In 1925 his only child, a daughter, was born. By then, Germany's internal problems, including violent strife and a hyperinflation, had abated, and normalcy prevailed.

Stability characterized also the life of Germany's Jews. "Stein" opened a law office with a Jewish colleague, Willy Wertheim, whom Dickinson calls "Werner Hagen." The partner, also a veteran, was four and a half years older. By reputation, "Hagen" was the sharper of the two but also more volatile, whereas "Stein" was calmer and more adroit in the courtroom. Both were liberal in their political views, "Hagen" a bit more so than "Stein." Yet the slightly more leftist "Hagen" would play cards with a man, Roland Freisler, who became a fanatical Nazi, known for having prosecuted the plotters who tried to overthrow Hitler in 1944.

As the partnership prospered, "Stein" moved into a better apartment. The picture drawn by Dickinson is that of a typical bourgeois life, with heavy furniture and the sort of books that many other Jews would have had on their shelves: a novel by the Norwegian Knut Hamsun, who wrote about hunger; the works of Heinrich Heine, the melancholy Jewish poet; Dostoevsky's *The Brothers Karamazov*, the massive Russian novel hailed as one of the most incisive works of fiction ever written; and a biography of Fieldmarshall von Hindenburg, the victor in the battle of Tannenberg in 1914 and the man who broke the French offensive in 1917.

What is most striking in this painstaking description of commitment and fulfillment is the degree to which it applies to the old established Jews of the western European countries in general. The First World War was a contest in which Jews fought in opposing armies, and when it was over, the photographs of the men in uniform along with their medals were not merely mementos but evidence of a price paid for acceptance in the society to which they returned. The Jews were now truly Germans, Frenchmen, or Italians. In this sense, the few hundred Jewish residents in the university town of Marburg on the Lahn river resembled the few hundred Jews in the university town of Pisa on the Arno. Still consciously Jewish, they were moving into the mainstream.

The periods of peace, Hegel once remarked, are the blank pages of history. Dickinson did not leave them empty. To the contrary, his emphasis on the expectable, commonplace, and slow-paced improvements in the life of "Sigmund Stein" fills almost half the text, and it is an essential foundation which marks the contrast with all that followed when the Nazis appeared on the scene. The emancipation that had brought security and respectability to the Jews in the course of a century was about to be reversed.

In the wake of the Nazi movement, self-confidence in the Jewish community began to erode. Dickinson recounts an incident involving a legal adviser, "Heinrich Wolff" (Ludwig Beck), who was a Jew but not always taken as one. Early in 1932 the man was accosted by a brown-shirted Nazi. A university student came to his aid and asked him why he did not defend himself. "Defend myself?" came the reply. "How could I? I'm a Jew." The story may or may not have been completely accurate, but it is a telling indication of a mind-set that had already surfaced in the Jewish community.

When Adolf Hitler rose to power on January 30, 1933, one could not be in doubt about the magnitude of the change. Nazism was based on a philosophy of "either-or," and this principle was applied to classifications of people. "Stein" resisted the idea that before long he might not be called a German anymore. In Germany he had been born, and German was the language of his thinking, speaking, and writing. Although the emerging separation of "German" and "Jew" could be recognized in countless ways, he approached it passively, rooted in his city and profession, and hoping that the Nazi regime would collapse. It did not disappear, and the mounting pressure of its actions affected him in a matter of months. On April 7, 1933, the Law for the Restoration of the Professional Civil Service was signed. It mandated, with certain exceptions that included war veterans, the dismissal of "non-Aryan" civil servants, among them the judges and prosecutors. Complementing this law, a second measure, signed on the same day, provided for the disbarment of non-Aryan lawyers in private practice, again exempting the war veterans. The two partners in Marburg appeared to be saved because they had been in the war, but "Hagen" had rendered services to a Communist party legal aid organization in 1932 and had enclosed a friendly note with his bill. This act was sufficient cause in the eyes of the Justice Ministry to deprive both partners of their right to represent clients in court. The successful practice they had built was demolished in a single letter from Berlin.

The events that followed the Nazi takeover produced an exodus of Jews from Germany that was larger than the outflow in each of the succeeding four years. The emigrants of 1933 reacted to an initial shock. For some it was the sudden realization that they had been rejected. For others it was the immediate loss of a career, a business, or the prospect of advancement. For still others, who were leftists, it was a fear that they might be specially vulnerable. To the large majority, however, a new life in a new country seemed even more onerous and more painful than staying with a lower status or a reduced income in familiar surroundings. Young adults without family responsibilities could start over, and those with a portable profession, like "Stein's" younger brother, who was a physician, had some realistic—if often difficult—prospects abroad, but lawyers could not simply make use of their knowledge in a foreign country with a different legal system.

"Stein's" law partner, Willy Wertheim ("Hagen") left in 1933. He had evidently concluded that his Iron Cross and the head wound he had sustained as an infantryman would not guarantee his personal safety. In Paris he operated a small bookshop. As it turned out, he had not fled far enough. We know now that he was deported on March 4, 1943, in a transport of a thousand Jews, almost all of them men, to the Lublin area of Poland. After the end of the war, only four men of that transport were still alive. They were in their early twenties.

The legal adviser Ludwig Beck ("Wolff"), who did not defend himself in 1932, lost his position and in the summer of 1938 was arrested as an "idler." Transported to the concentration camp Buchenwald, he died there of an illness and neglect.

Hermann Reis, the "Stein" of this book, remained in Germany. The family had some capital, and he could continue to earn money by counseling fellow Jews who had difficulties with the avalanche of new regulations. At the beginning, opposed to emigration, he advised everyone to stay. In 1938 he did not accept his brother's suggestion that they leave together. Instead he accommodated himself to the growing multiplicity of restrictions, giving up the office and moving to a less spacious apartment in a house set aside for Jews. When, finally, he tried to emigrate and then to flee, he did not succeed. The Jewish community of Marburg had shrunk to slightly more than a hundred people when their deportations to the ghettos of Lodz, Riga, and Theresienstadt was about to begin. Toward the end he assumed the administrative responsibility for this remnant and participated in the bureaucratic preparations for its dismemberment. The reader watches helplessly as Reis, his wife, and his daughter are themselves engulfed. Dickinson traces their path until they vanish from view.

This then is the story, as Bruno Bettelheim noted in an endorsement of the book, of a man "who walked to his doom small step by small step." It is also an account of the behavior of some of his German acquaintances as they distanced themselves from him, and as they coveted during his last hours in Marburg some of his possessions for "safekeeping." Through the memory of the witnesses, this past and its atmosphere comes to the fore. One might have thought, after reading the book in 1967, that Dickinson's experiment would have been repeated in other places at a time when many people, who as grown men and women had watched the fate of their Jewish neighbors at close range, could still have related in abundant detail what they had seen. But hardly anyone wanted to hear much from such observers, and now the ideal moment for questioning them is gone. John Dickinson's work still is and will always be unique.

RAUL HILBERG

[Contents]

GERMAN
AND
JEW

[Jewish children in a Hessian village]

On September 6. 1896, Sigmund Stein was born in the Hessian village of Bachdorf-on-the-Frieden. The location of Bachdorf in the surrounding landscape can be seen clearly from the Jewish cemetery which lies well up the northern slopes of the River Frieden's valley, a few miles to the north and west of the village. Sigmund's birthplace is in the middle distance; the broken gravestones of his ancestors are on the ground.

The valley of the Frieden is a shallow concavity in the Hessian landscape, with the river meandering through it to the east. On both sides of the river the land rises gradually, ultimately becoming mountainous in the north. To the south the earth swells into the irregularly rolling terrain of Oberhesse. The view to the north from the graveyard is closed off; to the south is a blue confusion of distant hills. The Jewish graves are on the edge of the pine forest which covers the higher reaches of a slight spur—one of several which

3

push out of the highlands and determine the Frieden's major curves and sweeps.

On a more heavily wooded spur to the west stands the town of Weidenberg, with its castle ruin surmounting a craggy promontory. Directly south, about halfway between the cemetery and the river, is the village of Weidenfeld. A line of maple trees marks the main road from Weidenberg, through Weidenfeld, Bachdorf, Niederhausen, and other villages to the town of Friedenberg, seven miles east, where the tower of the church can be faintly seen.

The railroad, which skirts the southern edge of Bachdorf between village and river, angles across the highway between Bachdorf and Weidenfeld, and divides a short distance beyond the crossing. The main line parallels the highway toward Weidenberg and the west; the branch curves back a little toward Bachdorf, then turns north, resolutely, into the hills.

It is a panorama of settled beauty and of a centuries-wrought harmony between nature and the works of man. Sigmund Stein's ancestors had been a part of this compromise between man and nature, and his feeling for this, his *Heimat,* was emotional and therefore often expressed in ways too easily dismissed as sentimental. Sigmund's attachment to his native heath had its somber side: having been extended to include the whole Fatherland, it ultimately was a crucial factor in his misjudgment of a Germany bent on his destruction.

Bachdorf lies on the intersection of two highways. The one lined by maple trees connects Cologne with Kassel. The other leads south from the Ruhr to Frankfurt-on-the-Main, passing through Hochburg, a large university town. Since neither of these routes is the only, or the most important, connection between its terminal cities, Bachdorf is closer to the backwaters than to the mainstream of commerce.

It is farming country, and most Bachdorfers were, and are, farmers. In the late nineteenth century, commerce was represented, as it is today, by a woodworking factory, a weekly market, an inn—*"Zum Goldenen Löwe"*—and by the *Viehhändler,* or cattle dealer. (In 1896, the year of Sigmund's birth, his father, Isaac Stein, was the village cattle dealer.) Now as earlier, however, commerce plays a background role in Bachdorf. It is a village way of life and a rural economy that meet the eye.

Most of the houses in Bachdorf, for example, are farmhouses. Hessian villages, like the majority of villages in continental Europe, are centers from which people go out to their fields. Typically, Bachdorf is tied to its fields by numerous paths and small roads, independent of the two highways. It is bound to these fields even more vitally by the men and women with shouldered rakes or hoes who, each morning during the growing season, leave the village by those lanes. Toward evening the movement is reversed and the village contracts upon itself once more.

It is easy to idyllize this ebb and flow of village life as a mysterious pulsation touched with the rhythm of nature itself. But the peasant's consciousness of his life is prosaic and, within the sphere of his experience, realistic. As a farmer, he must be concerned with nature, for on it his life and well-being depend. He must be able to judge the state of the weather, the condition of his land and crops, and the health of his animals. Far from being a blind creature of nature (as the mystique of the idyll suggests), the peasant is nature's original exploiter and master. Both his conservatism and his sporadically passionate radicalism summarize the trial and error of generations.

Despite the catastrophic changes of the last half-century, the people of Bachdorf remain essentially the same. When projected back to the German Empire of 1896, their characteristics appear even more strongly as those of the typical villager, the eternal peasant. Not that Bachdorf was an isolated hamlet at that time: the railroad was already there, and the two highways were important enough to be used by the imperial mail. But the automobile had not yet made the stranger a commonplace, and two world wars had not yet thrown the insistent shadow of the world over the village.

It was here that Sigmund's father, Isaac, decided to set himself up in business upon finishing his military service. In his own eyes and in the eyes of his fellow villagers, he had established his Jewish identity in and around Niederhausen, ten minutes' walk from Bachdorf. He was following a long tradition when he came to Bachdorf to become a cattle dealer. This was a "Jewish business," and even today the cattle dealer is sometimes referred to as "The Jew," although the last Jewish cattle dealer in the area disappeared during the Nazi era.

Isaac Stein became a cattle dealer because it was the most natural thing in the world for him to do, and he became one in Bachdorf because the previous cattle dealer, Moses Liebman, was old and had no heirs who wanted to take over the business. Yet Isaac Stein also came to Bachdorf because it was not far from home. (There are many people today who remember how faithfully he walked to Niederhausen, his birthplace, every Saturday afternoon.)

Isaac was not wealthy, but he was diligent, and in 1893 he made a good marriage with a girl from Delbach, forty miles away in the hills to the northeast. The dowry that Dela Abraham brought to the marriage is spoken of with respect as having been ten thousand marks—sufficient, in combination with a mortgage, to purchase Moses Liebman's entire establishment.

The house and its adjoining buildings still stand. (It was perhaps a hundred years old when Isaac moved into it. The current cattle dealer has built a prim new house, and there are some villagers who say that it shows what a good man Isaac Stein was, since he never gave up the old house.) The old house, with its visible framework of great timbers, its stone foundations, its relaxed sags and unconcerned slants, is everything the meaning of which is obscured by the word "quaint." It stands on the east side of the well-channeled but swift and turbulent brook, or *Bach*, from which the village takes its name. At the end of the nineteenth century it was the northernmost house on its side of the brook. Today, there is one house beyond it: the neatly-stuccoed box of the prospering present-day cattle dealer, Herr Bonke. On the west side of the brook, the houses extend farther north. These are old, though one of them, a little upstream from the Stein residence, has been so remodeled as to look new. In this house lives Frau Dorothea Friebertshäuser, a good friend of the Steins.

On either side of the brook, between its built-up banks and the houses, is a dusty way, part dirt, part cobblestone. Hardly a road and more than a path, it is most importantly a thoroughfare. Children, geese, chickens, and dogs call it their own. Parked on it, close to the houses, are large and small wooden wagons. With their open-slatted, angled sides and wooden wheels, these wagons are ubiquitous in rural Germany. The large ones are pulled by cows, the small ones by people or goats. At least one of these wagons, with cow pulling and farmer walking alongside, is usually to be seen, and its creaking heard, on the way.

A few old women can ordinarily be found rinsing their washing in the swift, clean waters of the brook. They speak thick Hessian German and are dressed in the Hessian manner. They are likely to be friendly and matter-of-fact and to show a stranger a particular house by guiding him to it. In her day, Isaac Stein's wife, Dela, probably rinsed the family washing in the brook. To be sure, it was not long before she had a servant girl to help her, because Isaac's business prospered from the first. This is not surprising: his diligence and his devotion to his affairs still arouse comment from many villagers of today who speak of the family with esteem and affection.

Even now Germans do not always speak well of former Jewish associates. Patterns which have been centuries in the making cannot be covered up, and one can still hear stories of the *Halsabschneider* (cutthroats) among the cattle dealers—how they would put a skinny cow in the barn of the peasant who owed them money and leave it there until it had been fattened. Villagers will volunteer the information about how, in the latter part of the nineteenth century, the rural producers' cooperatives were formed with the explicit purpose of rescuing the peasants from the "clutch of Jewish capital." If there is seldom active bitterness in the telling, there often seems to be an echo of past bitterness and a naive refurbishing of uncritically accepted tradition and gossip.

Thus it seems remarkable that no such stories are told about Isaac Stein. On the contrary, all accounts of him are filled with affection, gratitude, and respect. It is unnecessary to assume that he had no enemies, but it can be assumed that the statements about Isaac tell something of his relationship with his fellow villagers.

There are other reasons for believing in the image of virtue which Isaac projected. He was an orthodox and pious Jew. He was known as such and literally seen as such, by Elisabeth Kohlhausen for one, from her house across the brook. He would stand at the window, phylacteries in place, praying on the evening of the Sabbath. Unsophisticated country people, Lutheran Christians, would be impressed by such contact with "mysterious" elements in the Jewish religious observance.

This image is important in connection with the extent to which the situation of the Stein family was typical. *Was* Sigmund Stein brought up in a typical German-Jewish environment? The question is a legitimate one, and if the contradictions to which it leads are dealt with, much can be learned about the web of Jewish life in Germany.

The position of the Stein family in Bachdorf was roughly similar to that of many Jewish families in rural Germany, particularly in rural Hesse. Most German Jews, of course, lived in the larger cities and towns. The fact that the Steins were the *only* Jews in Bachdorf was an unusual, though by no means unique, variation of the rural Jewish pattern. It was more common to find several families in a village; this was the situation in Isaac Stein's native Niederhausen, as well as in Weidenfeld, which was one of the centers of Jewish life in the area, containing as it did the Jewish primary school, the synagogue, and the Jewish cemetery.

These minuscule Jewish communities in rural Hesse were interacting nerve centers of Jewish rural life. The Jewish occupations traditionally demanded more regional traveling than the life of the peasant. In his cattle business, for instance, Isaac Stein regularly went as far afield as Dela's village, Delbach, and Talheim, twenty-five miles away, riding either on the train or, often, with one of his customers in horse-drawn buggy. Probably little thought was wasted on such activity in normal conditions, but on the level at which the peasants experienced reality, the trips lent psychological force to the stereotype of "International Jewry" when abnormal conditions made it opportune for anti-Semites to speak of it.

Furthermore, the situation of the Jews in rural Hesse was of crucial importance because of the immediacy with which Jew and non-Jew confronted each other. It may not have been statistically typical, but as far as that confrontation was concerned, it was a more pregnant situation than that in the larger cities, where the very size of the Jewish community provided insulation from the frictions—as well as, be it said, from the fruitful amenities—of contact between Jew and non-Jew.

It is not that there was no larger Jewish community; the active social intercourse among the scattered village centers was, after all, the framework within which the marriage of Isaac Stein and Dela Abraham occurred. A larger community was also created by the fact that the village centers, usually too small to have a rabbi of their own, were served in rotation by the rabbi of the most accessible large town, or by rabbis who did nothing but ride the circuit. An additional bond among the village centers was, of course, Judaism itself, and an attachment to its external forms. It is surprising to find that four and five Jewish families in a village, though unable to support a permanent rabbi, often established a tiny and ritually proper synagogue. Such miniature places of worship can still be found, and they often bear witness to the presence of Jews in a village since the eighteenth century.

There is no synagogue in Niederhausen, but there are other records there which carry the Stein family back to the late 1700's. In 1837 the Elector of Hesse-Darmstadt had decreed that a register of vital statistics be started for the Jews in every community of his small domain. Such measures had begun two decades earlier with decrees requiring the Jews to take German family names. The effect, and to a degree the purpose, was to prepare the way for a general emancipation of the German Jews in the late 1860's. In the records for the years prior to 1837, the Jewish residents of Niederhausen, Bachdorf, and Weidenfeld appear less formally, though with moderate frequency.

Thus the original Isaac Stein, grandfather of the namesake who settled in Bachdorf in the nineties, and great grandfather of Sigmund Stein, is mentioned as the director of the Jewish community of Niederhausen as early as 1828. Because the father of this early Isaac Stein had been compelled to replace an original Jewish name with a German name, and because the records of the change are obscure where they are not missing, it is hard to identify the early Isaac's parental family. There is some reason to believe, however, that his father was the *Schutzjude*, Solomon, who appeared in 1786 as a new member of the community. A Schutzjude was one who enjoyed the direct protection of the regional sovereign and ordinarily paid a high price for the protection. (The records are full of requests that the protection fee of a particular Jew be moderated. There is little evidence of malice in such transactions, but the context is clearly one of a discrimination in which the Jew is regarded as a tolerated heretic.)

The old Isaac Stein was a man of status in the Niederhausen Jewish community. This status seems to have been passed on to his son, Benedict, the youngest of three children, and the only one of his sons who survived to found a family. The tradesman Benedict Stein was apparently poor rather than rich, even though he owned some farmland in addition to carrying on his trade as a grocer. He died in 1910. His sister, Sara, was never married, and seems to have been a familiar, if not really well-known, figure in Niederhausen until her death in 1912.

Isaac, the father of Sigmund Stein, was born in 1864, Benedict's second son and the fourth child in a family of three sons and four daughters. Two sons and one daughter died within three years of birth.

During the lifetime of Benedict Stein, important changes had taken place in the status of the German Jews, the main one being the emancipation of the Jews from all legal disabilities in 1869. In Niederhausen and other Hessian villages, an important side effect of the emancipation was the development of ideological anti-Semitism. This is not to say that the Jews in this and other parts of Germany had escaped persecution up to this time, for the very form of their existence had evolved in a history of pogrom and violence. Yet by 1869 Jews and Christians in rural Hesse had arrived at something like a modus vivendi. The Jewish position in this accommodation was insulting to human dignity; it was, indeed, a humanistic reaction against this indignity which had finally led to the emancipation. But humanism and enlightenment were found primarily in the cities; they were only dimly evident, if at all, in the villages.

Nevertheless, the rural modus vivendi between the two groups embodied genuine, if entirely contingent, values. A false and inhuman picture of the Jews was accepted by the Christians and endured by the Jews in a situation which carried with it an absence of friction under normal conditions. This absence of friction may account for patently sincere statements by older Bachdorfers to the effect that distinction and discrimination between Jew and non-Jew had been absent in their childhood.

It is hard to present this insistence convincingly, because distinction and discrimination seem so obvious in retrospect. Often enough the insistence is explicit: no distinction was made between Jew and non-Jew. More often it is indirect: of course there were differences, just as there are always differences among people, but such differences did not matter for they existed in an atmosphere of mutual tolerance. It is important that both Jews and non-Jews insist on these points today.

The anti-Semitism of the peasants was so completely blended into the modus vivendi that it is indeed hard to distinguish it at times. It would be a mistake, for instance, to interpret every peasant remark about avaricious cattle dealers as the echo of a well-articulated anti-Semitism. It is much more likely to be the expression of a tradition, the vicious implications of which are lost on the peasant. Like many traditions, this one embodies an interpretation of reality which was false and ultimately disastrous, yet not because of malevolence or stupidity—but because the peasants' reality was so limited. Many of the obscenities of the Nazi racial program were implicit in traditional peasant anti-Semitism, but before these implications could be realized, the great world had to intrude itself upon rural Hesse more than it had in the late nineteenth century.

Benedict Stein died before this intrusion gained momentum. He may have noticed the beginnings of it, but in general they were masked to his contemporaries by the tangible realities of mutual acceptance in Niederhausen and villages like it. By Isaac Stein's time, the mask had begun to fall away.

The emancipation of the Jews in combination with the nationalism of Imperial Germany had also introduced an element of inner conflict among the Jews themselves in regard to their traditional mode of life. In such communities of the hinterland as Niederhausen and Bachdorf, the effects of this conflict were not immediately felt, for they tended to spread out gradually from the large cities. Benedict Stein probably died without having been seriously touched by them. Because of the traditional mobility of Jewish life, however, the spread of these corroding effects among the Jews was undoubtedly faster than the spread of liberalizing ideas and attitudes among the peasants. Thus, at a time when the attack on the Jews from without had not appreciably diminished, the internal solidarity with which they had earlier been able to meet the attack was being undermined.

The exposed position of the rural Jews was too obvious. In the cities, Jewish involvement in commerce was disproportionately great; in the villages, it was total. In the cities, too, among both Jews and non-Jews, religious sophistication had here and there been able to replace a tolerance based on forebearance with one based on mutual understanding: minds could meet on a ground removed from the more astringent orthodoxies of either Judaism or Christianity. In the villages, the Jews observed their religion in the face of a Christianity which preached little that could modify the ancient picture of the Jews as people who killed Christ. In fact, the relative harmony of relationships between the two religions in rural Hesse was a remarkable demonstration of how intimate daily contact can obscure religious differences without de-fusing them. That human relationships often bridged these differences may go far to explain why the period is seen as one in which there was no discrimination.

The economic position of the Jews in rural Hesse was created by an earlier, and contributed to the later, anti-Semitism. As a cattle dealer, Isaac Stein had to have cash on hand and had to maintain regular relations with a bank. The Bachdorf peasants had cash on hand only after they sold their crops, and even then not much. It was still enough of a subsistence economy to permit the peasant to get by with comparatively little cash under normal circumstances. When extraordinary circumstances arose, the peasants went to Isaac.

The peasants did not want to deal directly with the butchers. They preferred to sell their cattle to the cattle dealer, a more familiar figure than the butchers, and one from whom they could borrow money on occasion without undue publicity. The interest rate was fairly high because the risk was great, since it was seldom the industrious and often the lazy peasant who borrowed.

Such peasants often continued in financial straits, and in many cases the cattle dealer would finally—and with complete legality —have to dispossess the peasant. Understandably, this created a certain amount of primitive anti-Semitism among the peasants when the cattle dealer was Jewish, as he often was.

This oft-repeated story is a plausible, though incomplete, explanation of rural anti-Semitism in Germany. The picture of peasant antagonism toward the money lender is one which has its counterpart in lands where the money lender is not a Jew and the peasant is not a German. The thralldom of peasant to money lender, and the antagonism between the two, has been sharper in such countries as India and China than it was in Germany.

In Germany, however, the money lender and the peasant were members of two religious communities, and the conflict between them was a function of their historical development from a common source. The enlightenment of the eighteenth century—one thinks of Lessing's *Nathan der Weise*—had mitigated this conflict somewhat, yet the enlightenment shone only on small groups among both Christians and Jews, and too often it was distorted into a scientism which provided new and fashionable rationalizations for old prejudice. Many enlightened Jews ceased to find refuge in a confident affirmation of their faith. A few accepted the challenge of the new racial ideology and defiantly asserted their uniqueness and superiority as a chosen people. Others turned to Zionism and the dream of a Jewish homeland as a haven from Christian antagonism and their own spiritual insecurity. Still others became assimilationists who too often failed to realize that no nationalism, especially not the contradiction-ridden nationalism of Germany, provides adequate ground for mutual acceptance. Some Jews were converted to Christianity. Their tragedy was that, however sincere their personal motives may have been, the reality of the situation stamped the act with opportunism, and the accusation came most cuttingly from their own hearts.

Of course, such conscientiously reasoned behavior involved a minority of Jews, just as a conscientious racism or toleration involved a minority of Christians. But the Christian could live his life with a minimum of concern for such problems. The Jew, though he might wish to be indifferent, was never allowed to be.

This may account for the sometimes pathetic eagerness with which he accepted the illusion of peace. In rural Hesse, the normal condition of life was an outward tranquility, a domination by traditional rhythms and familiar deviations from those rhythms.

Isaac Stein's purchase of Moses Liebman's establishment was one such familiar deviation. As such, it could be an occasion for entertaining gossip—about Dela Abraham's dowry, for instance, or about the mortgage necessary to round out the purchase price. Inevitably there would be overtones which could be considered anti-Semitic—but which were less that than they were part of the texture of the picture: how Dela's father was a rich Jew in Delbach; how cattle dealers come and go, but the Jew remains; speculation about the kind of a bargain reached between two Jews; and perhaps mildly salacious comments on Dela's fruitfulness.

But with the actual arrival of Isaac and Dela Stein accompanied by Dela's sixty-five-year-old father, Levi Abraham, the gossip of anticipation died out in the face of accomplished fact. Personal and business relations were taken up with the family. In both spheres, the villagers, as well as their new neighbors, saw, acknowledged, and accepted the differences in pattern of life which separated them. The acceptance was deep and contained both good and evil. But it was an acceptance of a difference which had been made by human beings and would have to be unmade by them before the promise of good which lay in the acceptance could overcome the potentialities of evil.

In 1896, Sigmund Stein was the first son born to the single Jewish family living in Bachdorf. The birth of a first son is very often an occasion for special rejoicing. For Jewish parents as orthodox as Isaac and Dela Stein it means more: until a son is born, they have no one who can celebrate the faith by saying *Kaddesh* in the year after their deaths. Sigmund was therefore truly welcomed into the world, and the welcome persisted.

Within limits set by the social situation, Isaac Stein appears to have been a normal father. He was affectionate and amenable; he left the rearing of the children to Dela. This was not surprising, and in the main not different from the practice of the peasant husbands with whom he did business. He traveled more than any peasant did, but most of his trips were short enough to permit him to be home every evening. Besides, since the peasants had to adapt their work schedule to weather and season, Isaac probably was at home at least as regularly as they were.

Dela Stein was a different matter. She drew more attention to herself, and shreds of gossip about her still float around Bachdorf. These concern her person, her neighborliness, her openhandedness to the village children, her earlier life in Delbach, and her father, Levi Abraham. Levi, it is said, had had a number of wives. Resigned, finally, to being a widower, he decided to spend "the evening of his life" with Isaac and Dela, to whom he became something of a burden, contributing greatly to Dela's nervousness.

To be sure, this is gossip. But Lieschen Schmidt, who relays much of it out of an evident affection for the family, was a servant girl at the Steins from 1904 to 1914, and her sister—now dead—had worked there for the preceding seven years. Lieschen is one of a group of three living women—Trina Koehler and Hannelore Kraus are the others—whose collective service with the Stein family spanned thirty years. All three had been *Dienstmaedchen*, servant girls.

The Dienstmaedchen is usually a peasant girl who goes into domestic service in order to learn the arts of housekeeping and to earn a little cash, frequently in anticipation of her marriage. Ordinarily she takes service in town, yet she often visits her village, and eventually she returns to it to become a farmer's wife and the mother of a farmer's children.

Dela Stein herself was a country girl and she, like her servant girls, had taken a job in town—though, significantly enough, with relatives who ran a clothing store in the distant city of Metz, when Alsace Lorraine was German. Here Dela learned French and acquired skills outside the sphere of housewifely training. Her future was not quite as set as that of a Christian peasant girl, and yet for her, too, the possibilities of great deviation were pretty well nipped in the bud by the conventional marriage to Isaac Stein.

Of the four Dienstmaedchen, Lieschen Schmidt and her deceased sister had immediate and responsible contact with the young children of Isaac and Dela Stein. Meta Stein was a little girl of three when Lieschen's sister started working for the family in

1896. The need for her services had arisen out of the pregnancy of Dela Stein, who gave birth to Sigmund in September of that year. Eventually, Lieschen's sister was married, and Lieschen replaced her at the Steins' in 1904, when David Stein was four years old.

Almost all the villagers of Bachdorf who are old enough to remember the period have something to say about it; no one remembers everything, but all remember something. During interviews, these people were curious to know what David and Meta Stein say about their youth. For Sigmund's brother and sister are still alive, their homes standing within blocks of one another in Philadelphia. Remembering the Dienstmaedchen with affection, they provide a general picture of Bachdorf and their childhood in the village. Yet it is not as detailed a picture as that available in the village itself, for Meta and David have tried to convey, in relatively limited conversations, the whole situation of their family, their childhood, and their later experiences. There is a gulf between their present life on the one hand, and their childhood on the other. However well they may have repaired their life, it has been broken, and memories of it are covered with scar tissue.

The Bachdorfers are, to some degree, victims of a parallel cleavage, yet they are all living within the same surroundings and according to pretty much the same rules as when the Steins were their neighbors or employers. Lieschen Schmidt and Hannelore Kraus live in villages from which they can walk to Bachdorf; Trina Koehler, Dorothea Friebertshäuser, and Elisabeth Kohlhausen live in Bachdorf itself. They are surrounded by physical and cultural reminders.

Within the family itself, tranquility was blemished, without being destroyed, by the trouble Dela Stein had with her father. He was, after all, a man of seventy-two in 1900. He was ailing and senile, and he disturbed the orthodoxy of the household by his dietary needs. One of Lieschen Schmidt's chores was to help him dress in the morning. He had been an active man; confinement and disability did not improve his disposition. After his death in 1912, Dela Stein is supposed to have attributed much of her "nervousness" to the tribulations of taking care of him.

That may well be true, yet the pattern of her own ailments was such as to suggest that the care of old Levi Abraham was an aggravation rather than a cause. For Dela was not a healthy woman. In addition to her "nervousness," she had heart trouble and high blood pressure, the latter being associated with her complaint of swollen feet. Her ill health was genuine, and if she seems to have talked too much about symptoms and remedies it is probably because her difficulties were real enough to lead to her death in 1922 at the comparatively early age of fifty-seven.

While her own problems doubtless heightened her concern over other people's health, her charitable and nursing activities have a context over and above her own ailments. She often took kosher soup to ailing neighbors. While such visits gave her a chance to discuss her own ill health, they are linked with the fact that she was a Jewish woman and suggest beyond this that she was a genuinely considerate person. Isaac often left on Sunday morning to spend the day in Delbach. When he did so, Dela would regularly tell Lieschen Schmidt to take the day off. Just as regularly, Lieschen would refuse, for, as she says, Dela clearly needed help around the house. Later, when Hannelore Kraus was working for the Steins, a striking instance of Dela's thoughtfulness occurred. Isaac had acquired two fields which he planted and harvested each year. It was expected that Hannelore would help in the harvesting, which, one year, was delayed by bad weather. It began to appear as though they would be taking in the harvest on a traditional German autumn holiday. Hannelore and her betrothed were afraid that Hannelore would have to work on the awaited day. Two days before the festival, however, much to Hannelore's surprise, Dela told her that arrangements had been made to find other help on the holiday. In telling this, Hannelore and the man who is now her husband comment with a gentle amusement that Dela herself was not much help in the fields; she worked hard and meant well, but, as Herr Kraus says, she did not know how to handle a rake.

Details of this sort about Isaac's personality are harder to elicit. Isaac was the breadwinner of the family, frequently out of town on business, and scarcely expected to engage in the domestic activities by which his wife's kindnesses are revealed. Isaac's thoughtfulness emerges in the context of his own characteristic activities. The Bachdorfers tell how he would "put a cow in a poor man's stall."

The phrase, "to put a cow in a poor man's stall," has often served a pejorative function when applied by German peasants to Jewish cattle dealers. It is therefore significant that Bachdorfers do not accuse Isaac Stein of having forced indebted farmers to fatten cattle for him. During the growing season, of course, every farmer needed a draft animal, and a cow could act in this function in addition to providing milk. Not to have a cow was a serious handicap, and to buy one could call for money which the peasant did not have. Isaac would often meet this situation by taking a cow which had just come into his possession, and, instead of selling the animal immediately, put it in the poor man's barn. Then, at the end of the growing season, after the need for the cow's services had passed, Isaac would take her out and sell her. Some Bachdorfers may note that Isaac probably never lost out on such arrangements, but even these villagers do not doubt that Isaac's motive was to help the peasants.

Isaac seems to have been both successful and satisfied in his business, and Dela, in spite of her ill health, was a good housewife. Bachdorfers remember both of them as having been dedicated parents; the villagers also stress the harmony evident in the Stein household.

It was in this atmosphere that Sigmund Stein, his older sister, Meta, and his younger brother, David, grew up. The details of Sigmund's infancy are mostly inaccessible; its larger features are plain enough: a harmonious household mildly flawed by a cantankerous grandfather and the ill health of his mother; a sister not enough older than Sigmund to have acted as his nursemaid; a brother not enough younger to have burdened him with any real responsibility; a Christian girl from one of the peasant families in the vicinity who showed affection and competence in caring for the children, this girl being replaced by her sister when Sigmund was seven. Although it was a Jewish household in an immediate environment which was totally non-Jewish, Jewish friends and relatives were in villages within walking distance. It seems hardly surprising that this early childhood was experienced as a happy one. Many years later, the principals looked back on it with almost overwhelming nostalgia.

Yet it is not possible to overlook aspects of these early years which foreshadowed problems that maturity would bring. A photograph in the possession of Elisabeth Kohlhausen shows Sigmund at the age of four or five. It is a charming picture of the children in the Bachdorf elementary school: boys in knee pants and visored caps, girls in miniature versions of the traditional peasant costume. Seated on the ground in front are children of pre-school age who had been permitted to have their picture taken with the others, and at the extreme right in this front row sits Sigmund Stein.

The other children are smiling, more or less self-consciously, or staring blankly into the camera. But Sigmund is scowling—an intense child's scowl. Standing out as he does by his expression and his place at the end of the row, Sigmund cannot escape his "difference." The temptation to interpret such a picture in the light of hindsight is especially strong.

It was a good life for the Stein children in Bachdorf. Around 1900, the village must have presented magnificent opportunities to childish imagination and enterprise. Directly in front of the Stein home was the brook, too swift to play in during most of the year, but a natural stimulus for a child's fancy. Five minutes' walk along the brook, where it flowed into the River Frieden, was a grassy, inviting meadow. To the north of the village, again only a short walk away, were the wooded spurs of the Sauerland hills.

Because the village went out to its fields each day, the whole area would be sparsely dotted with adults, so that even the hair-raising exploits of the redskins—then, as today, German children played Indians as passionately as American children—took place against a background in which adults were present. But the children did not heed the workers. There were many opportunities for children to roam freely, exploring what was yet unknown to them, however familiar it may have been to the sowers and the reapers.

The village itself was small enough to be familiar in all its parts, yet complex enough to be a challenge. Such seasonal activities as planting, slaughtering, and the harvest established a rhythm which the child quickly heeded. The lively celebration of traditional holidays added color. Animals abounded everywhere— like the rest of the children, Meta, Sigmund, and David Stein had certain favorites in the barnyard menagerie which "belonged" to them, without quite being pets. The railroad still had a quality of novelty for the adults; for the growing child it is always new. In the winter there were sledding and ice-skating for the younger children and skiing on an abundance of slopes for the older ones.

None of this ensured an idyllic childhood. But it echoes with an excruciating poignancy in the novelette which Sigmund Stein was working on in the months before his deportation. It is framed in the security and the sense of measured, optimistic movement which could hardly have become the myth of the post-Wilhelminian era if it had not had a semblance of truth.

The Stein children played freely with the other children of the village. The Stein home had a dark and capacious cellar, where the children of the house played hide-and-seek with their friends. There was visiting from house to house—though "visiting" is probably too formal a term. Lieschen Schmidt used to bring her sister's children to play with the Stein children, whose infancy had prepared the sister for her own motherhood. Lieschen herself enjoyed warm relations with the family and the children. All of the Dienstmaedchen make much of the fact that they always ate at the same table with the family, and Lieschen says that Isaac was always worried that she might not eat enough. She insists that the Steins treated her like one of their own children and remarks that she learned to pray with the family in Hebrew. She recounts with obvious emotion how the children spoke of her as "our" Lieschen and how, when they were given chocolate, they would insist that she have some first.

The essential equality is complemented by the way certain religious differences were smoothly integrated into the common life of the village. The integration appeared in the interactions between the Jewish and Christian holidays, particularly Passover and Easter. It is not clear that Christian children actually liked the *taste* of matzos unless the wafers were spread with jam or jelly! But the *idea* of matzos, as something strange, foreign, out of the ordinary, obviously was intriguing. At Passover, the Bachdorf children came begging for handouts. As for the young Steins, anyone who has seen the way the Hessian peasants paint their Easter eggs will understand the appeal these eggs would have for children who normally did not have them. So at Easter time the three Stein children would appear at the door of a neighbor's house bearing pieces of matzos for the neighbor's children. They would say, "We aren't allowed to beg, but . . ." and the hint being taken, they would be given the coveted eggs.

Another occasion of interaction between Jewish and Christian holidays was that between Hanukkah and Advent. A more general interaction between Jewish and Christian customs occurred at the secular and irregular *Schlachtfest,* or slaughtering festival.

It is less noteworthy that the Stein children should have wanted a Christmas tree than it is that their father consented to get them one. The Christmas tree of course had its origin in Germany and was originally associated with pagan usages rather than with the birth of Christ. Even though the tree had by 1900 become thoroughly permeated with Christian tradition, it is conceivable that a German Jew who was concerned with assimilation and believed in the possibility of some sort of a fusion between his Jewish identity and the German framework of that identity would have felt the Christmas tree to be an innocuous pleasantry.

According to neighbors' statements, however, Isaac Stein does not seem to have been that kind of Jew. And even though David Stein suggests that perhaps his father was not as completely orthodox as his attention to ritual indicated, it would be hypercritical to discount Isaac's regular attendance at synagogue, his compliance with the dietary laws, his abstention from smoking on the Sabbath, and his refusal to make fires or cook on that or other holy days. Isaac was orthodox, and yet he went out and cut down a Christmas tree for his children and is described as having enjoyed helping them trim it.

In Sigmund Stein's novelette, his longing for childhood centers on Christmas, and he takes pains to explain the difference between purchasing a tree in town and going out in a horse-drawn sled to get one from the forest.

In a German village, the Schlachtfest is an important, if not strictly formalized, occasion. It is a time of activity and excitement. The men are busy with the slaughtering itself, while the women are involved in salting and pickling meat and in making varieties of the local wurst. The peasants slaughter only for their own use; the meat they sell leaves on the hoof, to be slaughtered in some nearby city or town. In Bachdorf at the beginning of the century, Isaac Stein was the agent in such transactions, yet like the peasants, he also slaughtered for his own use. In his case, the crucial work was done by a Jewish ritual slaughterer, so that the meat would be kosher. Unkosher parts of the animal and, on occasion, choice kosher cuts, would be given to friends in the village or, infrequently, sold.

Centuries ago such gift and sale had been a constant source of contention between the village Jews and the butchers' guilds in the towns. The German guilds bitterly resented the competition and went to extremes of anti-Semitic agitation to combat it. In 1900 much of this bitterness had died out. In Bachdorf itself, Isaac's slaughtering was accepted and aroused little more than gratitude for the gifts which were its by-products.

It was of course impossible for the peasants to offer similar gifts to the Steins. The peasants slaughtered by traditional rules, but the rules were secular. And even if the rules had been religious, the religion was the wrong one. Yet the children were invariably infected with the excitement of the occasion, whether it happened in their own *Hof* or that of a neighbor. As children do, they loitered about, going into neighbors' kitchens where pickling and sausage-making were in progress. And here they fell prey to temptation! Perhaps it was looked upon as something of a joke to offer Jewish children pork sausage. Or the lure of forbidden fruit may have been too strong. In any event, David Stein succumbed. His enjoyment was short-lived; in a flurry of indignation, Meta Stein caught him and dragged him home, his howls of innocence notwithstanding. Later on, Sigmund and Meta herself also fell from grace.

This incident was the first step in the abandonment of Jewish orthodoxy which all the Stein children were to show as adults. It was abandonment, not apostasy. Despite the accommodation, none of the three ever rejected, denied, or tried to conceal the tradition out of which he or she had come.

The children's first contact with the institutionalized and secular segregation of their tradition came at the Jewish elementary school in nearby Weidenfeld. The synagogue was, so to speak, the very embodiment of their difference from the rest of the population; it did not involve a segregation resulting from that difference. The same may be said of their family life in its uniquely

Jewish aspects: this is what they were. The school, on the other hand, was segregated.

Yet the meanings of segregation were deeply and obscurely buried in the very nature of the Jewish school. It was by no means an inferior school. Its physical set-up was at least equal to that of many of the non-Jewish elementary schools of the area, and the instruction was superior. (When Sigmund left it to enter the academically oriented higher school, the *Gymnasium,* in Hochburg, he was able to skip the first year there.) The Jewish school in Weidenfeld was not compulsory, although the Jews were taxed by the state to support it. While it was neither a Talmud-Torah nor a synagogue school, it was on the surface a concession to Jewish wishes. Why the Jews wanted such a school is not clear, but Hochburg, to mention only one other place, also had such a school.

It was located on the extreme northern outskirts of Weidenfeld, on the street which just beyond it became the path up to the Jewish cemetery. Except for the few Jewish children from Weidenfeld itself, pupils had to spend considerable time and energy in order to attend—it was about a half-hour's walk for the Stein children.

Sigmund Stein attended this school from 1901 to 1908. He had been preceded in the school by Meta and was followed by David, who is generally considered to have been brighter than Sigmund. Meta Stein appears to have surpassed both boys scholastically.

On the one hand, the Weidenfeld school offered a certain protection to its students. Where Jewish and non-Jewish children were in school together, fights in which one of the participants was Jewish would be punctuated with such epithets as "Stink-Jew," "Jew-Pig," and worse. And some teachers *were* anti-Semitic.

On the other hand, the school institutionalized a rivalry between the Christian schoolchildren and the Jewish children. Individual fights were rare, but snowball fights between Jewish and Christian schoolchildren appear to have been frequent in the winter, with race and religion playing an explicit vocal part.

Yet there were also friendships from group to group. These were commonly among children who lived in the same street or neighborhood. Sigmund Stein and the other Jewish children who, like him, came from outside Weidenfeld were at a disadvantage compared to the children of the Jewish families in Weidenfeld. In disputes with Christian children, the Weidenfelders among the Jews were much more likely to have friends and allies in the opponents' camp than were the Niederhauseners or the Bachdorfers.

The six years in the school at Weidenfeld made Sigmund Stein's subsequent schooling in Hochburg easier. Hochburg was far enough from Bachdorf to make it necessary for Sigmund to live in Herr Dr. Jungmann's Boarding Home for Jewish Students. Weidenfeld was much closer to Bachdorf, so Sigmund could live at home while he attended school there. In fine weather he walked to and from school; in bad weather he took the train. In this way, the ties to home were ever so slightly loosened.

When Sigmund left for Hochburg in 1908, it naturally did not mean that his connection with his family was broken. Attenuated it surely was, but there remained vacations and the many holidays of the German school year. Weekends, except perhaps in conjunction with a holiday, were not very practical for visits home since, then as now, German schools operated on a six-day week.

On his visits home, Sigmund found enjoyment in helping his father, particularly when he fed and cared for the animals. During the first year of World War I this activity was expanded; when he had vacations at this time he not only helped his father but also went to work on the farm of Lieschen Schmidt's sister, whose husband was away at the front.

Although his life actually became more and more remote from the soil, Sigmund apparently felt that his roots were there, and the pattern of returning to the soil gave an illusory vitality to this belief. It is certain that Sigmund's love for the simple life was genuine; it is much less certain that it would have been expressed as often as it was and in the ways it was if Sigmund's relation to the simple life had been direct, functional, and uncomplicated.

In the history of the family after Sigmund left it, there were events to which his reactions must have had important effects on his personality. In 1912 there was one death in the household itself and one among close relatives in Niederhausen. When, in May of that year, "Old Sara," Isaac's aunt, passed away, Niederhausen lost a familiar figure, and the Stein family lost a matriarch. And when, four months later, Levi Abraham followed her, the Stein children must have been faced with one of those puzzling situations where a death is mourned and, at the same time, all the adults breathe a sigh of relief.

The war of 1914–1918 and the tumultuous events which followed it in Germany seem to have left little trace on the Stein family in Bachdorf. There must have been anxieties, with the two sons away at the front. There was grief, certainly, when Meta's betrothed, a young merchant from a neighboring village, was killed in action. But both Sigmund and David came through without injury, and Meta's loss gradually faded until it was eclipsed by the joy of her marriage to Karl Fuerst of Kirchdorf, who had renewed an earlier suit after his rival's death.

The blow which struck the family with Dela Stein's death in October, 1922, was anticipated, if not softened, by her increasing ill health and by her premonitions of death. These anxieties never got the better of Dela. Instead of bowing before them, she acted. She said that she had never, in her adult years, taken a long journey, and that this was something she wanted to do before she died. So she went to visit relatives in Berlin and came back laden with gifts for everyone and convinced that she had taken her last journey. Her death came suddenly, of a heart attack.

Isaac mourned and did not remarry, but he did bring his maiden sister, Emma, from Niederhausen, to live with him as companion and housekeeper. Emma was apparently a more down-to-earth woman than Dela had been. Trina Koehler, who was maid with the family at that time, recalls how Emma kept such a firm hold on the purse strings that the family ate more simply than was necessary. She also describes Emma's complaint that Isaac always paid his dues to the local veterans' organization, but never attended the meetings. Yet Emma is remembered by Trina and others as having been especially open-handed with matzos for the neighborhood children at Easter, and her relationship with Isaac appears to have been a warm one. With the frequent visits of the children, whose affection for their father increased after Dela's death, the ten years from 1922 to 1932 were to all appearances happy ones for Isaac. His children were successful, but not so busy with their own affairs that they did not enjoy returning to Bachdorf.

From the assumption of power by the Nazis early in 1933 until

Isaac's death in 1937, it is impossible to believe that his life was other than a series of fears and disturbing incidents breaking increasingly often into an otherwise normal background. It was perhaps a sense of continuity with Jewish history which made him better able to appreciate what was happening than either his children or his neighbors. He told Elisabeth Kohlhausen that "they" were persecuting the Jews now, but that the Christians' turn was coming. It is certain that he retained a core of friends in Bachdorf. It is also certain, however, that the crescendo of official vituperation against the Jews and the intensity of Nazi appeals to the peasantry drove away many supposed friends and forced even the faithful core to express their friendship with depressing surreptitiousness.

Isaac's funeral was the last gathering of Jews in Bachdorf. It was attended—how closely?—by a few Christian friends and watched, with open curiosity or from behind curtains, by most of the people who thought of themselves as neighbors. A mere remnant of Jews attended, and the eulogy by the rabbi from Weidenfeld was hurried and anxious. As Isaac was borne to his grave in the cemetery above Weidenfeld, where vandals had broken headstones and gouged inscriptions—testimonies to the deathful world he was leaving behind—few of the mourners went the traditional last mile with him. When, on the day after the funeral, Elisabeth Kohlhausen cautiously crossed the little bridge and went to the Stein home to express her sympathy to Isaac's children, she found them in deep mourning. But no private grief was immune from the general atmosphere, and her visit was signalized less by the sympathy which lay behind it than by David Stein's question: "Weren't you afraid to be seen coming here, Betti?"

In the weeks thereafter, Sigmund was to come alone to Bachdorf to sell the property to Herr Bonke and the garden to the village. Henceforth Bachdorf was Jew-free.

2

[Doctor Jungmann's Boarding Home]

It is said that Hochburg-on-the-Felsen never really accepted National Socialism because the radicalism of the movement had little appeal for the conservatism of the town.

Yet in 1908, when the scene had shifted for Sigmund Stein from his home in Bachdorf to Dr. Jungmann's Boarding Home for Jewish Students in Hochburg, the town was permeated with a conservatism which was reminiscent of past and prescient of future radicalisms. Hochburg in 1908 was relaxing during a lull in German history. Its castle, which dominates the valley of the Felsen River and protectively gathers the town on the slopes beneath it, grew up in a thousand years of fighting and the anticipation of fighting The years are visible as an eleventh-century buttress here, a Gothic chapel there, a Renaissance frame about a walled-up door, and the seventeenth-century enfilades which sculpt the heights.

Hochburg's history has another side. The town is polarized between the castle and the Ursula Church, a jewel of early Gothic architecture. The side of Hochburg's history which it represents was an important one in the intellectual development of Germany and in the physiognomy of the town itself. For the Ursula Church was, through most of its seven centuries, a shrine to which pilgrims from all over Germany came to seek grace from the bones of the saintly and sainted Ursula.

Ursula was dedicated to charity. For the glory of God and the memory of her dead crusader husband, who had been the hereditary duke, she devoted herself to the sick in a small Dominican hospital located where the church now stands. In consequence of her willing exposure to contagion, Ursula the good died young, and a healing cult soon grew up around her remains. Following her beatification, the cult of Ursula flourished. The construction of the Ursula Church, which occupied the crafts and interests of the Hochburgers for nearly a century after her death, supplemented the trade which the pilgrims brought to the town. Trade was necessary to the community. Hochburg had earlier been important as an administrative center and as a place where a medieval wine route crossed the Felsen River. Shifts in patterns of trade and dynastic alliances during the later Middle Ages had robbed the town of such importance. In their economic function, Ursula's relics were a welcome substitute.

When the local sovereign was won to Luther's cause at the time of the Reformation, the cult declined. Without its pilgrims, Hochburg was an economic impossibility; without its cloisters, a cultural nonentity. What better cure for both these ills than to make it the center of the new Protestant learning? There is no record that Heinrich der Kluge earned his sobriquet, "The Clever," by figuring it out in this way. He may well have had nothing more than the interests of the new faith in mind when he expelled the Dominican Friars from their ancient cloister and founded the Heinrich Karl University with the cloister as its original building. With this one stroke, however, both the cultural significance of the town and the bustling trade in the local inns were effectively transferred from a Catholic to a Protestant context.

Heinrich's conversion to Lutheranism began in the ferment preceding the Peasant Revolts of 1525. These revolts can be denied neither the religious nor the political liberating spirit which they claimed, and to speak of Heinrich's introduction of the Reformation to Hochburg and the surrounding region as having been solely a matter of princely fiat is to neglect the way his awareness of the ferment had been sharpened by fighting against the revolts. He knew that some concession had to be made to the turmoil which produced them. His concession was religious instead of political and therefore preserved power at the expense of ideology. But it was a response to a movement of great popular vitality.

By 1908, both castle and Ursula Church had given way to the University as symbol of Hochburg's significance. In its importance as a center of Lutheran theology and in its faithfulness to the Kaiser and pride in the young German Empire, the University incorporated the meanings which church and castle had expressed. The town itself was much larger than it had been in the sixteenth century. Its focus was no longer the Old Town nestling under the walls of the castle. An important railroad, built in the middle of the nineteenth century, followed function rather than form and touched the town at what was then its periphery, near the Felsen River. The result was a drawing out of Hochburg along the Bahnhofstrasse down to the railroad station, and this new axis was soon at least equal in commercial importance to the Windstrasse and marketplace in the Old Town.

Nevertheless, with its 1,500 students, the University remained the pivot of the town's commercial existence. Hochburg had retained some administrative significance until Hesse was absorbed by Prussia in 1866, but even prior to that time the dependence of the townspeople on student room rentals and on catering to student needs or their often wild caprices had been growing. Fear of lessening Hochburg's attraction as a scene of happy, carefree, and frequently riotous student life was time and again advanced as a reason for tempering exasperation with moderation when it became necessary to discipline transgressions against University rule or local ordinance.

Entering the Gymnasium in October, 1908, as a Fifth Form student—he had been able to skip one year—and oblivious to the fact that the eight years of schooling ahead of him would be reduced to seven by the outbreak of the World War, Sigmund Stein naturally saw the life of the University from a distance. He did see it, however, not only because it permeated Hochburg life but also because Dr. Jungmann's Boarding Home was located in the Humboldtallee. This is a pleasant, tree-lined street where three Hochburg *Korporations,* the German prototypes of American fraternities, had their houses. One of these stood directly across the street from the Boarding Home, and Dr. Jungmann's oft-remarked discipline must have furnished a dour contrast to the colorful abandon which occasionally erupted from the Korporationshaus.

In 1908, certain currents, of symbolic significance for Sigmund Stein, formed a locally important vortex in Hochburg. In 1907, several Jewish students had applied for University recognition of a Union of Jewish University Students. During much of the following year this application was under consideration by the University authorities. Other German universities were queried on their experience with organizations of Jewish students, and the most influential professors at Hochburg were asked to submit their opinions on the matter. These opinions provide a fascinating glimpse of the way the academic mind was working on the Jewish Problem in Wilhelminian Germany.

The rector of the University accompanied his request for opinions with a short account of his interview with the leading applicants: "As far as nationality is concerned, they affirmed their adherence to Germany. When I asked them, that being the case, the nature of their Jewishness, they at first gave 'race' as the criterion, but then took that back and admitted that they couldn't give a clear answer to this question."

A professor of law was in favor of recognizing the organization because such recognition would be in accord with the Prussian Constitution. A professor of philosophy had this response for the rector: "I am basically against recognition of this organization. I acknowledge the formal right of these young men to join together, but see as a decisive objection the detriment to the University and the nation which might arise therefrom."

A professor of political science wrote:

> The inability of the young men to answer the question on their Jewishness which you put to them is for me proof that what we have here is an international, and therefore anti-German organization. . . . I consider it mistaken to look upon the Jew-

ish Question as a religious or racial matter; it is a Folkish problem. It is clear from the proposed rules of the organization that it will promote the interests of the Jewish Folk, and I see no reason to grant it a right which will permit it to appear before the public decked out in the dignity of a German student organization.

Sigmund Stein, of course, knew nothing of these remarks. It is probable, however, that he became aware of the Union of Jewish Students when it was granted University recognition in the year of his arrival in Hochburg. And it is highly improbable that he failed to hear of its suspension two years later in an affair which, except for its explicit anti-Semitism, was characteristic of such groups, Jewish or non-Jewish.

One evening several members of the Jewish Union were sitting in a Hochburg pub, drinking beer. After a while several members of another, non-Jewish Korporation came in and, with a mixture of malice and mischief, started singing one of their repertoire of anti-Semitic songs. The Union boys reacted in characteristic Korporation fashion by challenging the offenders to a duel. The latter, correctly claiming that the song was a traditional one, refused to construe the matter as an affair of honor. As a result, the Jewish students declared that their opponents were cowards. This led to adjudication in a court of honor. The judgment went against the Union, possibly because in the ornate honor code of the Korporations the Jewish boys were technically in the wrong. Or, more probably, because the court was more representative of the pervasive anti-Semitism of the Korporations than it was of the traces of fairness and liberalism which could be found in the University administration. The temporary suspension of the Union which resulted was unremarkable, although it did display the attitude of the Korporations and their power in the University context.

The dispersion of such attitudes is so evident in the records of this affair that it is no surprise when one of Sigmund Stein's classmates asserts that two of Sigmund's teachers at the Gymnasium (now dead) had been, as members of the German Folk Movement, anti-Semites. Another of Sigmund's teachers is now a remarkably alert octogenarian whose perspicacity and humanity have allowed him to register the anti-Semitic tradition and to devastate it with critical acumen and analytical skill.

Gymnasium authorities, as a matter of fact, did try to be fair toward their Jewish pupils. This is evident in the concessions made in the school routine to the Jewish Sabbath and other Jewish holidays. In recognition of the Jewish injunction against working on the Sabbath, the boys were permitted to bring to school on Friday the books which they would need on Saturday, and to pick them up late Saturday, after the Sabbath ended. They were also exempted from written exercises on the Sabbath; special oral recitations were occasionally substituted. Jewish boys of outstanding competence were permitted to be absent on the Sabbath.

Sigmund Stein was never one of these, although extant records as well as the accounts of teachers and classmates agree in describing him as capable, though not brilliant. He was near the top of the class in German and mathematics, and he alternated with two other boys as the best student in the class. He is described as ambitious and as a model student. Because there are gaps in the records—attributed to the depredations of the French troops billeted in the Gymnasium after World War I—it is hard to judge the reliability of such assertions. Yet they are consistent with several statements made about the desirability of copying Sigmund's papers. In his first years at the Gymnasium, Sigmund is said to have refused requests to copy his papers, because he did not want to share the plaudits they earned him. Later on he evidently changed his attitude in this connection and was more helpful.

None of six surviving classmates of Sigmund makes any connection between Sigmund's capabilities and the fact that he was a Jew. Two do say that Dr. Jungmann kept his Jewish boys in line scholastically; another volunteers the hypothesis that the reason for Sigmund's excellence was his being older than the class average.

Such comments seem to reflect a general lack of resentment toward "bright boys." This was also suggested by the fact that the recitations of the better students were felt to supplement a teacher's explanations. Thus the Jewish Boarding Home was a boon to all other students because the boys who lived there could be counted on to have their lessons prepared! The only student type for whom there was automatic dislike was the tattletale, and Sigmund was not one.

There were, apparently, only two respects in which Sigmund fell notably short of Gymnasium ideals. He lacked the mandatory enthusiasm for sports, and he was an awkward boy during his first years in Hochburg. Nevertheless, his shying away from sports did not make him unpopular, because he did support his class teams in their games with those of other classes.

In a class photograph, Sigmund does not scowl as he did nearly ten years earlier in Bachdorf. Now his face is round, somewhat contemplative, and unsmiling. He sits on the left of Professor Luther (the alert octogenarian and mentor of the class), in the second row, and wears a rather baggy jacket. Most of the boys wear knee pants, with open cuffs that hang slightly below the knee; Sigmund's hang the lowest, and his shoes are unlike others: laced around shiny hooks, they appear to have that spread at the top peculiar to boys whose ankles are a little too fat for the foot beneath.

Sigmund was not the only boy in his class who arrived in Hochburg from the more provincial milieu of village life. Each of the four Jewish boys at the Gymnasium came from a different village in the Hochburg area. (They all lived at the Boarding Home for Jewish Students.) Seven of the Christian boys came from villages. All the other students came from Hochburg.

It is doubtful that Sigmund's initial awkwardness exposed him to extraordinary teasing by his less countrified classmates. One says, "What could you expect of a boy from a village?" and another remarks, "But after all, that's why we were all going to school, why we all took dancing lessons . . . we all needed polishing up." Sigmund's Jewishness, on the other hand, did expose him to situations which, even though they may not have been basically malicious, must have kept his awareness of difference alive.

A proper assessment of anti-Semitic behavior which appears at an early age is difficult. On the one hand, it is particularly cruel, since its victims are youthfully sensitive to ridicule and rejection. On the other hand, borrowed from the adult world as it is, it may neither intend nor effect the rejection it so clearly implies. It need not, but it assuredly can develop into an adult anti-Semitism, the more virulent because of the depth of its roots, an anti-Semitism which sees in adult delusions a confirmation of supposed childhood insights. Among the worst things about childish anti-Semitism is what it says about the adults from whom it is borrowed.

Just prior to the First World War attitudes toward "the Jew" were part of the atmosphere in Hochburg. For two or three decades they had been swinging into the turn which, twenty years later, was to lead to disaster. The German Folk Movement, with its racist ideology, had come to be the intelligentsia's substitute for the crude religious and social anti-Semitism on which many intellectuals had been brought up. The creation of the German Empire in 1870 furnished a national stage for men who had grown up in provinces. Folk and race became necessities in a polity which never before in recent history had been a nation, and where crude anti-Semitism had never died.

During the years from 1908 to 1914, Sigmund Stein could not have remained untouched by the fact that he was a Jew. He lived too much in the presence of its effects. Precisely how, on any particular occasion, he accommodated himself is seldom known. That he did, in general, accommodate himself is certain. With his classmates, Sigmund took part in the polishing process of the dancing classes. In 1912 or 1913 there occurred in connection with them an instance where his accommodation is visible, however ambiguous it may seem to be.

Itzig Mandelbaum, a boy of about Sigmund's age, came from a family of Eastern Jews which had recently moved to Hochburg. The influx of Jews from the Russian and Austrian empires had not yet reached the heights to which the disturbances connected with the First World War would raise it. But spurred by such specific miseries as the pogroms of 1905, and by the equality and economic opportunity to be found in Germany, it had steadily increased. The German Jews were too unsure of their position to view the influx calmly, yet because of the traditional culture and dress of the Eastern Jews, the influx was conspicuous. Conscientious attempts by German Jews to deal with the problems they felt were arising out of the situation were hampered by their own problematical situation in German society.

Consequently, the Jewish philanthropist whose granddaughter

tells how he had overcome many barriers to attain a commission in the Franco-Prussian War; how he had endowed the synagogue as well as many non-Jewish institutions in his East Prussian home town; but also, how he would not have allowed an Eastern Jew to cross his threshold—this man is a pregnantly symbolic figure. Hochburg, the granddaughter's home, embodies the symbolism, and the Mandelbaums, though tolerated by the rest of the Jewish community, occupied the fringe of Hochburg community life.

This did not prevent Itzig from trying to find comradeship and acceptance. The dancing class was giving one of its regular parties. Each member had contributed his two marks, and the party was open to the public for an equivalent admission fee. Itzig, in a situation where time has obscured the misunderstandings which were probably involved, tried to get into the party without paying. This led to an argument, at the height of which Sigmund Stein is supposed to have demanded of Itzig that he pay his money like the rest. Itzig did not or could not or would not, and he was told to leave—by a non-Jewish classmate, but with Sigmund's approval.

Herr Kirschbaum, the classmate, stresses that he certainly did not identify Sigmund with those Eastern Jews and thereby exhibited a common kind of behavior: the acceptance of Sigmund Stein for his fine, middle-class, German characteristics and the simultaneous rejection of other Jews because of their "Jewish traits." This kind of acceptance of Sigmund inevitably maneuvered him into playing a role.

It was probably at dances such as this that Sigmund first met the girl he later married. Most of the boys did not take the same girl to these affairs all the time, "for fear they would get matrimonial ideas." Of the girls with whom Sigmund had attended the dances, one was from Dreistadt, a short train ride from Hochburg. Since there were few Jewish families in Dreistadt, and since Sigmund's wife was to come from that town, in Sigmund's case the dances may indeed have led to matrimonial ideas.

All of the girls Sigmund took to the dances were Jewish, for anything else would have been extremely unusual. This is true despite the fact that the frequency of marriages between Jews and non-Jews had already become a matter of concern to both Jews and

Gentiles. Later, the mixed marriage was to appear in Hochburg; indeed, the only Jews who remained in Hochburg during the entire Nazi epoch were two men and two women who had married non-Jewish partners around the time of the First World War.

After four years in the Hochburg Gymnasium and Jungmann's Boarding Home, Sigmund was joined by his brother, David. While they were in Hochburg together, Sigmund appears to have been very much the "big brother" in the eyes of his classmates and probably in his own. David himself tells the ingratiating little story of how a joke was made of this. If two of the older boys encountered David, one would ask, "Is that Stein?" The other, according to formula, would reply "No, that's Stein's Brother."

David detested the regimen at Dr. Jungmann's Boarding Home and lived for his vacations. His assertion that Sigmund felt the same way is undoubtedly colored by the strength of his own feeling. Nevertheless, everyone agrees that Dr. Jungmann was strict, and most sources make a point of his Jewish piety. It is hard to believe that any great love was lost between Sigmund and Dr. Jungmann, and it seems proper to ask whether the old-fashioned discipline of the boarding house may not have helped to corrode the appeal of the severe piety with which it was associated.

It is difficult to form a satisfactory picture of Sigmund's friendships and associations during his six years at the Gymnasium. Two of his classmates describe him as a good mixer; nothing in any of the accounts of this period contradicts this. One of these classmates, however, prefaced his comment with a qualification which reproduces the Hochburg atmosphere of the period: "Despite the fact that he was a Jew, he was still a good mixer."

In connection with Sigmund's friendships, one boy deserves particular mention, even though his association with Sigmund at this time must have been limited. This is Werner Hagen, in partnership with whom Sigmund was eventually to undertake the practice of law in Hochburg. Werner Hagen was two years ahead of Sigmund at the Gymnasium but lived at the boarding home, where his stay overlapped Sigmund's for about three years.

Regardless of the extent of their association at this early period, it is interesting to see how the same difference in personality which was to appear strikingly twenty years later is anticipated.

A contrast between the personalities of Werner Hagen and Sigmund Stein is always evident. In their law partnership the men were constantly together, so it is not surprising that people explicitly contrast them when speaking of the partnership. The earlier contrast is implicit, but plain to see.

Werner Hagen, early and late, was ready-witted, wry, humorous, keenly aware of what was going on around him and usually with an opinion on it. Possibly because of his size—he was a small man—possibly because of his pepperiness, he gained the nickname of "Wursht." He is said to have achieved a fame of sorts through a marathon feud of temperaments with one teacher of English. That a surviving member of Werner Hagen's class is known as a collector and purveyor of stories about him suggests that Werner Hagen's personality was striking in a way which Sigmund Stein's was not. This difference was to be evident in their later association as well.

Sigmund Stein's career at the Hochburg Gymnasium was cut short by the First World War. Sigmund had accommodated himself to the war during its first year by vacation work on the farm of Lieschen Schmidt's brother-in-law. In June of the second year of the war he took his *Abitur*, or graduation examination. For him, as for thousands of other boys in Germany, this was a special wartime examination which advanced the date of graduation by a year. The young men were needed in the ranks. Sigmund had tried to volunteer prior to graduation; after it, he went directly into military service.

This, then, seems a reasonable point at which to sum up the first nineteen years of Sigmund's life. It is not easy. The obvious circumstances which vitally shape the life of an individual are affected by important subtleties, and few men arrange their lives for the convenience of biographers. The most relevant information is often preserved by chance and sometimes not at all.

Certainly, it would help to know the daily minutiae of Sigmund's life as a child and youth, and yet no quantity of such detail could obscure the fact that he was born a Jew at the end of the nineteenth century in the German village of Bachdorf. In a real and consequential way this defines his development, shaping from the start his relationships to the intimate society of his family, the larger society of the village, and the encompassing society of Germany; for all the evidence which may be lacking on some points, there is enough to support the assertion that he was constantly confronted with the reality of the Jewish–non-Jewish cleavage and had to adapt his behavior and his consciousness accordingly.

The difference between Jew and non-Jew was more pronounced for the Stein family than it was for many village Jews, since the Steins were the only Jews in Bachdorf. Certainly, they got along well with their neighbors; for this very reason, the inevitable occasions of rejection and lack of communication must have hurt the more and been more puzzling to the children. Sigmund was close to the people of the village and he loved the landscape he had inherited from five generations. He was drawn to everything of which the cleavage was a part.

Born in the time and place he was, Sigmund inevitably found that most of the relationships of his childhood had a provisional character. On the one hand, the fact that he was a Jew set some limits on his childhood friendships; more than a Christian child, probably, he was thrown back on his family for the warmth and reliability denied him elsewhere. On the other hand, this intensified relationship with his family was destined to be broken into by the drive for schooling and attainment outside the family which was an aspect of German Jewish life in the decades around his birth. This general picture is given specific shadings and nuances by the Stein's isolation in the village, by the "nervousness" of Sigmund's mother, by his position between an older sister and a younger brother, by the presence of an ailing grandfather in the house, and even by the constellation of neighbors and households in which the Stein home was located.

When Sigmund left this constellation in order to spend most of his time at school in Hochburg, his world had not attained the simple stability of outlook which characterized the world of his non-Jewish companions. This suggests both a lesser security at the time and a greater receptivity to the securities which would be offered to Sigmund by the more rigid and history-ridden context of the Gymnasium. When we see, however, what the holocaust of 1914–1918 did to the security of Sigmund's non-Jewish contemporaries, we may conclude that there were advantages in the fact that life's foundations had not yet solidified for Sigmund.

The Gymnasium as well as the life around it were permeated by the ideology of the German Empire. Counter-currents were few, and the war was to show their weakness while fulfilling their object. The temptation for Sigmund to accept this ideology as Life must have been great, however conditioned by his peculiar relationship to it as a sensitive person and a Jew. It was still too easy to feel and experience—if not to see and recognize—the way in which his milieu regarded the Jews, for Sigmund to have had complete confidence in the rationalizations which he wanted to accept. With this unresolved tension between the need for a base and the nature of the bases which had been offered, Sigmund entered the German army in 1915.

3

[The Kaiser's gift]

The First World War seems to have given much of the real content to the patriotism, the "Germanness," that was so characteristic of Sigmund's subsequent career. He went into the war with a tension between his need for an ideologically settled outlook and the inadequacy for him of the Imperial German ideology. He came out of the war with this tension resolved.

The war was the first major opportunity for the German Jews to display their devotion to the nation which had made them equal before the law to other German citizens. And, to the degree that this legal equality was not matched by social equality, the war provided the German Jews with the opportunity to "earn" the latter. To be sure, the Jews of Germany had participated, a hundred years earlier, in the wars of liberation from the French. That had shown an even greater devotion to Germany, because the Jews of 1814 had been fighting against a complex of ideas—the French

Revolution—which had offered and temporarily given them an equality and sense of status as human beings previously as well as subsequently denied to them by the very society for which they fought. Many Germans, with a malice tinged by insight, had asked: "Why should the Jews fight for Prussia, for Hesse, for Baden against the Revolution?" And when some Jews, along with some Germans, chose the Revolution, the trace of insight was transformed into an anti-Semitic hatred for the Jewish converts to the Revolution.

Later on, when constitutions were being pressed on the more or less reluctant potentates of the miniature German states, the Jews asked for, and usually got, the privilege of being conscripted into the little armies of those states. So it was that in the play of tensions which preceded the unification of Germany and culminated in the Prusso-Austrian war of 1866, Jews were represented in most of the armies concerned. But not as citizens equal to other citizens. Even after the emancipation of the Jews in 1869, they still were not granted the social equality which would have given them the right to become officers in the Franco-Prussian War of 1870, and the Jew who did manage to obtain a commission could look upon it as a real triumph. It is no wonder that the achievement often became the source of a pride which blinded him to negative aspects of his position in the German Empire.

Such pride was an important component of the Jewish mood as Germany entered the First World War. The public expressions and statements which define the mood were filled with impressive devotion to Kaiser and Fatherland. This is startlingly evident in the writings of the German Jewish publicists of the period. From Orthodox Jews to Reformed, from Zionists to radical assimilationists there came articles, pamphlets, and books, all asserting with fervor and conviction the support of the Fatherland in its hour of crisis.

It would be false to assume that Sigmund Stein accepted this mood completely at face value. Sigmund, whatever his background, was a soldier among soldiers, experiencing the difference between the exalted patriotism of the pen and the dogged patriotism of the sword. Yet because such moods are likely to color the sentimental afterglow of a war, because in Sigmund's case the

German-Jewish mood of the time would shape the manner in which he later defined German realities, it is neceessary to look somewhat more closely at that mood.

Two characteristics of the literature in which the mood is expressed stand out. First, the argumentation is reasonable and the ethical thinking on a high plane. It is not, and seldom sounds like, blatant nationalism. It is not, though it occasionally sounds like, perfervid adulation of the Kaiser and the empire. Second, deep devotion to Germany is combined with a recognition of traditional anti-Semitism.

The role played by this Jewish ideology is a familiar one. It is the support of an embattled nation which is especially effective because it comes from those who have been disadvantaged by or in that nation. It is the patriotism of Negroes in all American wars, of German-Americans in World War I, or of Japanese-Americans in World War II. Support of this kind is always solicited more or less overtly by the state in danger; it is always given, more or less enthusiastically, because of the credit-balance it creates, and because there is scarcely a real alternative.

The mood was also one of unity among the German Jews, of reconciliation between Jews and anti-Semites. This denaturing of internal differences in the Germany of the First World War was given a label: the *Burgfriede,* or truce-within-the-fort. Cases where anti-Semites recanted their views in recognition of the Jewish contribution to the war effort were widely publicized, and the Jews were generous in their praise of military leaders who had been, and still were, anti-Semites.

Among the Jewish factions themselves there was a truce. Zionists, assimilationists, Reformed, and Orthodox—all praised each other's gallantry in action. As far as the specific meanings of the war for the Jews were concerned, each group had its cachet. The Zionists looked to an increased role in Palestine if Germany won. The Orthodox looked on the triumphs of German arms as proof of the virtues of obedience and extended this to their own position of strict obedience to Jewish ritual law. The assimilationists saw in the nobility of German war aims a justification for their adherence to Germany, and in their own sacrifices a proof of their right to full acceptance.

At the same time, of course, the Burgfriede covered up a considerable amount of sniping among the parties to it. This is most significantly true of the relationship between the Jews and the anti-Semites. For such a truce serves as a kind of general celebration which drowns out rather than destroys the real prejudices which continue to exist, since any serious examination of internal prejudices would be likely to have damaging implications for the prejudices which sustain national feeling against the enemy. German anti-Semitism had existed too long; its roots were too deep in tradition and had too many deceptive relationships with a parochial reality for it to be seriously affected by such a truce.

Among the Jewish factions, sniping was seldom more than a dig at the opponent's expense. Despite the Jewish joke, "Two Jews, three opinions," the existence of anti-Semitism has forced the Jews to live in a truce which has lasted for centuries as far as conflicts among themselves are concerned. In Germany, the wartime truce with the anti-Semites, by apparently removing the common enemy, fostered division among the Jews but threw this division into relief as a danger to the nation rather than as a danger to themselves.

In the awareness of Sigmund Stein and other Jews of his generation, the truce may well have seemed real. Yet the divisions which it obscured and permitted were part of the reality which he experienced at home, in school, and in the army. They made it possible for him to retain his Jewishness and impossible for him to accept it as an ideological basis for his life.

Sigmund seems to have gone to war without the flaming enthusiasm which possessed many other young Germans of the time. When he thought about it he doubtless found that he believed in what he was fighting for and found himself loyal to Kaiser and Fatherland. A Gymnasium classmate takes pains to point out that Sigmund did not volunteer as several members of his class did, but that when he was called up, he went willingly and without griping, "the way some Jews did." Sigmund's brother, David, is detailed and definite in his contradiction of the first part of the story, saying that Sigmund definitely did volunteer and had to visit the recruiting offices in two different cities before he was finally accepted. Yet David's explanation is prosaic and familiar: he suggests that Sigmund's volunteering arose from a feeling that he would eventually be drafted, as David himself was two years later.

That Sigmund was not very enthusiastic about the war is also suggested by the fact that, unlike many of his fellows, he seems to have felt no great disillusionment at the defeat of the Wilhelminian Reich. When pressed, people who knew Sigmund at the time say that he certainly did not *like* the defeat—but how could anyone who considered himself a good German feel otherwise?

Despite these indications of a less than total involvement in the immediate fate of Germany, Sigmund's life was decisively shaped by the experience of the war: it gave him Germany, in the sense of actualizing relationships with people, both Jews and non-Jews, who were Germans. Thus the war eliminated a void which neither the Imperial German nor the Jewish idea had been able to fill.

How often has comradeship been mentioned as the one positive aspect of the soldier's life? It is the common front against the human enemy and the enmity of conditions; the common front against the officers, and the common devotion to the officer who can surmount this antagonism; the closeness to one another in terms of *real* needs and threats, in contrast to civilian life, where both need and threat are often more tenuous and divide men from one another more than they bring them together; the tenderness among men which the absence of women both demands and permits; finally, the catharsis of bare survival. These are all real values, and Sigmund was neither the first nor the last soldier to have succumbed to their deceptive solidity.

Anti-Semitism, of course, did not disappear the moment one arrived in the barracks or the trenches. The Reserve Officers Corps in particular was a pillar of anti-Jewish feeling and was influential in keeping down the number of Jewish commissions. Sigmund made the grade to the non-commissioned rank and toward the end of the war was being considered for a commission. His brother says that the consideration was serious, since the family was investigated to ascertain whether or not Sigmund's background was appropriate for an officer. The commission did not come through. Under the circumstances, it would have been irrational of Sigmund to exclude anti-Semitism from the reasons for this outcome, though the end of the war itself may have intervened.

Nevertheless, in the extreme situation of the battlefront, the Jewish soldier had only to do his duty in order to have a substantial retort to anti-Semitic slurs—a retort which was occasionally useful with his comrades, but which was more important as an answer to any doubts which he might have about himself. This kind of an answer had become increasingly absent in civilian life, and it was the existence of it, along with the real comradeship of the trenches, which set off the military experience of the Jewish soldier from the experience which had preceded and would follow it.

These were the circumstances by which the war gave Germany to Sigmund Stein. For he had done his duty, and something beyond, fighting on both the eastern and western fronts in a field artillery regiment. He won the Iron Cross, Second Class, and while his brother deprecates the achievement, saying that the decoration was won by many Jews, there are others who insist that it was a noteworthy achievement for a Jewish soldier in the face of the persisting, if muted, anti-Semitism. There are even some in Hochburg today who are positive that Sigmund was decorated with the Iron Cross, *First* Class.

First or second class, the importance of Sigmund's decoration in relation to the National Socialists was to be great and typical, but it belongs to a later chapter. Important here is the total experience in the context of which he won it, for it made of him a man who, as a non-Jewish legal colleague remarks, "could sing *Deutschland, Deutschland über alles,* and really mean it from the heart. And yet, he wasn't a fanatical nationalist."

One detail of Sigmund's wartime experience is of considerable interest. This was his contact with one or more of the Eastern Jewish communities during his military service. He first fought in the Latvian sector of the eastern front and could hardly have been unaware of the many Jewish "little communities," or *shtetl*, in the area. Later on he was in Rumania, and he told David that he had attended the synagogue in Bucharest on Yom Kippur, after which, with several other Jewish soldiers, he had been a guest at the table of one of the members of the congregation.

At the time of the First World War, eastern Europe and western Russia constituted an area of depressed and oppressive living conditions which deteriorated as a result of being in a war zone.

The living standard of the Jewish communities of the region had long been looked upon as primitive by many German Jews, and the war had lowered that standard further. During the war years, the saying went around among the German troops on the eastern front that, however well disposed toward the *German* Jews one may have been, it was impossible not to be repelled by the surroundings and mentality of the Eastern Jews, where—according to a soldier's ditty—a father would invite one in for a cup of tea and then offer his daughters for one's enjoyment. Conditions in a war zone, of course, have a way of making the morally notorious commonplace, but the origin of this ditty may well lie in the impact which the squalor and misery of the area had on the traditional negative attitudes toward the Jews which were widely dispersed among the peasants and workers who formed the bulk of the German army.

In any event, Sigmund Stein's contact with and awareness of the conditions in the Eastern communities may explain what appears to have been his subsequent rejection of them. He is quoted as having once said, "It almost makes an anti-Semite of a person to see those Eastern Jews"—a remark which may have been an attempt at humor or the exercise of a prerogative, which he felt arose from his own identification as a Jew, to criticize other Jews; it may even not have been said. David Stein asserts that when Sigmund told him of his Bucharest experience, there was no trace of condescension toward the Eastern Jews connected with it.

Nevertheless, the attitude symbolized by the remark was common both before and after the First World War among the German Jews—who, during the war, unceasingly attacked the enemy Russian government for its treatment of their Eastern co-religionists. For all the tragic consequences such attitudes may have—and the orthodox self-righteousness of the Eastern Jews toward the *Daytsch*, or German Jews, must be included among them—in the perspective of human behavior they shrink to a common enough peccadillo which hardly justifies the suggestion made by some observers that the German Jews somehow deserved the fate which befell them.

Sigmund's experiences in the East may well have given his typical soldier's romanticization of home a specifically favorable coloring with regard to his situation as a Jew in Germany. He was given only two leaves during his three years as a soldier, and both were brief. Trina Koehler, who was maidservant in the Bachdorf home during this period, does not recall ever having seen him in uniform.

Because the war had cut deep into German manpower, almost all of Sigmund's later friends and associates were veterans like him. David Stein was called up at the age of seventeen, but peace came before he saw action. Werner Hagen, Sigmund's future legal partner, not only saw action but was wounded in the head; his later disposition was attributed to this wound by some of those who considered him irascible. Israel Stern, whose help Sigmund was to call on in 1942 in connection with the deportation of the Jews from the Hochburg area, probably owes his life to the fact that he had won the Iron Cross, Second Class. Sigmund's non-Jewish associates likewise tended to be veterans, and among these men there is the strong inclination, when speaking of Sigmund Stein, to jump back across the years from 1933 to 1945 and, giving them a wide clearance, to land in the comradeship of 1914–1918. In some cases the inclination arises from pain rather than guilt. Nevertheless, it can only underscore the manner in which the former comradeship was trodden into the dust during the Nazi era, when a common comment on Jews who hopefully displayed their Iron Crosses was, "Where'd he buy that thing?"

4

[Law student from Bachdorf]

Heinrich der Kluge, founder of Hochburg University, was a child of his time in his attitudes toward the Jews. He viewed them as infidels or heretics, generally bad but occasionally good. Sometimes he used them as foils to prod his Christians, saying that the latter were "worse than the Jews." He was not above exploiting the Jews financially as his brother princes did. He was, however, at times better disposed toward the Jews than the Lutheran theologians of Hochburg University were, for in 1539 he rejected the theologians' advice to expel the Jews from Hochburg, supporting his position with a multitude of biblical quotations.

In 1918, remnants of the University's earlier attitudes toward the Jews persisted in the Korporations and in individual members of the faculty and student body. But antagonism toward the Jew was no longer University policy, and among the many veterans enrolling in the winter semester, 1918–1919, were numerous Jewish boys, some of them from Hochburg itself, others from the towns and villages of the area. Two of the latter were Sigmund and David Stein. Because of the war, the brothers were matriculating at the same time in spite of fours years' difference in age and three years' difference in the date of graduation from the Gymnasium. Sigmund enrolled as a student of law, David as a student of medicine. Both thus chose professions which were popular among the sons of Jewish families in general and not unusual for the ambitious offspring of a Jewish cattle dealer in particular. It *was* somewhat unusual that Sigmund, as we shall see, entered Hochburg University with the idea that he would eventually settle in that town and not in some large city. During his first year, Sigmund lived the impecunious and somewhat isolated life which is still the frequent lot of the serious student. Until recently, the German university (and indeed those elsewhere in Europe) furnished little in the way of community institutions to its students. The students still organize most of their own social life, the traditionalists in the Korporations, the others in the groups of *Freistudenten,* who are unaffiliated.

For Sigmund and other Jewish students, of course, the traditional anti-Semitism of the Korporations made fraternity life all but impossible. This anti-Semitism had always existed, though not always at the same level of intensity which it attained in the years after the First World War, when it was "the thing to do" to badger the Jewish students. These were also the years when many Korporations which had previously admitted at least some Jews rewrote their constitutions to exclude non-Christians, frequently with explicit reference to "Non-Aryans" and "German Blood." Because of its romantic and tradition-steeped setting, Hochburg had always been a center of Korporation activities; consequently, when anti-Semitism festered in the Korporations it became evident in Hochburg.

One answer to this situation was the attempt to form Jewish organizations modeled after Korporations. An early attempt to do this at Hochburg has already been described. The success of the attempt and the demise of the organization in the face of antagonism from the other Korporations occurred while Sigmund was still a student in the Gymnasium.

The most important achievement in the revived efforts came

in February, 1919, two months before the end of the winter semester and Sigmund's transfer to the Josef Albrecht University in Augsburg. The Jewish Korporation which was formed at this time, Hessinia, was to survive only until the end of the winter semester 1921–1922. Sigmund had returned to Hochburg for this semester, at the conclusion of which he was to take his doctor's degree.

A few people say that Sigmund was a member of Hessinia, more say they do not know, and David Stein is certain that his brother was not affiliated. David's view is almost certainly correct, and not merely because he is Sigmund's brother. Hessinia was a copy of the non-Jewish Korporations, aping their concept of honor, sharing their predilections for the riotous and romantic aspects of student life, their devotion to the sabre and respect for the gashed cheek. Sigmund, for all his attachment to things German, was not riotous and was not that kind of a romantic. When at Augsburg he was faced with the choice between a Jewish Korporation similar in all respects to Hessinia, and one which not only rejected dueling and ritual drinking but also, in principle, accepted non-Jews as members and was aimed at fostering the intellectual and cultural life of those who joined, he became a member of the latter.

This was the *Akademische-wissenschaftliche Verbindung Minerva,* to give it its full, resounding name. (There is no significant difference between a Verbindung and a Korporation. Originally, the Korporations were composed of students from the same provinces, while the Verbindung was not geographical. This difference has practically vanished while others, less clear, developed out of the history of the two kinds of organizations.) Minerva clearly had intellectual pretentions; it was named after the goddess of wisdom and not after the gods of wine or war.

Among the traditional elements which Minerva retained was the pairing off of older and younger members as Fellow and Fox respectively. Traditionally, the Fox acts as the Fellow's batman while supposedly learning the arcana of the organization. In Minerva the rigid and hierarchical nature of the relationship was softened, and it had become one of comradeship and general tutelage.

It was, certainly, a friendly relationship which is reflected in the account of Dr. Bauer, who had been Fellow to Sigmund's Fox. In 1919, Dr. Bauer, fresh from the trenches, resumed his interrupted education at Augsburg as well as his membership in Minerva, and was chosen by Sigmund as Fellow. Even if it were true, as Dr. Bauer says, that the choice as choice had no significance, it was hardly true that it had no consequence, and it says much about Sigmund Stein that he had this man as his mentor. The doctor's insight and intelligence impress one as characteristics which survived the horror and chaos of the East, not as qualities which were created there. Bauer was a much younger and happier man when Sigmund chose him, yet he had a seriousness of outlook which suggested the significance the choice had for Sigmund, who became known in Minerva for his diligence and ability. These qualities were formally recognized in his second semester at Augsburg, when he was elected to one of the three presiding positions in the organization.

Minerva embraced all the trends in the German Jewish community except those—embodied in the Jewish "dueling" Korporation at Augsburg—which sought assimilation through meticulous protective coloration. There were, to be sure, exponents of assimilation in Minerva, but assimilation on the basis of what was felt to be intelligent assessment of self and society. This was the so-called "Central Union tendency," from the name of the organization which promoted it throughout Germany: the Central Union of German Citizens of Jewish Faith. The pre-Nazi history of the Central Union was one of earnest education toward a harmonious synthesis of Jewish with German life; this was followed by a post-Nazi history of intelligent and doomed compromise, not with Nazism as such, but with the illusion and reality of moderation in the Nazi party and of decency in the German people.

The other general tendency in Minerva was Zionist. A Jewish homeland in Palestine and the eventual salvation of the Jews by settlement there were clear principles. Despite their clarity and intensity, this current in German-Jewish life was to escape the moral and ethical miasma of the National Socialist era no more than the Central Union.

According to Dr. Bauer, the tendency to reject Judaism as a religion was entirely absent in Minerva, whatever modifications of Judaism's more stringent aspects may have been projected. Minerva provided an intellectually lively environment, as it was supposed to. There was formal and informal discussion, both of specifically Jewish problems and of matters of general cultural interest. Informal discussion took place in the group's *Stammlokal*, the coffee house where it regularly met, with the formal meetings being held in a private dining room of the same establishment. This room was rented throughout the year for the purpose and contained paraphernalia—trophies, group pictures of past members, and the like—similar to that which is found on the walls and shelves of an American fraternity house. The formal meetings centered on the reading of a paper on a scientific or cultural subject, but always in the background was another pragmatic function: to develop fluency and social ease in the members, many of whom, like Sigmund Stein, came from rural and provincial backgrounds.

The members of Minerva were eligible and available guests at entertainments given by the Augsburg Jewish families. These entertainments were not always exclusively Jewish; yet mixing entailed the obvious problem of the anti-Semite and the subtler problem of the Gentile who might end up by feeling that he was somehow on display. For its part, Minerva gave parties to which the daughters of the local Jewish gentry would be invited. To judge by Dr. Bauer's description, the fear of getting involved with the girls, mentioned in connection with the dancing classes in Hochburg, was absent, and several marriages developed naturally out of these parties.

Academically, Sigmund's two semesters at Augsburg were taken up with his continued study of law. The University archives reveal nothing about his abilities; a record of grades, such as exists in the registrar's office of any American university, is unknown in German universities. Sigmund, like other German students then and now, was on his own, held in line by his personal sense of responsibility and the knowledge that his career would depend on passing the two terminal examinations, one for his state certificate, which was indispensable, and one for the doctor's degree, which was desirable.

In the *Sommersemester* of 1920, Sigmund entered the Johann Wolfgang Goethe University in Frankfurt-on-the-Main. This was a major change. Hochburg and Augsburg represent one kind of German university; each has a long tradition and each offers the student the opportunity to partake of this tradition in a setting which conforms to the most romantic notions of German student life. The Frankfurt university is different. It is new, having been founded in 1914. It is located in one of the major commercial cities in Germany, where many wealthy Jewish families were among its leading early supporters. Perhaps as a consequence of this, the curriculum of the University has more ties with commerce than universities usually do. There are Korporations at this University, but their role is a subordinate and disputed one. The student is a recognizable but integral part of the metropolitan populace. He does not dominate the scene.

There was reason for Sigmund to attend Frankfurt in the summer semester of 1920. It is customary for the German university student to spend the summer semesters at the older, more congenially located universities. In the winter, on the other hand, many students hole up at a "working" university such as Frankfurt or Berlin. To enroll at Frankfurt for a summer semester suggests a drive or need to get something done. In Sigmund's case the suggestion is borne out by the fact that in September, 1920, at the end of the semester, he took the state legal certification examination in the district court at Frankfurt. Beyond the bare notice that he did so, however, there is nothing in the records. His subsequent career, plus his own statement that, because of his veteran's preference, the examination had been handed to him on a platter, are evidence that he passed.

During the next year, Sigmund was not enrolled at any university. Instead, he was working in the Hochburg law office of Dr. Mordecai Mannheimer. This was the period of the *Referendar,* or legal apprenticeship, and it is often confused with a later period, when Sigmund was dickering with Dr. Mannheimer for a partnership—a transaction said to have fallen through because Mannheimer, who had a reputation as a skinflint, offered too small a share in the business. Yet the early period at Mannheimer's had a genuine significance for Sigmund's later career, because it brought him into renewed contact with Werner Hagen. Werner had begun practicing in Hochburg a few years earlier. As Mannheimer's factotum, Sigmund had frequent occasion to confer with Hagen. Through such encounters and through meetings at Jewish community and family festivals, the earlier acquaintance became a friendship which subsequently brought Stein and Hagen together as legal partners.

Before any such partnership could materialize, of course, Sigmund had to complete his training. In and of itself, the Doctor of Jurisprudence degree which Sigmund was aiming at was not essential. Presumably the extra academic study it demanded had genuine value, yet its possession was largely a matter of prestige. Two other hurdles were unavoidable, however. He had to broaden his experience by an internship with the judicial organs of the state, and finally, he had to take the major and decisive examination by which he became an *Assessor*, entitled to plead cases.

A surviving brother-in-law of Sigmund Stein, Herman Klein, who went through the same training at about the same time, points out that Sigmund undoubtedly took his doctorate at Hochburg and got nearly all his practical experience in the surrounding area because he intended to practice there. Sigmund's doctoral dissertation, "The Essence of the Hereditary Right to Build," not only deals with a topic which is of primary relevance to the peasant household, but also and in particular draws on local Hessian court decisions for data and illustrations.

This "legal localization," as it might be called, was to become fateful for many German-Jewish lawyers. From province to province inside Germany, the advantage of practicing in the province where one had trained and the corresponding disadvantage of practicing elsewhere were relative. But from Germany to some other country the disadvantage was often so great as to be crippling. David Stein was to carry on as a physician and surgeon after his emigration in the late thirties—the adjustment was difficult, yet possible. But Werner Hagen would become the proprietor of a small bookshop in Paris, and Hermann Klein would replace his broken legal career by an only moderately successful one as manufacturer of ladies' garments. These were, of course, only shadows on the future in the spring of 1922 when Sigmund was preparing for his doctoral examinations and writing his dissertation at Hochburg.

Sigmund did not become a member of Hessinia, the Jewish Korporation at Hochburg at this time, yet despite his antagonism to its principles and practices he may, according to his brother and others, have given it some support and had some kind of an association with it. In any event, he was certainly aware of its final suspension early in the spring of 1922 and of the part which anti-Semitism played in this suspension. Even if he had had no contact whatever with Hessinia, the attitudes of the other Korporations were too much a part of the local scene to have escaped notice. Such obvious anti-Semitism may have had an effect opposite to what might have been expected. It showed itself as a discrete and visible entity, drawing attention away from the extent to which ideas of racial and group superiority were interwoven with, and had arisen from, the entire German experience, with which Sigmund and so many other Jews were proud to identify themselves.

Related to this is the fact that, in the Hochburg of 1922, anti-Semitic tendencies were embedded in a matrix of attitudes and activities which could be seen by Sigmund and his co-religionists as genuinely patriotic. In 1922 the French were fostering separatism in the Ruhr. The Poles were in Silesia. And the Communists were in Germany. The Hochburg Korporations supplied young volunteers who at one time or another fought all three. The patriotic rationalizations of these volunteers were scarcely impeachable, and like most of his contemporaries, Sigmund accepted the rationalizations. If he questioned them at all, his need to concentrate on the forthcoming doctoral examinations as well as the time and effort demanded by his dissertation were genuine obstacles to his thinking much about anything else.

When, finally, in April, 1922, he took his examinations and four months later submitted his dissertation, his solid if not brilliant success with both left little room for morose reflectio.is on the future.

The completion of his university requirements did not mean the end of Sigmund's training, for he now had ahead of him about a year and a half of internship in the judicial machinery of the state. This was a continuation, at a higher level, of the practical experience which had started in the law office of Dr. Mannheimer, where Sigmund had absorbed the atmosphere of a private attorney's practice. Now he would absorb the atmosphere of the courts and the state prosecutor's office. The bar and the bench in Germany are not as widely separated as they are in America, but important differences in purpose and function remain and carry with them important differences in routine.

The young lawyer is a minor workhorse of the court or district attorney's office in which he happens to be working. He must do the drudgery of analyzing and preparing cases for trial, and he soon comes to participate in the business of the trial itself. His position corresponds in many ways to that of the intern in the American hospital, with the major difference, however, that the Referendar is gaining insight into a side of the profession with which much later, as a practicing attorney, he will be jousting (unless, as he may at the end of his training, he decides to become a part of the judicial mechanism of the state). He comes to see the judge or the district attorney as a person who can be sized up for his habits and idiosyncrasies and will make use of these insights when he confronts judge or district attorney in the courtroom.

Sigmund learned the lessons of this part of his training especially well and thus became ideally suited to work with Werner Hagen. For among the people who knew both men there is unanimity on one point: Werner Hagen was a brilliant legal technician, a man with a remarkable memory for cases and precedents, but a poor courtroom personality, too hot-headed and sarcastic to permit his brilliance to take maximum effect. Sigmund, on the other hand, capable enough with his books, is always rated below Hagen as a scholar, but always recognized as superior to Hagen in courtroom conduct.

Sigmund went through this phase of his internship in courts where he was later to plead or to counsel. He was first in the lower district court at Weidenberg, not far from his birthplace in Bachdorf, and it is probable that he lived at home during this period. Thus, he was on the scene when his mother died, shortly after he started working at Weidenberg.

Her death added to the difficulty he was already having at court. For the presiding judge was an anti-Semite who resented Sigmund's presence and refused to let Sigmund into the judge's chambers where he properly belonged, demanding instead that he work in the outer office. This restriction had a fortuitously happy result in the form of an enduring friendship between Sigmund and the secretary of the court. This friendship with a permanent "lower" official of the court may well have contributed more to Sigmund's success as a lawyer than the more formal contact with a presiding judge.

In Germany, as in other countries, permanent civil service officials like the court secretary have a relationship to their work which can be of enormous value to the novice. The conscientiousness of such officials is often the other side of the rather grim stereotype of "the Official." As is true of most stereotypes, this one contains elements of truth: deference to superiors can be cringing and supervision of subordinates can be arrogant. Yet it need not be so, and in the relationship between Sigmund and *Gerichtssekretär* Kleinfeldt, these very elements may, anomalously, have contributed to making the relationship what it was. Sigmund, an academically educated man, had a claim to deference in the framework of the caste system. On the other hand, as a novice and as someone whom the caste system itself, in the form of the judge, had rejected, the deference could be offset by Kleinfeldt's secret sense of both cultural and professional superiority so that, in balance, as it were, the two men could react to one another as men. Had Kleinfeldt been a basically unpleasant person, the situation could have been doubly unpleasant for Sigmund. But the court secretary was not such a person. He showed Sigmund the ropes, and their friendship became such that many years later Sigmund's brother-in-law, who had worked at the *Amtsgericht* in Weidenberg a year or so after Sigmund, speaks of it as *the* relationship which distinguished Sigmund's life during this period.

Herr Kleinfeldt himself substantiates this account. In addition, he provides information about Sigmund's political activity at the time. Sigmund's lectures and talks given in the Weidenberg town hall on behalf of the Democratic State party would indicate previous involvement with this liberal, bourgeois, and republican political organization which supported the Weimar Republic against attacks from both right and left. While Sigmund was an effective speaker, his party was doomed, in spite of a transient popularity, to be overshadowed by the radicalisms of parties which were more permeated with the actual tensions and ideological cross-currents of a period which saw Walther Rathenau murdered by extremists of the anti-Semitic right and an inflation in which the mark, although still the legal means of exchange, was worth less than a billionth of a dollar.

That Sigmund seems not to have been contaminated by the extremities of the era may be to his credit, but it raises questions about his relationship to and understanding of his times. It was not a calm and intelligent period in Germany. The abortive Communist revolts of 1919–1920 had been smothered by the crumbling middle classes. There was an often witless longing for the discipline and order of Imperial Germany and a nostalgia for the peace, prosperity, and prestige of the good old days. Germany was being pulled and hauled in a manner as consistent with her history as it was surprising and demoralizing to her people.

No party in Germany or elsewhere excludes scoundrels who, in times of crisis, may be welcomed as effective and vigorous supporters—with no questions asked. The right and left radicalisms of the 1920's in Germany welcomed them in this way. But both radicalisms also welcomed and attracted individuals of idealism, enthusiasm, and sincerity. In such a situation, itself immoderate, the moderate parties give the impression of clinging to a remembered comfort in their acute discomfort at the shape of the world around them.

This is what was questionable about Sigmund's active commitment to the Democratic State party in the early 1920's. It was the party of the liberal, semi-enlightened middle class. It was of the lecture hall rather than of the street. It believed in Germany. Germany did not, and could not, believe in it. Sigmund's affiliation with this party was possible because the ambiguities of his experience had not destroyed his illusions. His childhood had been happy despite the fact that it was the childhood of a Jew in Germany. Later on, the anti-Semitic judge was so obvious and the court secretary so friendly that the situation did not seem especially portentous.

After six months in the court at Weidenberg, Sigmund transferred to the district court in Hochburg. During this period, his relationship with Werner Hagen grew because of their impending partnership. This partnership in particular, and the plan to settle in Hochburg in general, made a great deal of sense.

Hochburg at this time was a town of about 25,000 people. Before the First World War the lawyers of the town had formed what some referred to as an "exclusive circle"—sons of propertied families, genteel businessmen who cultivated a steady civil practice in trusts, guardianships, and estate management. Of lawyers for the "little man," there were few. One of these was Dr. Mordecai Mannheimer, with whom Sigmund had had his early practical training. Dr. Mannheimer was also one of the two Jewish lawyers in prewar Hochburg. He dealt mainly with the peasants and had the reputation of being a gouger. The other Jewish lawyer before the war was Dr. Emmanuel Hirschberg. He was already an old man and retired in 1929. He was liked by his middle-class clientele, and his achievement in overcoming his blindness was respected by his colleagues, though one of them did remove his portrait from the lawyers' chamber of the district court when the Nazis seized power in 1933.

Sigmund could look forward with confidence to the development of a good practice among the farmers and other "little people" of the area who, according to Sigmund's brother-in-law, Hermann Klein, preferred to go to the Jewish lawyers—whose background was so often interwoven with their own—rather than to the "upper-crust" lawyers whose understanding of the law was not likely to be matched by an understanding of the life situation of the peasants.

With such confidence, and with his partnership a settled prospect, Sigmund could intensify his courtship of Esther Mendel of Dreistadt, with whom he may have attended the dancing class parties, and whom he was to marry in early 1924.

During the six months in Hochburg, Sigmund continued his political activity for the Democratic State party and was involved in one incident which is of some interest because it seems so out of character. In August, 1923, Sigmund attended a joint meeting of the Democratic State party and the Social Democratic party in the Hochburg municipal auditorium in honor of the Weimar Republic. The Social Democrats had been assigned the task of preventing disturbances in the hall, and at the end of the meeting they were forced to form a cordon in the street outside in order to keep the exit free from a crowd of nationalistic university students. The

SDP men and the people emerging from the meeting were singing a popular republican freedom song, *"Brüder zur Sonne der Freiheit, Brüder zur Lichte empor."* To this the students mockingly responded with the "Internationale" and—since it was only four months after the Nazi, Leo Schlageter, had achieved a dubious martyrdom through execution by the French for sabotage in the Ruhr area—the "Marseillaise." In effect, the students were accusing their opponents of being both Communistic and pro-French. It was impossible to keep the two groups entirely separate, and several fist fights broke out, in one of which Sigmund Stein reportedly gave a good account of himself.

The episode is less remarkable as a sign of the times than as an apparent inconsistency in the image we have of Sigmund. Physical violence—and there may have been other incidents of this sort—runs contrary to the entire picture of his personality and behavior. An occasional comment on his "timidity" in later years could always be understood to arise from a misunderstanding and misinterpretation of his impossible situation in those years. Sigmund was not timid. But he was prudent, he was respectable, and he simply did not become embroiled in street fights.

Most Germans frowned, like Sigmund, on the disturbances created by the radicals of the right and left. Yet the Nazis seemed to be fighting for things most deeply rooted in the German tradition. Communism and Socialism offended the German's carefully fostered sense of property. Furthermore, at a time when German nationalism was glorying in its wounds, the two left parties were tainted with internationalism. To be sure, the Nazis also deviated at times from conventional German ideas about property, but when they did so it was in the direction of glorifying a vague and irrational Folk Community, the Blood Community of the Village, the *Band*, or the Youth Group, with frequent reference to the military comradeship which so many Germans could remember. The racial idea, which has always been harmonious with ideas about the Folk, added to the Nazi appeal. In sum, the Nazis had the advantages, partly because they ruthlessly pursued them, partly because Nazism managed to be an astute combination of several trends which had become influential in German ideology and popular in German culture. Hence, too many people were able to say to themselves that the rowdyism of the Nazis was the result of their willingness to fight the good fight, and that the instigators of the violence were the Communists and Socialists.

Sigmund was neither a politician nor a sociologist, and he was immersed in the events of the time. Especially in the spring and summer of 1923, in the midst of an inflation so fantastic that there was hardly room on the postage stamps for the zeros needed to express the millions of marks they were worth, it was obvious that something was wrong. Sigmund believed that radicalism was mistaken and recognized that the fanatical anti-Semitism of the Nazis made their error personally relevant. Yet the maelstrom of the times in Germany was such that radicalism was understandable. It is doubtful that he regarded Nazism as more or less a moral abomination than Communism.

Sigmund was influenced in his political perceptions by the sound observation that people as people are always more complex and variegated than their political labels would lead one to believe, and he had a good example of the point before his eyes.

In 1923 and 1924, Roland Freisler and Werner Hagen were friends, in a relationship which touched Sigmund. Freisler, the vindictive presiding judge in the 1944 trials of those who had conspired against Hitler, was already anti-Semitic in 1923 and already had leanings toward the Nazis. But "some of his best friends were Jews," and the situation in 1923 was by no means so far gone that an unqualified anti-Semitism was the royal road to success. Freisler was at the time a young lawyer assigned to the Hochburg District Attorney's office. He, like Hagen, was an enthusiastic Skat player, and they often played together, with Freisler on occasion borrowing money from Hagen. Freisler is supposed to have spoken of Hagen's partner-to-be, Sigmund Stein, as a capable lawyer; this may be legend, but in the middle 1920's it was perfectly possible.

It is easy to ask why Sigmund and his fellow Jews did not see how the situation was shaping up, and easy to condemn the Germans for failing to anticipate the course National Socialism would take, especially when it assertedly was there for everyone to see, in *Mein Kampf*. Yet experience—which is all we have to go by— has repeatedly shown the danger of projecting the future on the basis of a political platform or program, and only realistic assessment of political developments can give a more or less reliable basis for guessing the direction in which a program may be changed.

But the predominant German thought of the early twentieth century contained a major false assessment of reality. This was the belief that human groups have a transcendent character unrelated to the historical context and social environment in which they develop. It was the belief that mystically hereditary "blood" characteristics shaped the connection between the peasant and the soil, the craftsman and his tools, the Jew and his money. This mystique, of course, was widely held outside Germany and was shared by many of the Jews in Germany.

Thus it was possible for a Jew like Sigmund Stein to look upon anti-Semitism (embedded as it was in Folkish sentiments and nostalgic ideas about a society where everyone was supposed to have and know his place) as part of an essentially unobjectionable drive to give to each his own. A drive it was, certainly, with its violent and extreme supporters, yet it was hardly different in this respect from other ideological movements.

So it was that in the political confusion after the First World War, German anti-Semitism was seldom seen, even by the Jews, as something which in and of itself made a man a scoundrel; that therefore Werner Hagen could play cards with and lend money to Roland Freisler; that Sigmund could tolerate the rejection of the anti-Semitic judge; or that the same judge could later show professional respect for the attorney he had earlier decried as a Jew.

Sigmund Stein was well aware that anti-Semitism surrounded him, but he could not think of himself as separate from his society. He was a gracious and congenial person who never limited his associations on the basis of ethnic affiliation, just as he never lorded it over classmates who had not gone to the University. Unlike so many "educated people," says the wife of a worker, Sigmund Stein could relax over a friendly glass of beer with a working man.

Werner Hagen was in much the same position as Sigmund so far as a sense of belonging was concerned. Some people thought

Werner was irascible and, as we have seen, attributed this to the head wound he received in the war. This irascibility, examined closely, reveals a humor and peppery aggressiveness which were already evident in the Gymnasium. Both traits come out in a story about an incident which occurred in the early 1920's. Frau Huss, a woman we shall hear more about, first met Hagen when she and her husband retained him as legal counsel in a case involving their effort to evict a roomer. Their daughter was getting to an age at which, the Husses felt, she should no longer sleep in their room. The tenacious roomer had the only other room available. Since their arrangement with the roomer was a contractual one, they called on Werner Hagen for advice. A meeting of the Husses, the roomer, and Werner Hagen was arranged. The Husses argued that it was not right for the child to remain in the parents' room at night after she was old enough to be aware of "things." To this the roomer replied that he had slept in his parents' room until he was twelve years old, and it certainly had not done him any harm. Whereupon Hagen remarked, "Well, some children just aren't as alert as others."

Werner Hagen was not as popular as Sigmund Stein, the extent of whose tact sometimes masked the degree of his humor. But the two men were well suited to one another, and when Sigmund left Hochburg late in 1923 for his final period of training in the court of appeals at Kassel, he could look forward with confidence and a sense of belonging to his return to Hochburg and his partnership with Hagen. The future must have seemed secure, despite anti-Semitism, Nazism, and the economic uncertainties of the era.

["They were practically fellow citizens"]

Late in May, 1924, Sigmund Stein, temporarily of Kassel, and
Esther Mendel, of Dreistadt, were married in Hochburg. Werner
Hagen was the best man; David Stein was present and says that
Werner was truly resplendent in his tuxedo. Sigmund and his bride
went to Gottschalk's Hotel in Wiesbaden, a popular watering place,
for the "tinsel week" of their honeymoon. Following this, they returned to apartment living in Kassel for several months while Sigmund finished his legal internship at the Court of Appeals. They
then went to Berlin, where Sigmund took the final state certification examination. He passed, and thus they could move to Hochburg, where they took up housekeeping in an apartment on the
Bergsteigweg which Sigmund had rented and furnished earlier in
the year.

Esther Mendel was the oldest of three daughters of Jakob
Mendel, a well-to-do dealer in pedigreed cattle. She was a woman

64

whose delicate beauty was associated with a refinement which came close to isolating her from her surroundings. It is her aloof beauty and its contrast with her later fate which dominate all recollections of her. Sigmund quite literally adored her; she seems to have accepted his adoration as a matter of course, without seeing the gulf it implied. To be sure, Esther's fantasies of being above it all never interfered in any real way with her being a wife and making a home. Instead, they expressed themselves in mild social climbing, a tasteful elegance of dress, and a drive to conform to the respectable rather than the merely conventional aspects of town life.

Today when people speak of Sigmund there is a warmth in the voice—warmth which is often genuine and which, even when it seems forced or exaggerated, still manages to evoke the many facets of Sigmund's character which were the natural occasions of warmth. Sigmund valued the role of solid citizen, but he could drop it and be natural and down to earth—*volkstümlich,* as the Germans say, meaning "homely" or "folksy."

Sigmund rose above his background but never rejected it. Esther, one feels, rejected her background without ever rising above it. When the two went to the milk store together, Sigmund would wait until Esther had bought the proper items. Then, as she was on her way out, he would slip behind the counter, quickly take and pay for a quantity of the dubiously fragrant Hessian *Handkäse*—or farmer's cheese—and then rejoin his wife, who preferred to take no notice of what she knew full well he had done.

There is friendliness and often considerable sympathy when people speak today of Esther. But there is little warmth. What there is appears in tributes to her comeliness, and some insist that she was once the most beautiful woman in Hochburg.

Eleven months after their marriage, Marion, their only child, was born. The *Standesbeamter* is the town official who registers and keeps records of births, deaths, and marriages in a German town. The Hochburg Standesbeamter, in commenting on Marion and her parents, and the Hochburg Jewish community, said, "Yes, they were quite thoroughly assimilated. They were practically fellow citizens."

Who were these Hochburgers who were "practically fellow

citizens"? How long had it taken them to attain this status, and what were the circumstances of its attainment? What was the background of the Jewish community of which Sigmund Stein and his wife had become members, and into which their daughter was born?

The Hochburg Judengasse, "Jew Lane," was where the Jews lived six hundred years ago; it continued to appear on the maps of the town until as late as 1930. How long the Jews had been in Hochburg before 1325, the first documented date of their presence, is not ascertainable, but it had been long enough for the establishment of a synagogue. During the persecutions associated with the Black Death of 1348–1349, the Hochburg Jews fared better than their fellows in the surrounding countryside. This was in keeping with the generally rural character of these persecutions: the towns and cities offered a protection to the Jews which, however shaky, was non-existent in the open countryside and the villages.

In the middle of the fifteenth century, a monk, John of Capistrano, wandered through Germany, preaching nominally against the heresies of John Huss, but actually, and with grim effectiveness, against the Jews. There is no record that he came to Hochburg, but his fame and his teachings did. The result was the destruction of the synagogue, the stones of which now form part of the foundation of the regional health office.

The Jews were repeatedly harried out of the towns; just as repeatedly, they came back. Except when persecution was general, they were usually able to stay in the villages or in some temporarily more lenient town. They were never barred from Germany as a whole during this medieval period—as they were, for instance, from England. Some did leave the area, often emigrating to Poland and eastern Europe. But more of them remained.

In its own way, the nobility was glad to have the Jews around. Under the "sponge policy," the Jews, forbidden all occupations except trade and usury, would amass ready cash. Then, under one pretext or another, the princes would extort from the Jews what money they had, demanding special payments over and above the large number of taxes and fees which the Jews, for being Jews, had to pay regularly, and which made life without money impossible for them.

In 1524, Heinrich der Kluge decreed the eviction of the Jews from Hochburg; eight years later, needing money, he admitted them again on payment of "protection."

The sponge policy of the nobles, which was shared by the authorities in the towns, forced the Jews to exploit the common man—the peasant in the villages, the craftsman and small businessman in the towns. This use of the Jews blackened their image in folk cultures throughout Europe and created the feelings inadequately described as anti-Semitism. Later, when religious rationalizations for these feelings had been undermined by enlightenment, the tradition would find a new, racial basis.

Neither aspect of the Reformation—the social as embodied in the Peasant Revolts, the religious as embodied in the theological disputes—left the Jews of Hochburg and central Europe unscathed in the sixteenth century. The seventeenth century brought the Thirty Years' War, an entire generation when the religious, dynastic, personal, and nascent national interests of all Europe ground together where they came together: in Germany.

In the grinding everyone suffered, but the lowliest suffered the most. The population of the villages around Hochburg was halved and quartered by the ravages of one army, one mob of underpaid and underfed soldiers, after another. It was further reduced by disease and by flight to the comparative safety of Hochburg's walls and dominating fortress. Among the refugees were Jews from the villages, and in the complaints of the townspeople against the "beggars and Jews who have sneaked into our town" can be seen the harassment of the townspeople by conditions, as well as an irritability and insensitivity to the suffering of refugees which are still widely observable attitudes in men of the twentieth century.

The effort to expel the Jews from Hochburg continued in the years following the Peace of Westphalia which in 1648 ended the Thirty Years' War. How successful this effort was is not clear. It was revived repeatedly by groups like the Butchers' and Tanners' guilds which stood to gain from the removal of Jewish competition. It was supported by the municipal council and usually opposed by the officials of the Hessian Dukes. This opposition to expulsion has most often and with good reason been attributed to the financial interest of the state in the protection money pressed from the Jews.

Nevertheless, the appearance on the scene of a man like Karl, successor to Heinrich der Kluge, suggests that attitudes may not always have been as ignorant, insensitive, and piously narrow as they certainly were in the main. For Karl was a humanitarian who understood the causes of anti-Semitism among the people as well as the profound and petty malice of those who preached it. At one and the same time he recognized and disposed of the religious pretext for expulsion by arguing that one could not expel people for failing to accept Christ until they had been given a chance to see the light and *then* had rejected it.

Toward the end of the seventeenth century, the theory of the absolute state—with a powerful sovereign, a strong central administration, and an effective bureaucratic apparatus—took hold in the conglomerate of states which made up Germany. It seems almost ridiculous to associate this theory with these minuscule principalities, and yet what was possible in these tiny states then, as a consequence of their very smallness, has become possible in mammoth states now, as a consequence of technology.

The German Jews benefited from having the state replace local nobility as their protector. The Jews' financial burden continued heavy, but a degree of stability was introduced which was obviously preferable to the whims of a country baron or a town council. The upper bureaucracy became sure enough of itself to begin to acquire attitudes of tolerance and humanity, previously stultified by extreme localism. The Jewish community benefited directly by acquiring greater mobility among fewer barriers to commerce; indirectly, but significantly, by the increased importance of the *Hofjude,* or court Jew. Trusted adviser and often friend of the sovereign as he was, he was able to aid his fellow Jews more and more with the consolidation of the sovereign's realm.

These stabilizing trends are reflected in the growth of the Hochburg Jewish community over the late seventeenth and eighteenth centuries. In 1657 there were five Jews in Hochburg, and in 1700 only two families. By 1776, the number of families had increased to eight, three of which were still in Hochburg 150 years later. The prospect of sudden, mass expulsion gradually died out, though the threat of individual expulsion remained. The comings and goings of Jews (as of others) continued to be controlled. Near the end of the eighteenth century, the Hochburg municipal authorities decreed the removal of protection from any Schutzjude who gave lodgings to an out-of-town Jew, unless it was during one of the seasonal fairs and the outsider had notified the authorities in advance. It is interesting to learn that the resident Jews often supported such regulations and protested the granting of residence rights to new Jewish families or individuals.

Indeed, the anti-Jewishness which seems unmitigated from a distance and was, of course, real enough, is frequently qualified by details. Thus, the Hochburg town council supported the cases of particular Jews on occasion, sometimes against the citizenry as a whole, more often against the narrowly monopolistic tendencies of the guilds. Or, as happened in 1797, the Hochburg town council and leading citizens in the nearby village of Steindorf could combine to recommend that "an honorable and skillful cattle dealer from Mainz" be granted residence rights in Steindorf because an outbreak of cattle sickness there found no one competent to treat it. The "honorable and skillful cattle dealer" was, of course, a Jew.

The spread of the French Revolution into Germany and the incorporation of Hesse into the Napoleonic Kingdom of Westphalia confronted the Jews of Hochburg with the competition of loyalties mentioned earlier in connection with the Jews of Germany as a whole: how to respond to a foreign domination which gave them so much? The entire legal basis of all the restrictions and indignities which have been described was wiped away in December, 1808. Shortly thereafter a Jew was even named to the town council. It is no wonder that individual members of the Jewish community responded with loyalty and enthusiasm to the Napoleonic regime. After all, even the non-Jewish residents of Hochburg went to great lengths to celebrate when Jérôme Bonaparte did them the honor of spending the night in the town, and the one insurrection against French rule which was attempted in Hochburg was a comic opera affair, so little response did it awaken among the townspeople.

By and large, however, the Jews, like their non-Jewish townsmen, looked upon the French as intruders and occupiers. Among the rights of citizenship which the Jews obtained from the French, of course, was the right to be conscripted into the Napoleonic armies. However valued this may have been as a symbol of emancipation, it created disturbances in the family and home which the Jews had not previously known. In the end, the Hochburg Jewish community showed where its predominant loyalties lay when, in 1813, it sent sons, husbands, and fathers to fight along with the Prussian armies of liberation.

What this liberation meant soon became clear. The emancipation was castrated and the old business of protection, acceptance, and expulsion began again; that things never went back completely to what they had been before the French could hardly have been a great consolation. Emancipation continued to be in the air, and the fight against it had retreated to a last line of defense: "They aren't ready for it yet." But they were ready for it. The reaction to the revolutionary and Napoleonic epoch was a bigoted and short-sighted exploitation of resentment against French rule and of irrational and sentimental nostalgia for a very dead past. The reaction to the reaction came in the revolutionary ferments from 1825 to 1850.

It is not surprising that in this quarter-century of turmoil the Jews were viewed with suspicion by the powers-that-were. The Jews clearly wanted emancipation and were clearly destined to get it. Most of them minded their own business and viewed the radicalism of a relative or friend with as much discomfort as the next man. Often, in fact, their distress was greater, for the wayward individual Jew nearly always provided an occasion for general anti-Semitism. Nevertheless, the evident trend of the times had an unmistakable meaning for the Jews. Some of them, like Moses Goldstein in Hochburg, could not do other than commit themselves. Moses was convicted of hoisting the revolutionary banner over his house in the Schloss Strasse. He denied doing so, but the strength of his denial rested, ironically, on the incriminating fact that he was generally known to favor the revolutionary party; he argued that the flag had been hoisted over his house by provocateurs desiring to smear his philosophical radicalism with treason.

However painfully and grudgingly, society was opening up

for the German Jews. Their dependence on ways of life and thought that had been formed in isolation, exclusion, and persecution was diminishing. The gradual crumbling of non-religious barriers in combination with the emphasis which the post-Napoleonic reaction placed on the notion of the *Christian* state, threw the religious uniqueness of the Jews into bold relief; it assumed the character of the single remaining barrier to full participation in the rights and duties of citizens. Latent schismatic pressures were strengthened and new ones created. In Hochburg, where the Jewish population in 1850 consisted of between sixty-five and seventy-five individuals in fifteen families, such pressures had resulted in two sectarian offshoots from the old community. In the turbulent year 1848, the "New German Faith Comrades" and the "Convinced Believers" were formed. The three-way schism did not last long, at least officially, since in 1852 the regime required that all the Jews of a locality be registered in one and only one community. Because the reduced "old" community had not been able to keep up payments on the synagogue in the Schloss Strasse after the schism, the building had been sold. Now, with the reunification, it had to be repurchased—at some disadvantage, since the merchant who had bought it insisted on maintaining storage rights in the cellar.

During this same period, an obscurely interesting situation turned up in the vicinity of Hochburg. This was the presence of Jews in the robber bands of the area. These bands—one of them led by a man who called himself the Turnip King—had a vaguely Robin Hood character, preying on the rich and helping the poor. At one time, sixteen out of sixty members were reported to be Jews, and this suggests an extreme rejection of a social system which in all sanctioned ways was progressing with frustrating slowness toward the acceptance of the Jews as human beings. Chucking the whole thing over for a life outside society may well have had an appeal to which a few men, out of the idiosyncrasies of their development, responded.

The presence of a few Jews among the "foreign agitators" who were constantly and unconvincingly being turned up by the Hochburg police lends itself to a similar interpretation, but the fact that there were only four Jews among those uncovered between 1830 and 1848 suggests what was without doubt the truth: the large majority of Hochburg's Jews were God-fearing and law-abiding people who, like their fellow citizens, obeyed and believed in obeying.

The absorption of Hesse by Prussia in 1866 as a consequence of the Hessian Duke's having taken the Austrian side in the Prussian-Austrian war, and the full legal emancipation of the Jews three years later marked the beginning of a period during which the Hochburg Jewish community rapidly increased until it numbered 420 persons in 1900. With this growth—which occurred in the face of the strong tendency to use administrative prerogatives as a means of nullifying the emancipation of the Jews—the synagogue in the Schloss Strasse became too small, and a fine new synagogue was erected on the Landgraf Heinrichstrasse near the Phillipsplatz and the bridge which crosses the Felsen to the Felsendorf quarter.

By 1908, when Sigmund Stein came to Hochburg to attend the Gymnasium, a Jew was on the town council for the second time in municipal history. The development of the Hochburg Jewish community from 1800 to 1900 had been one from isolation to a definite, if still problematical, integration. The domestic inadequacies of the German-Jewish relationship were closely connected with the major questions which could be raised about Germany's position in the world community. Until that position had been established, there could be no guarantee of German-Jewish integration in the future. The First World War found the Jews heart and soul for Germany. The Weimar Republic presented them with a situation which, deceptively close to complete social emancipation, was actually the beginning of the end.

When the Standesbeamter said that the Jews were "practically fellow citizens," he did not realize the extent to which the truth of the statement—after six hundred years the Hochburg Jews still were not accorded complete acceptance—belied the gloss of his intention in making it: we really got along very well with the Jews.

Many Jewish children were born in Hochburg during the 1920's, and despite all the uncertainties of the time their parents looked to the future with the same confidence as Sigmund and Esther Stein. A place for Jews in the community seemed assured.

It was not unexpected, perhaps, for a Jew, Willi Schoenbaum, to have been the highly respected head of the local merchants' association. It *was*, however, surprising that old Meyer, the jeweler, should have been director of the *Turnverein*, the very Folkish gymnastics association. But Meyer, after all, was generally active in Hochburg affairs, and his shop was patronized by those who were interested in quality, fine craftsmanship, and fair prices. With Meyer, even the anti-Semites among his competitors kept their mouths shut until the Nazis were practically in; those who began talking then were the exceptions. People stuck by Meyer a long time. It was the ex-policeman, Schumann, who pointed to a handsome, deep-chiming grandfather's clock and said, "That's from Meyer. So is our silverware. We always traded at his place, even after '33, and finally Meyer used to come to us at night, as he did to other customers."

Other Jewish businessmen elicited the same degree of feeling. Frau Schmidt, wife of the baker in the four-hundred-year-old house in the Stadtplatz was first a lukewarm Nazi and then a lukewarm anti-Nazi. She had obviously accepted the traditional picture of the Jews as it had been further distorted by specifically Nazi retouchings. Just as obviously, she had always had reservations in favor of the Jews based on particular personal experiences.

"No Christian," she says, "would have treated my husband and me the way Herr Solomon did. He had a grain business in the Flachstrasse. My husband and I were engaged to be married just before the First World War, and in order to start up the business he borrowed two thousand marks from Herr Solomon. Well, the war came along and my husband had to go. When he came back, we wanted to get married, but there was all that money to repay. We decided to call on Herr Solomon, and we did and we talked and Herr Solomon didn't bring up the question of the money at all. So finally my husband did and told him how worried we were about getting married and all. Well, Herr Solomon just said, 'In heaven's name, don't let that stop you from getting married. You just go ahead and pay back the money as you can.' So we got married and the business did pretty well, and when we had paid off an amount equal to the capital, what did Herr Solomon do but say we shouldn't pay any more!"

"Of course," she adds, "Herr Solomon also traded in brown coal briquets, the kind we had to use for our ovens. We had bought them from him from the beginning and naturally we continued to do so, so I don't suppose he lost anything in the long run. We continued to buy from him after the Nazis came in and were called 'Jew-lovers' for doing so, but we had a perfect right to, and he had been awfully nice to us."

The shoemaker, Johannes Kaiser, a Social Democrat and long-time member of that party's militia, the *Reichsbanner*, also has good words to say for Herr Solomon because of the kindnesses which Solomon showed toward Kaiser's father. It is Kaiser who says that he had never heard the word "anti-Semitism" until his father went to work for a professor in Hochburg University who was a known anti-Semite.

There were anti-Semites among both students and faculty at the University in the twenties. But there were also Jews, and the position of the Jewish faculty members in the Hochburg Jewish community merits consideration.

One Jewish professor is said to have been both nationalistic and anti-Semitic, and if the combination is bizarre, it is also suggestive. Another, Professor Mendelsohn, head of the Near East Institute, was not anti-Semitic and only mildly nationalistic. He was a cultured man and a profound scholar, the son of a Prussian army officer who had been one of the few Jews to attain that rank during the Franco-Prussian War, was inordinately proud of that fact, and saw in it a confirmation of his faith in Germany as well as of his rejection of Eastern Jews. The son was more tolerant, though *his* daughter describes him as having been unable to stomach the orthodoxy of the Hochburg synagogue community. Both before and after 1933 there were repeated contacts between the Mendelsohn family and Sigmund Stein, who always addressed the professor as "Herr Professor" but who was addressed by the professor as "Herr Stein" and not "Herr Doktor."

Frau Professor Mendelsohn was a Christian, her husband Jewish. With three other leading Hochburg professors it was the other way around: the professors were Christians, their wives Jewish. With each of them it seems to have been a matter of the poor but promising young scholar who married a Jewish girl of wealth and social standing.

Professor Wilhelm Stadtmaier brought numerous honorary degrees to himself and fame to Hochburg University by his brilliant researches in the physiology of aging. He was a scholar of conscience, skill, and insight. Nevertheless, his productive devotion to his studies would have been difficult had it not been for the financial security which his wife, Hermione, born Rothschild, had brought him. He himself acknowledged this frequently, publicly, and without embarrassment. It was a known and accepted fact in Hochburg. Professor Stadtmaier died in 1929. His wife survived him by eight years, and when she passed away even the enthusiastically Nazi paper, the *Hessische Landeskurier*, had good words to say of her.

Frau Professor von Schlegel, wife of a renowned chemist, was regarded by most people in Hochburg as having been a lovely woman who never thrust herself forward and who ran the big house on the hill with gentleness and consideration for all who worked there. In the early thirties the landscaping of the Castle Park behind the von Schlegel mansion was one of the public works which were being used to absorb the increasing number of unemployed. Frau Professor von Schlegel used to go out every day to invite the men on the project to come to her yard for *Butterbrot* sandwiches with wurst and coffee. "And probably," adds the wife of the man who was caretaker of the von Schlegel house and who herself was housekeeper and governess, "there were men among those unemployed who later joined in the persecution of the old lady which the Nazi louts began after the professor's death in 1936." Frau Dienstbach speaks with undimmed bitterness. She hated and she hates the Nazis, both for what they did to the von Schlegels and for the way they tormented her and her husband, who was a Communist. She was especially bitter about the "Aryan" lawyer patronized by the von Schlegels for years. After the old professor died, the lawyer became apprehensive and refused to represent them any longer. The result was that the family took on the services of the defrocked lawyer, Sigmund Stein, developing a connection which was to have fateful consequences for both parties.

Frau Professor Stadtmaier, Frau Professor von Schlegel, as well as the wife of the less eminent professor of political economy, Karl Gottfried, were not and are not looked upon as members of the Hochburg Jewish community. This is chiefly a matter of social status. Professors and the wives of professors formed the elite of Hochburg. The two prayer leaders in the synagogue were a paint merchant and a shoe wholesaler. But when it came to the Jews, the Nazis were great levelers, and after 1933 the barriers of status among the Hochburg Jews were cracked and broken if never entirely destroyed.

The Jewish members of the Hochburg academic world excepted, the Jewish community of Stein's time presents an appearance of cohesiveness which is deceptive. One reason for this is the bleak fact that it is no longer there to be seen in its variety and human complexity. Another reason is the fact that the community had a legal embodiment as the synagogue congregation, so that the synagogue itself was a concrete and meaningful symbol.

Perhaps the most important reason for the apparent cohesiveness of the Jewish community was the attitude toward the Jews which prevailed in the twenties: the deeply rooted, vaguely negative view of them as a group apart, as tolerated heretics in a culture which thought itself Christian. This was not the anti-Semitism of the Nazis: it was compatible with friendly relationships with Jews as individuals and lack of malice toward them as a group. But it was the soil out of which Nazism, fertilized by a conjunction of other factors, had been able to grow.

The Hochburg Jewish community that Sigmund knew, of course, contained the splits which always hide behind the façade of human institutions. That the community is generally described as having been very orthodox is certainly consistent with Professor Mendelsohn's rejection of it. Sigmund Oppenheimer, one of the two Jews who remained in Hochburg during the entire Nazi era, was a humanist and non-doctrinaire Socialist. The other, a tailor, Casimir Dombrowski, retains an inclination toward the orthodoxy brought with him when he came to Hochburg as a Russian prisoner of war in 1916. He looks upon the Hochburg community as not very pious, saying, "In other places they used to go to the synagogue every morning, but here they went only on the Sabbath and the feast days." Yet it was the fact that both these men had married Christian women which was primarily responsible for their later escaping the Nazi net.

Many members of the community were relatively orthodox; adherence to the dietary laws was usual as was the avoidance of work on the Sabbath. One thing, however, was clear: the Eastern, the Caftan Jew was rejected by the community, and this rejection, motivated as it was mainly by social considerations, could not help rubbing off on the Eastern Jew's strict religious orthodoxy.

In the twenties, there were several Eastern Jewish families in Hochburg. Some, like the family of Itzig Mandelbaum, had been in Hochburg prior to 1914. Others had come after the end of the First World War. They are described by Jewish and non-Jewish Hochburgers alike with condescending tolerance, though there is often a surprising admixture of warmth from many non-Jewish Hochburgers of the lower classes.

For instance, Isidore was the youngest of the three Morgenstern brothers. The father and the two older brothers peddled soap, but Isidore is said to have been touched in the head and, because of his shambling figure, his hands forever in his pockets, and his whistling, he was teased by children—and remembered with sentimental affection by the adults who were those children. It is clear that the tolerance and affection of Christians for the Mandelbaums and Morgensterns were greatly aided by the extreme social distance from these Eastern Jews with their strange ways and dress. For the other Hochburg Jews, very many of whose fathers or grandfathers had been just as "strange," there was no such social distance. The Jews from Poland and Galicia could only represent a regression and threat, their social and religious customs an embarrassment and an unwanted reminder.

From 1919 to 1935 the synagogue community was led by Rabbi Levy, who was also head of the Hochburg Jewish Community Board of Governors, the official embodiment of the community. Assisting the rabbi, as advisers and delegates from the people in the community were, for most of the period, Dr. Mannheimer, the lawyer; Willi Schoenbaum, the merchant; and Tannenbaum, the banker. The Board of Governors met once a month with the *Landrat,* or District Commissioner, who was also in charge of official relationships with Protestants and Catholics in the Hochburg area. During the late twenties and until the Nazis took power in 1933, Landrat Staerke, a Catholic anti-Nazi, held the office. Staerke asserts that there was "a certain rivalry" for his attention and favor between the orthodox and religiously conservative members of the community, as represented by Rabbi Levy, and the more liberal members, as represented by Tannenbaum the banker. The conservatives had the advantage in this rivalry because the nature of Staerke's position demanded more contact with the Rabbi than with other members of the board.

Landrat Staerke remembers the name of Sigmund Stein and the fact that he had been a lawyer; he thinks he had met Sigmund once or twice at meetings with the officers of the Jewish community. He is sure, however, that Sigmund was not regularly connected with this body.

Sigmund Stein and Werner Hagen of course *did* belong to the Hochburg Jewish community. Their membership was both social and religious, though in each of these respects the two partners differed appreciably from one another. By all accounts Hagen was a devout and conscientious Jew, even though, as his widow says, he was practical about it and, for instance, avoided wearing a beard, since he felt it would not be proper for him to appear in court with one. Descriptions of Sigmund Stein's religious position show great variation. Esther Stein is said to have adhered strictly to the dietary laws, but all sources agree that Sigmund believed in eating what was available when he was hungry. He was never described as orthodox, though some say he was truly, if informally, religious. Others, however, say that he was a free-thinker, and some go so far as to assert that he was an atheist. A rabbi who knew and liked him spoke of him as "a Jew in name only." He attended the synagogue on the Sabbath and the high holidays only and not always then.

Yet the nature and strength of Sigmund's commitment to his Jewishness appear in several ways. School Inspector Wiegand, Sigmund's onetime associate in the Democratic State party, points out an interesting contrast between Sigmund and Herr Mannheimer, owner of the Mannheimer drygoods store. Speaking of the way Sigmund combined his Jewishness and his Germanness, Wiegand says, "Oh yes, he had a wonderful way of somehow harmonizing these two aspects of his life. Some of the Jews seemed unable to do so. Take Mannheimer, for instance. He was always telling stories which showed the Jews up in a bad or ridiculous light. It was painful to see because it seemed so obvious that he was trying to ingratiate himself with the non-Jewish world. Sigmund never told such stories."

Herr Franz Wilhelm had been a social worker in Felseneck, a town about ten miles up the Felsen River from Hochburg. As such, he had first encountered Sigmund in the early thirties, when the latter occasionally represented the accused father in paternity cases. A friendship grew up which was to survive many of the difficulties of the Nazi era. Wilhelm is fond of referring to Sigmund as *"ein geschulter Bauer,"* a peasant with schooling. Nevertheless, he asserts, Sigmund was insistent on one point: the undesirability of intermarriage between Jews and Christians.

For Sigmund to have denied his Jewishness would have meant denying his family. And it was especially in the late twenties and early thirties that his attachment to his family, his widowed father, and his Aunt Emma in Bachdorf was underlined by his frequent visits to the village. These were the years when, according to Trina Koehler, there were almost daily telephone calls from Meta, or David, or Sigmund, and when, during visits, "it was Papa this and Papa that all the time." Sigmund made such visits more often than the others, since he was able to combine them with professional appearances in the District Court at Weidenberg. But they all came, sometimes alone and sometimes with wife or husband and children. And if Sigmund's Esther was "a little bit too refined for the Dienstmaedchen and the villagers," Sigmund himself was not and pooh-poohed the attempts of the villagers to call him "Herr Doktor."

Politically, the Hochburg Jewish community was middle class —at least this is the image it left behind. The image is unquestionably accurate in a general way, as is indicated by the jeweler Meyer's leadership of the Gymnastic League, Willi Schoenbaum's respected position as head of the merchants' association, and the presence of Jews in important positions of the veterans' organizations and the board of education. Perhaps most striking in this regard were the many community activities of the banker Tannenbaum, as detailed in an adulatory article in Hochburg's Social Democratic daily, the *Taegliches Hessenblatt,* early in 1930. Tannenbaum, it seems, was a director of the home for the aged, the local Group Health Board, the Chamber of Commerce, the Hochburg Tourist Association, and the Museum League!

One or two Jews in Hochburg are said to have been members of the extremely nationalistic and conservative *Deutsch-nationale Volkspartei,* or DNVP. This was unusual, not only because of the racist innuendos which were current in this German National People's party, but also because the national outlook of the Jews was ordinarily broader than the narrow one represented by the group. Nevertheless, it is possible that the individuals named were members of the DNVP. The party did have Jewish members, and its leader and presidential candidate in 1932, Duesterberg, was the great grandson of a Jew—although this came as an embarrassing revelation rather than an attempt to lure Jewish membership.

Heinrich Preusser, who was active in the Hochburg Communist party both before and after 1933, shares the opinion that Hochburg's Jews had been middle class, "although," he adds, "they —and especially Hagen and Stein—were friendly toward the working man." Nevertheless, Johannes Kaiser, the shoemaker and old Reichsbanner man, comments on how many of the Hochburg Jews supported that militantly republican organization, some of them with active participation, more with financial support, and a few, such as Werner Hagen and Sigmund Stein, with both.

Friedrich Michael, who for several years up to 1933 was regional adjutant of the Reichsbanner, says that Sigmund was active in the organization, and tells of Sigmund's swapping tales of his World War experiences with other members at the meetings. "Of course," Michael explains, "Sigmund was not a Social Democrat, but was instead a member of the Democratic State party. He was in any event a sturdy and able supporter of the democratic ideal." Michael's opinion of Hagen, on the other hand, is a friendly though critical comment to the effect that Hagen was more of a materialist and kept an eye out for profit and loss.

Heinrich Konrad, who was treasurer of the Reichsbanner, gives a somewhat different picture. He describes Werner Hagen as the more active Reichsbanner man, and Sigmund as a comparatively passive participant. But both men, he asserts, had a little money to spare and that had been welcome. Herr Konrad attributes Sigmund's less active participation to his greater bourgeois respectability. Sigmund belonged, according to this extreasurer of the Reichsbanner, to that group of people who believed in democracy and the republic—the only prerequisites for membership in the organization—but whose chief contribution was financial.

Certainly the German Jews were patriotic; they may even have been more genuinely so than their non-Jewish fellows. Sigmund Stein, attached as he was to his village roots, had developed above and beyond them, and this was characteristic of many Jews of his and the preceding generation. Under the often reluctant aegis of the German state, the Jews had made gains in fifty years which had surpassed those they had been allowed to make in ten centuries by German local principalities. There was gratitude for this, and this gratitude was turned toward the state and fostered patriotism to that state; it did not refer, except by indirection and reflection, to local conditions. The patriotism of many non-Jewish Germans, on the other hand, tends to be an inflated and projected home-town spirit.

Sigmund Stein loved the country around Hochburg and Bachdorf; he was nostalgic for the village life of his childhood, both as it really was and as he imagined it to have been. Yet his connection with his childhood was less genuine and less immediate than that between most Hochburgers or Bachdorfers and their childhoods. He collected paintings by a well-known Hessian genre artist: landscapes, costumed peasants, the typical timber-framed houses. But the peasants were peasants, worked in the landscapes, wore the costumes, and lived in the houses. Sigmund was a Knut Hamsun enthusiast, yet much as he went beyond the books to the soil itself, he was not "of" the soil as were the peasants who could not read.

There is little question but that Sigmund Stein and Werner Hagen felt that they were integrated with the Hochburg scene, and by the round of their daily activities contributed to the overall integration of the Jewish community with that scene. It is a moot point as to which contributed more: the business associations of the lawyers, Hagen and Stein, the friendliness of a Herr Solomon or of the storytelling Herr Mannheimer, or the leading position of a man like the banker Tannenbaum. Officer Schumann recalls the name and the importance of Tannenbaum, but he becomes sentimental over the way Herr Mannheimer would stand in front of his drygoods store of a morning and, seeing Schumann, would call him over, offer him a cigar, and be ready and willing to while away a half-hour or so with a chat.

In the end, however, all such integration was insufficient to stave off the coming catastrophe, and Officer Schumann did his duty as correctly under the Nazis as he had under the Republic. The Jews were able and willing to be fellow citizens; it was the environment which added the "almost."

[An airy ghetto]

When Sigmund Stein moved to Hochburg with his bride, Esther, he was settling in a town where the Jews had long since ceased to live in any one section, let alone in the vicinity of the Judengasse, which nonetheless still bore this name so reminiscent of the crowded ghettos of earlier times. Sigmund and Esther first lived in an apartment on the Bergsteigweg. That is what the street does— it climbs the hill, circuitously, through the old part of town to the castle. It is a residential street, though no location on it is far from the Kirchdorfstrasse where Hagen and Stein's first law office was located, or from the center of the old town, the Markt-platz. Like so many other streets on the hill, it affords the man walking to work or the casual stroller repeatedly changing vistas of seasonal greenness on the nearby hills and the more constant blueness of the distant reaches of the northern Felsental in the billowy Hessian landscape.

Sigmund's landlord was not Jewish; there were, of course, Jewish property owners in Hochburg, and Jewish families, if not concentrated in any one part of town, did occur in clusters. Yet isolated families and individuals were common enough, and Sigmund's domicile in a non-Jewish house was scarcely exceptional. People in Hochburg, then as now, live mostly in apartments; both home ownership and mortgages are less frequent there than in a comparable American town. Apartment or single-family home, most dwellings in Hochburg have their student "digs"—a single housekeeping room almost always let out to a University student, thereby adding to the family income as well as compensating for the scarcity of dormitories at the University.

Jewish addresses were scattered over the whole town, and their locations varied across the entire spectrum of "niceness." Herr Meyer, the jeweler, had a fine mansion in the Dominikanerstrasse, which leads out of the old town through what was once one of its main gates. It is still a good address to have in Hochburg, but in the twenties it was an even better one. The Mandelbaums, on the other hand, together with relatives more recently arrived from Poland, lived in the Enggasse, the appropriately named "Narrow Lane." Crowded though it is, this street is neither dirty nor run down. The Enggasse is on the opposite side of the castle hill from the Bergsteigweg, and is closer to the marketplace. The slope of the hill is steeper on that side, and the cobblestones of the Enggasse were on about the same level as, and not far from, the dome of the "new" synagogue in the Landgraf Heinrich Strasse.

Many Jews in Hochburg lived in or near their places of business, but this is not mentioned by residents of the town, perhaps because it was by no means unique to the Jews. Naturally, since most of the businesses in Hochburg are concentrated along the Windstrasse, the Bahnhofstrasse, or around the Marktplatz, most of the Jewish businesses appear in these areas.

But the Hochburg Jewish community did not have a geographical center residentially or commercially. The Jewish *Volkschule*—Esther Stein was to be on its board of directors along with the wives of Tannenbaum the banker and Meyer the jeweler—was a common concern of Hochburg's Jewish residents in the twenties. Small as it was, however, and located in the building which served as the Catholic parish house and parochial school, it provided no strong focus of community interest—and it prepared the children who attended it for their entrance into the entirely non-segregated environment of the higher schools.

Sometime in the twenties, the Boarding Home for Jewish Students in the Humboldtallee had become the residence of the rabbi who served Hochburg and the surrounding area. The place of the Humboldtallee Boarding Home was taken by a newer building in the Helenastrasse, closer to both the synagogue and the Gymnasium; gradually, in the years before 1933, it became less a boarding home for pupils of the Hochburg area than a home and school for crippled and defective Jewish children from all over Germany. Werner Hagen was elected to its governing board in 1931 along with Banker Tannenbaum.

There were other organizations devoted to Jewish community affairs: the Association of Jewish Men, the Association of Jewish Women, the Jewish Charitable Committee, and an Association for the Promotion of Jewish History and Literature. Existence of such other organizations as a Jewish Veterans League is asserted but not recorded. The record of the Central Union of German Citizens of Jewish Faith in Hochburg does not begin until after the Nazis had assumed control, at which time Sigmund Stein appears as the director. The later record nevertheless suggests that a Hochburg chapter of the organization was founded in the late twenties.

It is difficult to know how active these organizations were; on the one hand, the widow of the man who had been teacher in the Jewish elementary school writes that she was forced to leave a community which she remembers as blooming with institutional life and activity. On the other hand, Frau Hagen reports that the Jews in Hochburg had always been a little reticent, and several non-Jewish residents supported this opinion.

The Jewish religious community was physically represented by the imposing synagogue on the Landgraf Heinrich Strasse, which forms the effective boundary between the flats of the Sumpf-viertel on the one side and the foot of the hill which rises up through the old town to the castle on the other side. The synagogue was on the hill side of the Landgraf Heinrich Strasse; directly behind it and looming over it was the massive base of what had once been part of the town's fortifications. The masonry of this base fronts a natural or man-made cliff and shows at one point a cylindrical swelling which must once have been the base of a tower. The length of this masonry, which runs behind the open space where the synagogue stood and the Landgraf Heinrich Institute of the University next to it, is topped by houses which face on the Enggasse, and the structure of many of these houses incorporates material which became available when the upper-works of the old wall were torn down in the eighteenth century. Some of the houses are newer, and here and there narrow streets between them give the effect of crenellation. Before the synagogue was destroyed in 1938, these little streets permitted an occasional view from the Enggasse directly to the dome and topmost walls of the synagogue. The Landgraf Heinrich Strasse was a part of Hochburg's only tramline; hence the synagogue was especially accessible. It was a fine site for a synagogue or any other public building.

In this airy ghetto Sigmund Stein started out by supporting his family and went on to become a successful attorney. His progress is indicated by his changes of address.

In 1927 he moved from the apartment in the Bergsteigweg to the Oberteichstrasse, which is nearer to the outskirts of the town and a pleasanter place for a three-year-old-girl than the Bergsteigweg. In Hochburg, however, differences of this kind are not great, and it cannot be assumed that this was the chief reason for the move.

The Oberteichstrasse, being fifteen minutes' walk from Sigmund's office in the Kirchdorfstrasse, was practically suburbia for Hochburg. It was a somewhat "nicer" address than the Bergsteigweg and in it, for the first time, Sigmund had a personal, residential telephone. This improvement in neighborhood and the larger living space were among the chief reasons for the move.

A second move, in 1931, to the apartment in the Dietrichstrasse was a definite residential step upward. The building in which the Stein apartment was located was a new and pleasant one, and the site, on the corner of the Dietrichstrasse and the main route south from Hochburg, the Mainzerstrasse, was both respectable and convenient. It was about as far from the center of town as the Oberteichstrasse address, but on the opposite side of Castle Hill. The apartment itself was appreciably larger than the one just left, more comfortably appointed, and—a real hallmark of modernity— had central heating.

The success of Hagen and Stein's practice justified these steps up the residential ladder, although they were undoubtedly aided by the modest wealth which Esther Stein had brought into the marriage. The frequent comment that Sigmund did well enough not to need his wife's money is given some support by the fact that each of his residential moves was paralleled by a change of business address. The office in the Kirchdorfstrasse was small and not really set up for two lawyers in partnership. Hence, even before Sigmund moved his family from the Bergsteigweg to the Oberteichstrasse, he and Hagen had concluded that their business quarters were inadequate and had transferred them to a larger, if somewhat less centrally located, address in the Hospitallerstrasse, which continues the Teichstrasse beyond the square in front of the Ursula Church through the lowland at the foot of Castle Hill to the Felsen River.

This new office was next to the chocolate wholesale business of Johannes Huss, an old friend of Hagen's and a client of Hagen and Stein as he had been of Hagen before the partnership was formed. Johannes Huss's widow is a source of many stories about Hagen and Stein and about their partnership. It would almost appear that the Husses became better friends of both the Hagens and the Steins than these two families were of each other.

In the same block of buildings with Hagen and Stein and the Huss business was the office of the Social Democratic daily, the *Taegliches Hessenblatt*. The man who was printing this paper when Hagen and Stein moved to the Hospitallerstrasse, and who was to become its owner and editor in 1930, was Konrad Muenschner. Johannes Huss was an active Social Democrat. Konrad Muenschner was Social Democratic in his sympathies, which were reinforced when he took over the paper. Werner Hagen was a Social Democrat and Sigmund Stein, however his love of country and his attitudes toward "blood and soil" may have shaded his political commitment, was a Liberal Democrat. Thus it is hardly startling that the physical nearness of these men to one another came to increase their ideological proximity.

In contrast to the friendly familial relation with the Husses, however, Sigmund's connections with Konrad Muenschner seem to have remained at a professional and ideological level. The *Taegliches Hessenblatt,* although it had been in existence for fifty years and had a core of faithful subscribers, was not flourishing. Expansions and improvements were made less out of skimpy or nonexistent profits than out of gifts and interest-free loans from those who supported its policies. Both Hagen and Stein were among those who contributed in this way, and both came to participate to some degree in the management of the paper. Understandably, there were occasional references to both men in the regular court reporting which the paper offered. This feature was character-ized by the fact that the names of the litigants and attorneys were mentioned only in important cases. Muenschner says that this reticence was customary and accorded with the desires of both the court and the participants. Fortunately, Hagen and Stein were in-volved in enough important cases so that newspaper accounts form an important source of details about their professional activities.

Shortly before or after Sigmund moved from the Oberteich-strasse to the Dietrichstrasse, he and Hagen moved their office once again, this time to the corner of the Bahnhofstrasse and the Wiesenstrasse near the bridge which carries the former over the Felsen River and not far from the main railroad station. This of-fice was even less centrally located than the Hospitallerstrasse, but both commercially and professionally it was a better address.

Soon after the move to the Bahnhofstrasse, both Hagen and Stein passed an important, if undramatic, milestone in their legal careers. They acquired the status of notaries and were therefore allowed to certify wills, deeds, and other legal documents. Hagen achieved this status in the normal course of events, because in Germany all lawyers automatically become notaries after ten years of practice, and in 1931 Werner Hagen had been practicing for that length of time. Sigmund Stein had not, but was permitted to count his war service in establishing his eligibility.

No man's life is defined by his addresses, yet Sigmund Stein's changes of address are important interactions between Sigmund and the community in which they occurred. All of them produced at least some resonances which would echo into the future.

7

[The law firm of Hagen and Stein]

In the early thirties, Sigmund Stein, Werner Hagen, and Mordecai Mannheimer were the only Jewish lawyers in Hochburg. Sigmund and Werner were partners; they had a flourishing general practice and an excellent reputation. Mordecai Mannheimer had been established longer, with a more specialized practice and a poorer reputation. Politically, Mannheimer's interests and activities were few and contrasted in their conservatism with the known liberal leanings of Hagen and Stein.

There is no need to doubt the statements which are now made about Hagen and Stein's popularity as lawyers. They were respected by the courts, where Sigmund's moderate and down-to-earth presentation of cases was complemented by Hagen's legal acumen and frequent sharp in-fighting. Generally, they were known for their vigor in pursuing a case.

Real as this situation of the partners was, a closer look dis-

89

closes shadows, which cluster mainly around the figure of Hagen. When these shadows are associated with specific complaints, they have their source in the legal community, in men who came up against Hagen in the courts. Hagen's general reputation was less favorable than Sigmund's, but this general reputation revealed little of the bitterness which appeared in some of the statements by his legal colleagues.

A few of these erstwhile colleagues had been on friendly personal and professional terms with both men. As far as Hagen was concerned, however, they did not deny the fact of his less favorable reputation but merely showed a willingness to look behind and around it. They agreed that Hagen was a sharpshooter whose quick and bitter tongue sometimes got the best of him in court. But they were willing to attribute this to his wartime head wound, willing to acknowledge the benefit to his clients which often went with Hagen's aggressiveness. And they suggested that the most rancid opinions of Hagen would come from lawyers who had lost cases to him. This seems to be true, yet the sins and lesser failings of which Hagen was accused had at most an indirect relation to his position as a lawyer.

One of these sins was avariciousness. At some point, Hagen and Stein are supposed to have had only one set of judicial robes between them. These were in such tatters that the judge at the Hochburg District Court asked Hagen if he could not, please, get a new robe, since it hardly befitted the dignity of the court to have lawyers appear in rags. The narrator of this story, now district attorney in a large West German city, had been a young Referendar at the time. Unresponsive to the humor in the story of the robes, he went on to tell of a party he had attended at the Hagen's. At the end of the evening, when the departing guests went to the bedroom to get their coats, Hagen drew attention to the finely carved and crafted bedroom set and explained how a client had made it for him as a way of paying his bill.

Frau Kuerschner is not an anti-Semite; she is mainly concerned with the fact that Hagen had been her dead husband's boss. Until his death in 1929, Herr Kuerschner was office manager at Hagen and Stein's. According to Frau Kuerschner, Hagen held the purse strings of the firm, and it is probable that up to 1929 he did have more of a say-so in financial matters than Sigmund, the junior partner. Kuerschner had gone to Hagen and Stein because they paid well.

Sometime in the mid-twenties, Hagen suggested that he pay a portion of Kuerschner's salary in stocks and bonds. Kuerschner agreed to this and by the time of his death had accumulated a modestly substantial interest-bearing nest egg. However, when Frau Kuerschner went to Hagen to take possession of the capital, he laughed in her face. Doctor Stein was friendly, she says, but his hands were tied.

This is Frau Kuerschner's story. In her telling of it, there is neither explicit nor implicit reference to the fact that Hagen was a Jew. But there is vast bitterness at his avarice. Yet the clue to the situation is obvious. She went to Hagen not with her husband's will, but with the record of the payments. And the reason she didn't go with his will was that he was not her husband! He was her brother-in-law with whom she had been living in a common law arrangement since her sister's death.

The evidence for Hagen's "avariciousness" is not always so transparent. Sometimes it is opaque. Frau Wolff-Foerster is a Jewish woman who, as the wife of a Christian physician, survived the Nazi era in Hochburg. She remains angry and resentful about the way Hagen, as she claims, defrauded her father out of a large sum of money. Unquestionably, there was an arrangement between her father and Werner Hagen, with her father thinking that Hagen had welshed on it. Yet he never brought suit, and the accusation of fraud could easily come from a situation in which one loses the dice when the lights are low in a sharp deal.

Frau Wolff-Foerster's father, Heinrich Wolff, was a legal adviser, a recognized status in Germany attained without university training or apprenticeship, by passing an examination. The legal adviser's lack of academic training means that he is not a respectable member of the legal community. Herr Wolff's reputation and activities will continue to play a role in the context of Sigmund Stein's life. That reputation is one of many hues, and Hochburg newspapers of the early thirties contain material which suggests that Wolff's fringe position in the Hochburg legal community was not an easy one to sustain without getting mixed up in dubious transactions.

He was also on the fringe of the Hochburg Jewish community and was one of two people whose status as a Jew was not generally known in the town. Werner Hagen's widow expressed surprise upon learning that Wolff was a Jew, and while she is aware that her husband had had dealings with him, she says that she had little contact with business associates of her husband other than Sigmund Stein.

Heinrich Wolff was one of the least respectable members of the Hochburg legal community. Mordecai Mannheimer possessed the golden key of academic training and was a bona fide lawyer; yet his respectability in the Hochburg legal community was marred by his reputation as a skinflint and gouger. Only lack of the right family background kept Hagen and Stein from complete respectability.

It was the custom of the Hochburg Lawyers' Association to hold a ball each year, the announcement and invitation being posted in the lawyers' room of the Hochburg District Court. One year, Hagen, Stein, and Mannheimer decided to attend this festivity. Together with their wives they did so, and the experience was so unpleasant that this first time became the last. Frau Hagen, Konrad Muenschner, and Dr. Muehlenbach, dean emeritus of the Hochburg legal community, all comment on the bravado of Hagen, Stein, and Mannheimer. Frau Hagen notes merely that the Jewish lawyers had never before attended the ball. Muehlenbach, who as a Freemason seems to have retained decency if not asserted heroism during the Nazi period, says with a revealing innocence that he does not think anti-Semitism was involved but simply the fact that the non-Jewish lawyers were not accustomed to having their Jewish colleagues attend.

Muenschner, as ex-editor of the *Taegliches Hessenblatt,* is more sophisticated. He relates his assertion that it was "daring" of the three men even to think of going to the ball to his belief that the Jewish lawyers were looked upon as "intruders" who were "proletarianizing" the exclusive circle of the Hochburg legal profession. Muenschner says that Hagen and Stein were definitely better lawyers than the rest of the lot, whom he described as a lazy crew. He deals with criticisms of commercialism and the handling of dubious cases when he says, "Sure, Sigmund and Werner got mixed up in messy affairs. They were the only ones who'd take the case of a man who obviously didn't have a cent to his name. They were human, and over the years they made money, but they were the only ones in town who adjusted their fees according to a man's ability to pay. That bed business is a good case in point. The man needed a lawyer; he was unemployed and couldn't pay. But he was a good carpenter and felt he had something to offer in return for legal services. Hagen and Stein were the only ones who would take it."

Muenschner's view of the difference between Hagen and Stein is atypical, though not inconsistent with the more common views on this point. He says that it lay in the extent to which the two men were absorbed in their practice. Hagen was all business, on the street as well as in the office. Sigmund, Muenschner says, left the business behind when he left the office. Hagen was not choleric or irritable; on the contrary, he was always master of himself—too much so, perhaps, but it paid off. Once, Muenschner was in court with Hagen and Stein as his counsel. The opposing attorney made statements which were so farfetched as to be ridiculous; Muenschner and Sigmund laughed heartily at them. But not Werner Hagen, who instead went on busily taking notes which then enabled him to make a devastating rebuttal by quoting word for word the fantastic statements of the opposition.

There is disagreement about the details of the "difference" between Hagen and Stein, with some sources going so far as to assert that Sigmund showed a growing dislike for Werner during the years leading up to the Nazi coup. Otto Knopf, who inflated his position as a long-time clerk in Hagen and Stein's office to that of office manager, but whose statements otherwise have proved reliable, says that there was no rift between the two men during this period. Yet he does say that Sigmund was not happy about their taking as many political cases as they did.

Most of the cases handled by Hagen and Stein, however, had no political applications. Some of them are notably typical of the era and of the Hochburg region.

The region is mirrored in the predominantly rural setting of these cases. There was, to be sure, crime in Hochburg itself, and Officer Schumann's nostalgic reminiscences about the "good old days," when order prevailed and one could walk alone from Hochburg to Berlin with a bag of silver and never be molested, are thrown into proper relief by Schumann's own accounts of the three murders which occurred in thirty years, of the bicycle thievery, of the petty larceny of food for sustenance, and of the two instances when Meyer's jewelry store was robbed. There was crime in Hochburg itself. But not much.

Most of the cases which appeared before the Hochburg courts had their origins in the villages of the region, where policemen were scarce and where the village lads occasionally got fed up with bucolic peace—a boredom which must not be overlooked as adding to the appeal of the Nazi agitation in the countryside. Perhaps their boredom explains the relatively frequent paternity suits and the occasional case in which incest figured. Crimes of violence —often assault and battery with fatal consequences—seem to have been numerous enough.

The era is mirrored in Hagen and Stein's cases of the early thirties by the extent to which they show the effects of the depression and by their increasing political coloring. In 1931 and 1932 the number of "politically motivated breaches of the public peace" shows a drastic increase.

One locally famous case was that of the Mühlhausen Spotlight Poachers which Hagen and Stein carried through the courts from early 1931 until late 1932. Game has always been strictly protected in Germany, and poaching has always been punishable. It has, however, always existed. In the village of Mühlhausen, among the hills and forests between Hochburg and Bachdorf, the people said there had never been so much poaching as in 1930. Chances are that most of them knew who was doing it, but what were foresters for if not to attend to such matters?

And indeed, the foresters were on the alert. All during November, 1930, shots had rung out at night in the forest; carcasses of animals killed illegally with buckshot had been found, along with blood and drag marks in the early snows. In December, the chief forester reported that he had had to shoot a deer which seemed to have a broken leg; on superficial examination, however, he found that the leg had been injured by shot. He concluded his report by writing, "A more careful examination was unfortunately precluded by the fact that the leg, which I had cut off in order to dissect and examine it, was eaten by my dogs."

Often, when blood and drag marks were found, they led to a road and then disappeared. Eventually, a light snowfall enabled the forester to make a rough sketch of the tire tracks left by the car which had apparently been used. One evening, during a dance in a Mühlhausen tavern, the forester checked his sketch against the tires of the three or four cars parked in front of the place. Those on Hugo Schaefer's car seemed to match the sketch, and during the next few days the forester was able to penetrate the taciturnity of the villagers sufficiently to confirm his suspicions of Schaefer. One of the details he ferreted out became a journalistic hallmark of the case: the use of a car spotlight as a lure. The forester concluded that he had sufficient grounds for questioning Schaefer and invited the latter to his office. The questioning was productive, and at this point Schaefer realized he needed legal help. He turned to Hagen and Stein.

This was presumably one of the cases referred to now when Hochburgers say that Hagen and Stein sometimes accepted cases that were not quite "pure." The irrelevance of the accusation is seen in the record, for the efforts of Hagen and Stein to see that their client got all the benefits of the law were those of any good lawyer. This meant a detailed reading of the law, to which any subjective impression of guilt or innocence was immaterial.

When questioning Schaefer, the forester had confronted him with the penalties for poaching. Consequently, on the advice of his lawyers, Schaefer repudiated the partial confession he had made as having been extorted illegally. The law also decreed certain limitations on preliminary imprisonment for investigation. Schaefer's wife had recently had a miscarriage, so she needed his physical and financial help. Since he had not yet been found guilty, Hagen and Stein requested his release. That they failed to obtain it does not prove the impropriety of the request.

The lawyers made a strong argument against the assumption of guilt in the indictment, which had declared that knowledge of

Schaefer's poaching was general in Mühlhausen. Since Schaefer had not been proved a poacher, the indictment assumed what the trial was supposed to prove.

At the end of his trial, Schaefer was found guilty and sentenced to nineteen months' imprisonment; two accomplices got shorter terms. The state's attorney had asked for thirty months. Hagen and Stein had sought acquittal, or, in case of conviction, clemency.

Sigmund Stein had the reputation of being a lawyer who inquired about the social and economic circumstances surrounding the crime of which a client was accused, and the comment has its relation to the case of the Mühlhausen Spotlight Poachers. Because of his large rural clientele, Sigmund was aware of the manner in which the depression was strangling the rural economy and of the growing desperation of the farmers. A few weeks before his involvement in this case, there had been much local publicity about the dynamiting of fish for food in the River Frieden, at a point between Bachdorf and Niederhausen. Sigmund and Hagen came from backgrounds of intimate familiarity with the peasants and knew the rough directness with which the villagers could meet a frustrating and threatening situation. It may well be, in fact, that this very knowledge let them minimize the meanings for themselves of the political brawls and crude anti-Semitism which were soon to spring up in the villages around Hochburg.

The partners' reputation as lawyers grew with their business, and their business grew with their reputation. A continual flow of non-political cases passed through their chambers between 1930 and 1933. Considering the vast amount of paper work, legal research, conferences with and visits to clients which lay behind each case, the two men may well have been so busy during these years that they were unable to give much calm and deliberate thought to the storm which was rising around them. To be sure, harbingers of the storm came through, even in the non-political cases, as when— early in 1932—they defended a Jewish cattle dealer against charges of assault and battery which had arisen from his attempt to protect himself. Two young fellows from his village had been plaguing him for months trying to make him give the Hitler salute. They finally went so far as to threaten him with a beating as he was driving past in his buggy. When they tried to climb into the buggy, he beat them off with his whip.

Hagen and Stein's burden of case work in this period provides an excellent example of the way in which one's ability to analyze and deal with a crucial situation is limited by the routine demands of everyday life. Both men, it would seem, had the intelligence to deal with the developing situation, at least insofar as its personal impact was concerned. Yet it is especially the intelligent man who likes to base his actions on information which he feels is reliable. The anti-Semitism of the Nazis and its implications for the Jews were clear enough. But the Nazis were not yet in power and were faced with determined resistance from various quarters. Sigmund and Werner could see only the conflicting and confusing newspaper headlines and below them stories of greatly varying plausibility. Because of the press of professional activities, the two men could not inform themselves to the degree they recognized as necessary in order to make valid judgments about the rapid course of events.

The two lawyers conducted non-political cases to the very end. In their correspondence with the court about such cases, one begins to see slight traces of the gathering storm in the first months of 1933. Faintly but unmistakably, the purely functional and businesslike tone begins to reveal an element of pleading: even though we are what we are and the country is turning against us, could not the case of our client be expedited?

Hagen and Stein, of course, had come to be known as "the" Jewish law firm in Hochburg. Like Sigmund Stein and Werner Hagen, Mordecai Mannheimer was attacked as a Jew by the burgeoning Nazi movement. Because of his political conservatism and his caution, however, his business did not extend into the same political crossfire.

Yet direct attacks on the firm of Hagen and Stein were surprisingly few in the local Nazi press and rhetoric. This appears to reflect a tendency on the part of the Nazis to bypass less vulnerable positions on the assumption that if their assault on the more widely dispersed weak points was successful, the strong point could be taken care of later.

The *Hessische Volkshut,* a National Socialist paper founded in 1930, shows how this tactic was applied. The general anti-Semitism of this *"Hessian Folk Guardian"* is almost totally unrestrained. It reveals a sure, firsthand knowledge of traditional attitudes toward the Jews, complete confidence in the wide distribution of these attitudes, and a ruthless determination to state them in such a way that their implications appear as part of the attitudes themselves. Thus, elimination of the Jews from German life was not merely advocated; in addition, age-old anti-Semitic canards were seen as expressions of the impulse to eliminate the Jews. This was ominously clever, for it subtly transformed the peasant or clerk or laborer who read the paper for a variety of reasons, who was not disturbed by the traditional prejudices (because they were usually his own) and who had never thought about their logical consequences—it transformed him into an accomplice. The paper succeeded in showing that what had been absorbed without awareness was actually a commitment. In a perverse way, it called on its readers to live up to their beliefs, to follow their consciences.

This drumming on a generalized anti-Semitism was sharpened by specific attacks on individual Jews; not on the well-known and respected firm of Hagen and Stein in Hochburg, but rather on some little restaurant owner in the large city of Kassel, or perhaps on a cattle dealer in one of the villages. Such attacks had two advantages: since the victim was not well known, there would be few witnesses who could say anything about the accuracy of the charges. In addition, it was in the nature of things that by sifting through all the numerous little Jewish businesses, the National Socialists could usually find one or two which were guilty of some major or minor impropriety.

At the same time, like other Nazi papers of the era, the *Folk Guardian* had a sure source of news in the activities of the Nazis themselves. As hard as it is to capture the more subtle moods of such a period, it is clear that in the early thirties unsubtle moods of fear, hatred, distrust, and uncertainty were being aroused. Such sheets as the *Folk Guardian,* the Communist *Worker's Voice* (a mimeographed weekly), or even the more respectably leftist *Taegliches Hessenblatt* and the more moderately rightist *Hess-*

ische Landeskurier, give an all-too-chilling sense of the mood of the time. It becomes clear that under the stress of economic depression, widespread hardship, and the lingering consequences of the lost war, the moral and philosophical uncertainties of the twenties, which had been glossed over by a brief period of prosperity, were beginning to ferment into violence. The Nazis were part of this violence, and in their press their "heroic" and "defiant" exploits made exciting reading.

Any account of the manner in which this violence and excitement overflowed into the chambers of Hagen and Stein must be prefaced by a rehearsal of the "differences" between the two men, since these bear on the political involvement of the firm.

Otto Knopf's assertion that Sigmund was reluctant to become involved in the political cases has been mentioned. Knopf also says that Sigmund once made the statement, "If it weren't for the anti-Semitic nonsense, I might have voted for Hitler." Knopf's story may be questioned, yet there is no need flatly to disbelieve it. One has only to turn back to the German Jewish literature of the First World War to see that Sigmund Stein was not the only Jew whose beliefs and commitments tied in at various points with the ideas about the Germanic Folk Community. Sigmund's continued contact with his native village as well as familiarity with his peasant clientele would have made him respond to those components of the folk-community idea which do, in fact, make sense: the organization of peasant life around fundamental needs and processes; its freedom from urban artificialities and tensions; and—complementing that freedom—the directness and vigor of its self-expression. Sigmund not only saw these things and was impressed by them in the years before the Nazi takeover, but he was also to retain his respect for them through the bitter and terrible insights gained in the course of the Nazi years.

Sigmund was probably deeply opposed to the image of Communism that he knew. In part this image was one which still pre-.ails in Germany and is related to the type of people who are thought to be Communists. They are "the scum of the Hochburg populace," "disgruntled misfits," who believe that "if you won't be my brother, I'll knock your head off." They are everything other than the "decent, hardworking, true-hearted people" who made up the German middle class, according to its own mythology. If Sigmund was willing to and did defend the Communists in the courts, it was in large part out of belief in the universality of legal protections, in part because he did not reject the Communist as a human being just as he did not reject a village ruffian whom he might defend as a human being.

Sigmund was also the junior partner in a law firm where the senior partner was politically more radical and personally more aggressive than Stein himself. Werner Hagen was no Communist. But he was a Social Democrat and seems to have lacked Sigmund's basic psychological antagonism to Communism. Nevertheless, there is no hard evidence which would indicate that Sigmund ever had serious second thoughts about his association with Werner Hagen, whereas there are abundant records to support the belief that the two men did work harmoniously and effectively together. There is nothing to indicate that Sigmund's participation in the political cases was halfhearted, or that his fundamental sympathies lay anywhere else than with German liberalism. It would be a mistake to ignore the hints which point to a division between the two men as 1933 approached, but it would be a greater mistake to conclude that this shadow became a substantial antagonism.

It will be recalled that Werner Hagen is remembered by some sources as having been more religiously orthodox than Sigmund. There were other Jews in Hochburg in whom a strict religiosity seems to have been combined with political radicalism. This suggests that the Jew who wanted assimilation in German society would be tempted to adopt the most common social attitudes of that society. No matter what they were or did, the Jews could not escape the venom of the National Socialists. But within the framework of its overall strategy, every political party adapts its tactics to the particular demands of time and place. Jewish piety was mocked and ridiculed in the vilest fashion, but in its traditional forms it was already strange, and identification with its adherents already difficult. The adherents of assimilation, the Jews who wanted to look upon themselves as Germans and not merely as Jews, were the ones who had to be made strange, had to be thrust back into the ghetto.

Hochburg was the center of Nazi agitation in the towns and

villages around it. In 1935, the party celebrated the tenth year of
its existence in Hochburg. It was an occasion for exultant and sentimental reminiscence, exemplified by this description of election
activity in 1932, in a pamphlet prepared for the event:

> What an election that was! Evening after evening we were on
> the road, usually to our own meetings, but often enough to
> those of our opponents. Almost everywhere we went there
> were brawls. We had long since accustomed ourselves to the
> saddles of our steel "horses" and were virtuosi in speedy
> emergency trips and in pedaling hell-bent for election without
> let-up. . . . I can still see Mother Schmidt standing in the
> doorway, wiping the kitchen dampness from her hands on her
> apron before shaking hands with each of us. "Good luck,"
> she'd say as we were getting on our wheels, "I'll have a pot of
> coffee on the stove for you when you get back. Heil Hitler!"
> "Heil and Sieg," we'd reply, "we'll make out, don't worry."

The opponents might be the "Reichsbananas," as the Reichsbanner men were called, the "Sozis," "Commies," or, more in-
clusively, just "the Reds." And always the Jews, though not in the
same political sense. This anniversary pamphlet gloated over recounting the fact that the brawls might involve a "belly kick at
the Horse-Jew Mannstein of Kirchdorf," whose protests at the insults hurled against the Jews had threatened to become violent.

Such activities rose to a new peak of violence in each of the
eight major elections between 1928 and 1933. Nor was there any
real respite in the intervals between elections. As the most active
opponents of the Nazis, the Communists and Social Democrats
were also involved in the fever of agitation. Friedrich Michael,
who provides much information about Sigmund's connection with
the Reichsbanner and was described as an "incurable blabber-mouth"
in the anniversary pamphlet of 1935, is proud of the sobriquet and
proud, too, of the fact that, however the leftist parties may have
maneuvered their political alliances on the national level, around
Hochburg they had often made common cause in the scutwork of
local meetings and demonstrations.

All of the non-Nazi parties were active in their opposition to
the Brownshirts, and the opposition was often enough strategically

principled and tactically astute, however tragically inadequate. Yet such inadequacy must be measured against the magnitude of the challenge, and in Germany the challenge of economic circumstance and political mood was without parallel.

The *Taegliches Hessenblatt* did not carry advertisements or announcements of Nazi meetings. The *Hessische Landeskurier* carried both and heralded a climax of activity in the third week of February, 1931, with the announcement of a lecture in the municipal auditorium by one of the Nazi philosophic lights, Johannes von Leers. The day after this meeting, the *Landeskurier* carried a report which described how von Leers spoke in a "factual and lively way," and along with this, the announcement of a Nazi meeting in nearby Gosmarshausen the following week.

The *Taegliches Hessenblatt* gives a much different picture of the von Leers meeting, reporting fights before and after, accusing the police of favoring the Nazis, and running an editorial in which it jeers at *von* Leers, a Prussian aristocrat, as representative of the German National Socialists *Workers'* Party. The editorial asserts that the *Junker* came through when von Leers called on the SA to take action against hecklers, and then stood silently with folded arms while the rough stuff was going on.

As a result of the fighting during and following the von Leers meeting, feelings were running high when the Gosmarshausen meeting took place one week later. Gosmarshausen is a village which had been merged with Hochburg in 1930. It was something of a Communist nest, one of the three voting districts of the town where the Communist vote had approached the national figure of about 12 per cent. The meeting was held in the main hall of an inn belonging to a Nazi of some years' standing. The Nazis looked on the meeting as an invasion of enemy territory, and the trouble which was joyfully anticipated did, of course, come.

While the Nazis were still arriving at the hall, threats and ridicule were heard from the crowd waiting to get in. The Nazis who came from Hochburg in uniform did so in groups, since the danger of coming alone was too great. When the meeting opened, it was apparent that most of audience were opponents—chiefly Reichsbanner men and Communists. But in addition to the Nazis on the platform and those in the audience, there were forty-eight SA men lined up in front of the podium, facing the first row of seats.

"The speaker started off calmly," says the anniversary pamphlet, "but soon went over to the time-honored tactic of setting Sozis against Commies." This time, the tactic did not work, producing instead an angry furor directed at the speaker. It is characteristic that the pamphlet relates what happened next with a smug sense of "our" cleverness. During the furor the speaker kept banging on the order bell and was finally successful in quieting down the audience somewhat. Then it "was the only chance, and our leader seized the opportunity by giving the signal. Then he himself picked up a chair and waded into the first row of Reds." The other SA men immediately followed his example, and the whole line of forty-eight chair-swinging Nazis moved slowly along the hall, driving the audience before them.

Naturally, there was resistance; naturally, the audience grabbed chairs. The SA men, however, had timed matters well for their purpose, and their opponents were surprised and confused. As they fled out the doors and through the windows they were collared by the police, according to the account in the *Hessenblatt*.

As was customary at such meetings, two policeman, one of them Officer Schumann, had been present as guardians of the public peace. The *Hessenblatt* complained bitterly of their failure to put a timely end to the meeting and of the asserted readiness of the police generally to arrest Socialists and Communists in preference to Nazis. Schumann is victim of an illuminating confusion concerning the meeting. He remembers it as having been organized by the SPD, which was false; at the same time, he recalls the Nazis as aggressors, which was true. His main concern is to deny the partisanship of the police, and his admission that the police used their blackjacks embarrasses him because it is obvious that this meant using them primarily on the leftists.

The accounts of this meeting indicate that both the Nazis and the Reds were definitely looking for trouble in Gosmarshausen. The latter were bent on disrupting the meeting but were routed by the Nazis' timing. It is also reasonably clear that after the meeting, when the police were escorting the Nazis back to Hochburg by a roundabout way, the Reds did initiate various actions such as rock- and garbage-throwing, beating up of stragglers, and general harassment of the column.

The uncertainties about the affair must be stressed, however, because it is in court action brought by the Nazis against the Communists and Socialists for "politically motivated breach of the public peace" that these uncertainties appear most clearly. The discrepancies in the various partisan accounts were not resolved by the trial but simply brought into sharp focus by conflicting testimony.

Hagen and Stein, along with an able woman lawyer from Frankfurt, were the defending attorneys. There is no question where their general sympathies were, but there is a very large question as to whether or not a lawyer taking either side's part could be assured of his client's virtue and the opposition's villainy. There was no dispute over the willingness of both sides, like sovereign nations, to use force when they thought it was *necessary*. There was no doubt that both sides would, in a situation like the "Gosmarshausen Schlägerei," seek to capitalize on their opponents' use of force, presenting their own recourse to it as provoked.

In fact, the trial was a complex of trials, consisting of one main and several satellite trials, each with its progeny of appeals and counter-appeals. Of the twenty defendants in the main trial, eleven were acquitted with the aid of Hagen and Stein and their female associate. The luster of these acquittals is somewhat diminished by the fact that the prosecutor himself agreed to eight of them; on the other hand, the impact of the nine "guilty" verdicts was reduced by reversal or reduction of sentence on appeal. A Hochburg University student, for instance, was at first given one month in jail for possession of a blackjack. He was, however, able to convince the court that the weapon was not really a blackjack but rather a chair leg which he had grabbed in the excitement of the moment. On appeal, the jail sentence was eliminated and a 100-mark fine imposed.

There were other cases, such as the brawl in the Tannenbaum Workers' Settlement, in which Hagen and Stein defended the anti-Nazis against charges growing out of a situation where the virtue of the anti-Nazis was even less obvious than it had been in the Gosmarshausen affair. The brawl occurred on the last Sunday of July, 1932, when the voting in the first of that year's two parliamentary elections was to take place. The Tannenbaum Workers' Settlement was a small, low-income housing project on the outskirts of Hochburg, literally and figuratively on the other side of the tracks. Middle-class Hochburgers look down their noses at it today as they did in the early thirties as a section where "the wrong kind of people," mostly unskilled laborers, live. In the summer of 1932, both Nazis and Communists lived in the settlement, and the situation of the Nazi family Grundbach, whose apartment was next to that of the Communist family Schnitzler, was not exceptional.

Early on the morning of election Sunday, Father Grundbach and his son Hans were on their way into Hochburg where they had SA duty—slapping up last-minute posters, handing out literature, and the like. As they were crossing the railroad tracks, they met Bertram Schnitzler who was returning home from a night of *his* electioneering, having rewarded himself with an undetermined amount of alcohol. Herr Schnitzler greeted the Grundbachs with such epithets as "Nazi bastards!" and "Rats!" He also drew a dire picture of what would happen to them when they returned to the settlement. At this point, however, no blows were struck.

When Schnitzler arrived in front of the building in which his own and the Grundbachs' apartments were located, he directed loud insults at the latter, and then went in to sleep it off. He was still sleeping when Hans Grundbach came home for lunch, which passed without any of the dire threats materializing. Young Grundbach then left for poster-watching duty at the voting place for the district in which the Tannenbaum Settlement was located. Shortly thereafter, three workers came back to the settlement from the Teichstrasse where they had been beer-drinking at the annual Teichstrasse fair. They may or may not have been Communists— during the trial, the Nazis referred to all of their opponents as such —but the three men were certainly anti-Nazis and began insulting the Grundbachs from outside the kitchen window, saying what they would do to Hans when he returned.

Frau Grundbach was frightened and upset, and managed to send her daughter out to warn Hans. Hans got in touch with the SA headquarters which gladly provided him with an escort of fifteen Brownshirts, and the whole troupe paraded to the big fir tree at the entrance which gives the settlement its name. Taking three SA men with him, Hans started to go toward the building in which his family's apartment was located, leaving the other Nazis waiting at the tree, their heavy belts in hand, ready for action.

It is at this point that the report in the Communist news sheet begins. The *Landeskurier* and the Nazi *Volkshut*, on the other hand, were able to present a somewhat more complete version of the affair, simply because this was an instance where they could capitalize on an approach to the truth; they played up the events of the morning and early afternoon in order to present the "attack" itself as justified self-defense.

One of the anti-Nazis had been posted to watch for the return of Grundbach, saw the four men coming, gave a whistle, and yelled, "Workers out, here they come!" Whereupon Hans Grundbach signaled the SA men waiting at the tree, and the two groups, the Nazis running into the settlement and the anti-Nazis running out of their apartments, met in a short, hard scuffle, from which the SA retreated in good order.

This is more or less what actually happened, and the Nazis this time had a fairly defensible case, even if the events described do not exhaust the causes. Hans Grundbach had not forgotten the meeting at the railroad tracks early that morning and had mentioned it to his comrades shortly after it happened. The touchy situation in the settlement, especially that between the Grundbachs and the Schnitzlers, had not sprung full-blown from the events of election Sunday. The three workers had made their threats on the spur of the moment, to be sure, and old Schnitzler had been drunk, but the whole turmoil out of which these threats grew had been fermenting vigorously in the steamy political atmosphere of the preceding months.

Hagen and Stein probably did not know all the events of those preceding months, but they knew that such events were there, that many of them were political, and that the Tannenbaum brawl was embedded in them. Hence, when it came to the juridical aftermath of the brawl, they knew that their task was to probe the framework in which the matter was set. They did so, and Hans Grundbach himself, the chief plaintiff, though encouraged by the court not to be confused by the questioning, became involved in lies and the contradictions growing out of them, with the result that the cases against nine of the fifteen defendants were dismissed, while the remaining defendants got six months each for breach of the public peace combined with assault and battery. Hagen and Stein were able to get an appeal for them, but were unable to win it.

The months between the "Gosmarshausen Schlägerei" and the Tannenbaum brawl had been filled with similar incidents and their juridical consequences. Many of these cases grew out of the Nazi propaganda outings which became a feature of the Sunday countryside all over Germany during this period. Usually the Nazis would go from village to village by truck, dismounting at the outskirts to march, with colors flying, pipes playing, and slogans rampant, through the ordinarily sleepy ways and lanes. These were peaceable occasions—the Nazis were not out to beat anyone up. Unless, that is, they were intolerably provoked, and they were experts at being intolerably provoked. In some of the villages there were determined contingents of Socialists and Communists. In Hugelsdorf, pleasantly located in a shallow valley about eight miles east of Hochburg, one of the former was Herr Kleppner, a disabled veteran of the World War—he had lost a leg on the western front.

As the Nazis passed an inn where Kleppner and other villagers had gathered to jeer or cheer, Kleppner was on his crutches in the middle of the road attempting, according to his account, to reach his house on the other side. T˙ Nazis claimed that he was defying the column and that he struc ˍhe standard bearer. Whereupon he found himself roughed vˋ and down flat, *knocked* down by the Nazis, he said. The Nazis said that he was pushed out of the way and fell. They said that they tried to help him up. Perhaps this was true, because when he had gone down onlookers had cried, "Shame, a wounded veteran!" And the Nazis ordinarily flaunted their special love for veterans. But Kleppner insisted that the "helping up" was merely a continuation of the knocking down.

At that point the matter went no further, and the column of marching Nazis proceeded on its way. Fifteen minutes later, having paraded all around the village, the column came back by the same route, on its way to the waiting truck. When the column passed the inn a fight ensued in which the Nazis fought with flag-poles and belts, while the anti-Nazis used stones, firewood, and fence palings.

Hagen and Stein were called on to defend Kleppner and associates against the charges of politically motivated assault and battery. They lost the case in the trial itself, for the court believed the Nazi contention that Kleppner and his friends attacked according to a plan hastily organized between the first and second appearances of the marchers in front of the inn. Kleppner was sentenced to five months in jail, his comrades to three. Hagen and Stein appealed, emphasizing the extent of Kleppner's disability and introducing witnesses who said that when Kleppner brandished his crutch at the returning column his purpose had been to underscore Nazi cowardice in having knocked down a disabled veteran; there was no threat in the gesture. Such arguments as well as the counter-arguments of the opposition were summed up by the appellate court in a verdict of acquittal for Kleppner but confirmation of the original sentence in the case of his comrades.

Hagen and Stein did not always appear in court together, and were occasionally retained as individuals. Thus, Sigmund appeared as counsel for the young die-maker, Johannes Krebs, who had been beaten up by a group of SA men. This was not an important case, and its outcome is unknown. Nevertheless, its significance cannot be neglected. Krebs was the plaintiff, the SA men were the defendants. Krebs was not Jewish nor was he, according to all accounts, a political person: not a Social Democrat, or a Communist, or a member of the Reichsbanner. But his lack of political identity was of no help to him when he happened to be overheard as he commented that a nearby column of SA men looked like a bunch of overgrown boy scouts. The opposition lawyer was a Dr. Kutscher, who had defended and counseled Nazis as regularly as Hagen and Stein represented their opponents. In the beginning his activity, if not his point of view, could have been admired as a willingness to jeopardize his career in defense of a party which was then small, unpopular, and too scornful of the regime to be an easy client in the courts.

In December, 1932, however, when this case occurred, he and his clients were representatives of a movement which was surging toward success. Sigmund was Jewish, but his appearance at this late date as counsel for Krebs does not necessarily prove him a hero. Nevertheless, it was a time when some kind of victory for the Nazis was in the offing, and it followed by a few months Werner Hagen's response to a young colleague's question about what the SPD ought to do: "It's all up with the Social Democrats, the Nazis are not to be stopped, and it's all up with me as a Jew, and I'm getting out as soon as possible."

At such a time, for Sigmund to have taken on the representation of Krebs against the SA required an assurance which is hard to comprehend in the light of what Sigmund already knew about Nazi policy toward the Jews. Yet in spite of the lateness of the hour, and in spite of Hagen's foresight—but was this foresight in terms of what eventually came, or simply a clear analysis of his own position as a Jew and as an outstanding political opponent of the Nazis?—the immediate effects of an assumption of power by the Nazis were still unpredictable and the more remote consequences undreamed of. In December, 1932, Sigmund was doing no more than acting like the conscientious lawyer he had always been.

Naturally, Communists, Socialists, and the more conservative parties also held meetings and carried on propaganda activities of various kinds. In fact, it was a reference to a Reichsbanner parade as "that herd of swine" which, according to the *Taegliches Hessenblatt,* had been the initial provocation at the Gosmarshausen meeting. Werner Hagen was definitely seen in such parades, and probably Sigmund also participated on occasion. Sigmund was a Democratic party man, and even in this party his activity was less in 1931 and 1932 than it had been ten years earlier. But membership in the Reichsbanner did not imply commitment to socialism—except to the Nazis, for whom all cats were red— but only to the Weimar Republic. By choice and by preoccupation with other things, Sigmund had become less active politically. But the threat to the Weimar Republic was growing and may well have led Sigmund into occasional active participation in spite of himself.

In these political cases, as in non-political ones, Sigmund and Werner played substantially equal roles. Sometimes their roles were *seen* differently. For instance, although the records and accounts of the Tannenbaum Workers' Settlement brawl show no distinction between them it was Werner Hagen who was singled out for praise by the Communist *Stimme der Werktaetigen* and pointed out as the lawyer who had been retained by the Communist legal aid organization, *Rote Hilfe,* in this and other cases.

The "equality of roles" of course was almost inevitable in the partners' method of operation. When a client visited their chambers to discuss a case with them, he was as likely to talk with the one as with the other, depending on who was free at the moment. If both were free and if, as Konrad Muenschner put it, a client were a "friend of the family," he would talk to both.

Otto Knopf is one of three or four people who say that new clients tended to ask for Sigmund Stein rather than for Werner Hagen. This is explained on the basis of Sigmund's greater "respectability," although it is clear that in 1932 the firm as such was continuing the climb in prominence which had characterized it from the beginning. Early that year the two men opened a part-time branch office in Weidenberg. The move was a response to rather than a bid for new business, and Sigmund had for several years been combining visits—sometimes accompanied by his wife and daughter—to his father in Bachdorf with appearances in the court at Weidenberg. In the late twenties he had ceased making the trip by train and had become a regular customer of a Hochburg car livery. Sigmund, unlike his partner, did not have a car of his own and did not enjoy driving, since he always hired a chauffeur along with the car.

Sigmund seems, in fact, to have been content to do little traveling. In the summer of 1929 or 1930 he did take his family to the Dutch seaside resort of Scheveningen, near The Hague. Here Esther Stein is supposed to have enjoyed herself greatly, taking the opportunity, it is said, to show off herself and her clothes a bit. Sigmund was less enchanted with this vacation. When asked about it later on, he replied that the Dutch coast was all right, but that Hochburg and the surrounding countryside were more beautiful. Dr. Bauer, Sigmund's mentor in Minerva, remarked that he had seen Sigmund two or three times at yearly reunions, but aside from these occasions Sigmund's traveling seems to have been less than what might have been expected of a person of his growing affluence.

Werner Hagen, on the other hand, traveled all over Germany, alone or with his family. He had his own car, and, as a sports enthusiast, would drive to Frankfurt simply to see a major soccer match. On these trips he often took one of the subordinate officials of the Hochburg District Court with him, and this man tells of these excursions with enthusiasm. Other people make a point of the fact that Hagen traveled not only by car but by train, by bus, and even by air—certainly indications of a lively enterprise and prosperity.

The growing stature of the firm of Hagen and Stein is visible not only in the extent to which it prospered but also in the ways that recognition was being accorded to the partners by the Hochburg Jewish community. Sigmund, as has already been suggested, may have come into the chairmanship of the Hochburg Chapter of the Central Union of German Citizens of Jewish Faith in late 1931; this was the period when Esther Stein was elected to the board of the Jewish grammar school—an indirect tribute to Sigmund, since all other members of the board were wives of men with an established community status. This is also the period when, Landrat Staerke recalls, both Sigmund and Werner were playing a part in the affairs of the official community, and when Hagen was elected to the Board of Governors of the Home for Crippled Jewish Children.

For Hagen and his family, this eleventh-hour attainment of influence and affluence was to have little significance. For Sigmund, however, these developments and the growing prestige he enjoyed as a lawyer were all steps toward an entrapment which would make a mockery of the status they carried with them.

8

[The flood of Nazi power]

Early in March, 1932, the *Taegliches Hessenblatt* carried an appeal to German voters by twenty members of the Hochburg University faculty. The forthcoming election was for the president of Germany. The incumbent, von Hindenburg, was a candidate, and it was the support of this aging general, hero of World War I, which the faculty endorsed. Throughout Germany, von Hindenburg was favored by the center and by the moderates of left and right. The other candidates were Hitler, backed of course by the NSDAP but by no other party; Duesterberg, the candidate of the German National People's party; and Thaelmann, a Communist, backed by his own party and by the left Socialists.

The tone of the Hochburg faculty appeal is solemn, concluding with the words, "This is the only man whose personality, granted by Destiny to the German people in their hour of greatest need, is above all criticism and calls forth supreme respect." Among the signers were the Jewish professors as well as the professors whose wives were Jewish.

There is little doubt that von Hindenburg, former commander-in-chief of the German armies and the victor of Tannenberg, was a sacred cow. His status as such is practically clinched by the appeal's assertion that he was above criticism. Even the Nazis hesitated to attack him directly, limiting themelves to the assertion that he was surrounded by Jewish advisers, a propaganda line which the *Hessenblatt* had reported a few days before the faculty appeal. This line was paralleled by the locally attractive assertion that 60 per cent of the faculty and students at Hochburg University were Jewish. The truth of both claims corresponds to that of the statement, made by the Nazis in the same campaign, that Christ was a German.

Still, the presence of the names of the Jewish faculty members among the signers of the faculty appeal was symptomatic; so too was the fact that the biography of von Hindenburg, along with volumes by Knut Hamsun and Heinrich Heine, occupied places of honor atop Sigmund Stein's bookcase. Von Hindenburg was a figure around which the German middle class could rally. The trouble was that such unity was attained at the sacrifice of insight into his weaknesses and those of the regime he headed. It was hailed as a triumph that so many party lines could be crossed in the support for von Hindenburg; as often happens, however, the tactical unity so obtained had to be emotionally and ideologically inflated into a diapason of unity, which it was not.

In this campaign, the "Iron Front" was formed. This was not a party or union of parties, according to the announcement, but a welding together of all republican-minded people in Germany. Johannes Huss, Werner Hagen, and Konrad Muenschner were instrumental in founding the Hochburg unit of the "Iron Front." Heinrich, son of Johannes Huss, says ruefully that it had been a good idea but too late. In retrospect, it gives the appearance of an attempt to use a symbol to impose on the anti-Nazi forces a unity which they simply did not possess. The three arrows of its emblem soon were emblazoned on various articles such as cigarettes.

It really was too late, and it was also an attempt to compete in an area where the Nazis, with their brassiness and lack of scruple, had already established themselves as hucksters extraordinary. A roll-your-own tobacco labeled *"Anti-Semit"* had been on the market two years when the "Iron Front" was formed, and there were cigarettes with the trademarks *Sturm* and *Neue Front* to compete with the *Drei Pfeile* (*Three Arrows*) brand.

Furthermore, the "Iron Front," in spite of its avowed republican universality, was too obviously sparked by the Social Democratic party and the Reichsbanner people; hence it was easily lampooned by the Nazis in such doggerel as the following:

> Three Arrows they've dragged out again
> And brushed off every mothball
> Freedom, Beauty, Dignity of Man—
> The Socialists have got gall!

> Three arrows are but camouflage
> To hide their greedy swindling.
> Don't be fooled, tear off the mask
> And soon we'll have them dwindling.

As soon as the "Iron Front" appeared, the Nazis accused it of relying on Jewish gold, and the only reason that the lampoon above contains no explicit reference to Jews is because it was no longer necessary. Words such as "greedy swindling" and "mask" had become anti-Semitic passwords to anyone who read the *Hessische Volkshut,* where the lampoon was printed. Of course, as a consequence of the way in which the situation had developed, there is little question but that the "Iron Front" did get support from Jews.

The German Jews, believing they had the right of self-defense, were caught in a trap, the spring if not the teeth of which had been centuries in the making. Underlying attitudes toward the Jews were too deeply rooted in the history of Germany and the histories of Germans to be shaken off in a period when they were being exploited with fanatic and ruthless sincerity. The Nazis themselves could thus exploit these attitudes and gain a propaganda bonus by taking advantage of Jewish reaction to the primary anti-Semitism.

As early as 1929, for instance, the Nazis were urging sympathetic innkeepers to publicize their wish not to serve Jews. In response to this the *Israelitisches Familienblatt,* a widely distributed Jewish periodical, adopted the practice of publishing lists of such inns. One motive for this was the desire to spare their readers the embarrassment of going to an inn where they were likely to be discriminated against. The lists were also designed to apply economic pressure. The request for an explicit statement of his anti-Semitism—and no inn was included on the list without such an explicit statement—from an innkeeper who was wavering between it and his desire not to lose Jewish trade was an effective suggestion to put up or shut up. The threat of a loss of Jewish clientele was obvious and not "veiled" or "underhanded" as the Nazis would have it.

The *Volkshut* in the Hochburg area made a great play of these listings on occasion. Usually it published the "shameless" and "presumptuous" letter from the Jewish periodical, along with the "courageous" and "forthright" response of the innkeeper, who "proudly" demanded the "honor" of having his name included in such a list and "thanked" the management of the periodical with heavy irony for informing him about the list. The risk of such irony was surely foreseen by the *Israelitisches Familienblatt.*

The exploitation of reaction to prejudice in ways which furthered that prejudice was not new, not peculiarly German; its importance in the crisscrossing of factors which led to Nazi success should not be exaggerated. In many other European countries the underlying attitudes toward the Jews were as strong and as warped as they were in Germany. In their own conjunctions of time and circumstance they had produced pogrom and violence fully as terrible in their immediacy as anything the Nazis were able to whip up. The ultimate horror of Nazi anti-Semitism surpassed anything that had gone before. This does not imply the innate perversity of the Germans; it is not explained by any one tactic or group of tactics.

It is possible that the Jewish foresight, which reckoned with the consequences of such measures as the publication of a list of anti-Semitic inns but discounted the impact of these consequences, was inadequate. It is possible that many Jews had a mistaken idea of their institutional strength and influence within a German culture so dominated by tradition, history, and the traditional distortions of history.

Overconfidence carries with it the dangerous possibility that, as awareness of the actual situation grows, despair and resignation will take the place of effective attempts to grapple with the problem. By 1932 this process had gone far in the case of both the German Jews and the German liberals, and it could be seen in the reports on the organization of the "Iron Front" which appeared in the *Taegliches Hessenblatt*. Despair is not overt in these reports, but it is implicit in the playing up of the "Iron Front," the playing down of the inevitable brawls it got into, and in the petulant, belittling tone taken toward the much greater Nazi activity which was going on at the same time.

There was, for instance, the time when Hitler came to Hochburg in the spring of 1932. He was to speak at the Citizens' Assembly Grounds between the Sumpfviertel and the Felsen River, where a huge tent had been pitched. It was clear beforehand that it would be a big affair—the *Hessenblatt* had to print the mayor's public notice which gave the rules of traffic flow in and out of the area. The meeting lived up to expectations: the *Hessenblatt* reported twenty thousand in the audience, the *Landeskurier* estimated forty thousand. But Hochburg at the time was a town of thirty thousand people in a generally rural area! The *Hessenblatt* waited two days to comment on the occasion, and when it did so it contrasted its rampant emotionalism and demagoguery with the quiet rationality of a rally of Sigmund Stein's Democratic party which had taken place a day or two earlier. The attendance at the Democratic party meeting was not given, but anyone reading the article would have known that it was well under five hundred.

The *Hessenblatt* also made a perfectly good debating point out of a blooper that Hitler made in the course of his speech when he asserted that in 1918 "the republican leaders took over a flourishing state." Flourishing, as the *Hessenblatt* correctly snorted, in a pig's eye! Unfortunately, the time for debating points was nearly over, and the sweet reasonableness of the Democratic party had a built-in weakness factor of 500/20,000. This sweet reasonableness had, moreover, its genuine rational weaknesses (Hindenburg was "above criticism") just as the demagoguery of Hitler had its genuine rational strengths (what Germany needed was a revolution). Debating points are slender reeds in a strong wind.

The *Hessenblatt* and those it represented can hardly be blamed for grasping at straws when there was so little else to grasp at. But these desperate gestures betrayed the crumbling of illusions about Germany, illusions which reappear in an article several months later, when the writer complains of the Nazi uniforms and "their un-German character."

The despair of the Jews is heard in a comment by the legal adviser Heinrich Wolff. Early in 1932 he was beaten up by an SA man near the Old Bridge, which crosses the Felsen in the vicinity of the South Side depot. A student at Hochburg University came to his aid and afterward asked him why he had not tried to defend himself. "Defend myself?" he replied. "How could I? I'm a Jew."

Despair is expressed less eloquently and more problematically in Sigmund Stein's withdrawal from political activity in these years, a withdrawal which must be inferred. There is both comment on and evidence for his continued participation as a lawyer in the political trials of the era. But in contrast to the fact that Hagen's activity in the "Iron Front," his marching in demonstrations, his participation in the Reichsbanner are repeatedly remarked upon, there is near silence on the extra-professional activities of Sigmund Stein. He was definitely a member of the Reichsbanner and may have taken part in some of its parades. He was seen at one or two Democratic party meetings.

In combination with the hints of underlying differences between Sigmund and Werner Hagen, the silence about Sigmund's behavior at this point strongly indicates his having concluded that the Nazis were in the ascendant and would probably achieve their goal of political power. He also believed—and is frequently and explicitly quoted on this point from a somewhat later period— that having gained power the Nazis would then demonstrate the emptiness of their political pretensions by muffing the responsibilities of power. It is likely that he disagreed with aggressive Jewish efforts to defend themselves against Nazi scurrility, considering the way in which such efforts had been exploited around Hochburg.

Such an analysis is encouraged by all the positions he had previously taken. As an assimilationist, faced with the fact of accelerating Nazi strength, his only alternative to a complete about-face was to look upon the situation as a temporary aberration. This permitted him to believe that the madness he saw about him was a superficial disease brought on by the real difficulties in which Germany found itself; thus, he could still preserve his love for the "real" Germany. It is, after all, a common enough experience to have to watch one's friends doing things he does not approve of; especially common, perhaps, when only certain particulars of the behavior elicit our disapproval—that "anti-Semitic nonsense," for instance.

The desire to avoid immediate unpleasantness was probably an element in Sigmund's withdrawal. There is a tendency to react to such avoidance with impatient moralism, to contrast it unfavorably with the activism of a Werner Hagen. Yet the desire to avoid unpleasantness is as universal as definition can make it. That Sigmund acted out this desire in one way and Hagen in another is a function of the separate histories of the two men, as symbolized by Werner's aggressive argumentativeness in the Gymnasium twenty years earlier and Sigmund's somewhat passive agreeableness at that time. Similarly, when the Brown Wave finally broke, the resolution with which Hagen took himself and his family out of Germany, so easily seen as wisdom and foresight, is little more than a touchstone for his history at this stage. Hagen was not only a Jew but also a recently active Socialist: he had marched in many processions and fought the Nazis in the streets as well as in the courts. He *had* to get out. The alternatives were too plain.

Sigmund's withdrawal from politics in the early thirties and his notion of Nazism as a temporary aberration in the German people are touchstones for his history, which did not and could not develop an insight sufficient to penetrate to the dangers which threatened himself and his family in his love for Germany. He could not see—for his whole development obscured it—that his human and perhaps ultimately reasonable belief in the better qualities of the German people, his faith in the many friends he had, would envelop and trap him. Had he been able to see it, he would have fought, for he was no coward and his final entrapment was not something he would have accepted had he been able to anticipate it in 1932.

The presidential election of March, 1932, resulted in the failure of von Hindenburg to receive the majority necessary for his re-election. Out of a total of 37.5 million votes he had a plurality of about 7.3 million over the runner-up, Hitler, who had attracted 11.3 million votes. The next largest total, five million, went to the Communist candidate, Thaelmann. Duesterberg of the German National People's party ran a poor fourth with 2.5 million. The atmosphere in and around Hochburg can be seen from the fact that, in contrast to the national figures given above, Hitler led von Hindenburg in the town itself, 6,400 to 6,330. Distressing as this contrast was to the anti-Nazi forces in Hochburg, it had to be weighed against the fact that there was a contrast almost equally as great, and in the opposite direction, between the outcome in Hochburg and that in the rural area surrounding Hochburg, where Hitler led von Hindenburg 12,000 to 6,500.

Von Hindenburg's failure, in the nation as a whole, to obtain a majority, required a run-off election one month later. In this second election Duesterberg dropped out, and it is interesting to note that despite later Nazi attacks on Duesterberg's Jewish antecedents, there is reason to believe that his supporters transferred their strength to Hitler. Duesterberg was the national commander of the *Stahlhelm,* the largest and most respectable veterans' organization. In the later Nazi attacks on Duesterberg, his organization supported him, but the extent to which this support was already corroded shows up in the way the rank and file of the Stahlhelm turned to Hitler in the run-off election.

It may have been a mistake for Sigmund Stein to draw back from politics at this time, but there is little doubt that he was correct in his observation of what was happening. Even the Communist electorate got cold feet. Thaelmann himself did not drop out of the election, but many of his supporters dropped away in order, by supporting von Hindenburg, to vote against Hitler. These realignments enabled the old general to get his majority on the second ballot, but, taken together with the fact that the total vote declined slightly, they also betray the desperation and lack of confidence among the anti-Nazis. Much was made of the victory, but it sounded hollow. Von Hindenburg's support was too clearly a shaky coalition of three major and several minor parties whose chief point of agreement was opposition to Hitler—an opposition determined enough at its Social Democratic core but doubtful and weak among the peripheral parties. Von Hindenburg got his majority, yet the increase between the first and second elections was two million for Hitler, 700,000 for the incumbent von Hindenburg.

In Hochburg things went from bad to worse—from an anti-Nazi viewpoint—with the second ballot; Hitler increased his lead over von Hindenburg from less than a hundred to more than a thousand. This change was more favorable to Hitler than either that for the country as a whole or that for the countryside around Hochburg, due probably to the disproportionately large number of erstwhile Duesterberg supporters in the town. Hochburg was known as the "National Town," and the Stahlhelm and its ideology were very strongly represented there.

These two votes for the presidency of Germany were the first of five nationally important elections which were held between March and November, 1932. The detailed results of these elections were not irrelevant to anyone in Germany, least of all to Sigmund Stein and his fellow Jews, but it is the general picture coming out of the details and out of events related to the elections which is clearest in its significance. This general picture shows four major features: a regular decrease in the total number of votes cast, reflecting in part the growing extent to which people were becoming fed up with politicking; an absolute and relative rise in Nazi and nationalist strength; a decline in the strength of the Center and the Social Democrats; and an increase in the Communist vote. The increase in Nazi strength must be qualified by the fact that in the "last free election," the secondary parliamentary election of November, a Nazi decline in strength occurred which was greater than that suffered by the Social Democrats and the Center, while the Communists increased their strength, both absolutely and proportionately, topping for the first time the number of votes given to the Center.

The first parliamentary election came at the end of July, 1932. (It was on Election Sunday for this ballot, incidentally, that the

Tannenbaum Settlement brawl occurred.) The Nazis emerged from this election as the dominant party in parliament, with 230 seats, a plurality in the total of six hundred.

It is often said that the Nazis were never able to muster a majority until the "unfree" elections of March, 1933, when the effective, if not always the actual, power of the Nazis extended itself into the voting booth. This is true. It is also true, however, that the Nazis received more votes than any other party in the several free elections which preceded their assumption of power. The Nazis were willing to exploit any and all motives to sell their product. They were able to capitalize on the almost unbroken increase in strength of the Communists from election to election, holding up the thin specter of Communist power in order to pretty up the ominous reality of their own. They needed no motivational research because, fifteen years after defeat in the first World War, in a period of severe economic depression, and in a land where the buffeting of history had intensified the mutual reinforcement of common European prejudices, the country's motives were obvious. And big money, so necessary for an effective advertising campaign, was behind them at critical junctures.

The German people responded because their needs were real and their views of reality distorted. They saw reality from the cranny of the social structure into which they had been born. For a time, during the Wilhelminian era, things had been well organized, and it had been possible to spend a whole lifetime in that cranny without coming out except to look around and see how strange life in the other crannies was. Identification with that life had been impossible except through one or another of the proffered intoxications.

With the First World War, the structure cracked; it ceased to be a whole, even though certain relationships remained the same, like a bathtub jutting out of a pink tiled wall high up in a bomb-shorn building. Life forced the abandonment of the native crannies, and this first step toward seeing reality was cursed with the nostalgia for security, for the real comforts that once were. In retrospect, the events of the autumn and winter of 1932 make it seem obvious that the Nazis would assume power, and there were others beside Werner Hagen whose comments at the time sound prophetic. Yet to most of those who were living through the events with Hagen and Stein, it was not obvious. The Nazis were to suffer a loss in 1932's second parliamentary election in November. And their audacious parliamentary maneuvering in the fiasco by which the Reichstag elected in July was dissolved, had caused many people besides Sigmund to rejoice and say, "They've gone too far this time!"

Political activity in Germany during the fall and winter of 1932 took place in a framework which had already been decisively shaken. For, shortly before the July elections, the entire cabinet of the dominant state of Prussia had been dismissed by a presidential decree in the nimble hands of the federal chancellor, von Papen. This was done on the pretext that the cabinet was able to function only with the support of the Communist party, a subversive organization, said von Papen in the radio address by which he explained and excused his action. This fact, he went on, made Prussia a danger to the Reich and justified intervention by the federal government.

This move was an important factor in the tangle of events which led to Nazi power. Coming as it did shortly before the elections, it was well timed, because an effective reaction on the part of the Social Democrats and the Democratic party liberals would have looked like an alliance with the Communists. Since both these groups had buttressed their genuine anti-Communism with continual reference to the sins and subversions of the Communists, they were in no position to challenge von Papen's pretext.

The move was also important because it ousted the Social Democrat and loyal republican, Severing, from the key post of Prussian Minister of the Interior—the ultimate head of all the Prussian police. After a short pause during which no adequate reaction to this measure developed, the process was carried further and applied to high police officials throughout Prussia, replacing men of proven loyalty to Weimar—usually Social Democrats—by their immediate subordinates, who were almost always career officials with more nostalgia for the monarchy than loyalty to the republic and who were, to say the least, susceptible to much of the Nazi argumentation. This action by von Papen had been urged by the Nazis and was welcome to them: no matter how unpartisan the police may be, it is a distinct advantage if they are headed by one's friends.

This "purification" of the police, as it was called, along with the defamation of the Communists, paid dividends to the Nazis, since the blacker the hell to which the Communists were relegated the easier the attack on the left generally became. It was especially easy in Germany, for the Social Democrats were not yet ashamed of their Marxism, and the fight was not on a level where the refined distinction between Communist-Marxist and Socialist-Marxist meant anything except to those who were divided by it.

Hochburg is in Prussia. Indeed, two-thirds of Germany was in Prussia. The brawls continued, but the elections which, as the liberal *Frankfurter Zeitung* pointed out, would have been endangered had the non-Communist left objected too strongly to von Papen's ploy, did take place. The Center and the non-Nazi right were willing enough to form a coalition with the Nazis, but the Brownshirts did not reciprocate. As the strongest party in the Reichstag, the Nazis enjoyed the prerogative of filling the chair. In the September fiasco by which this Reichstag was dissolved, their man, Goering, chairing the session, exercised his functions with bold ruthlessness. To this day there remains some confusion about just what happened. Did the government fall by the Reichstag's passage of a no-confidence motion, or was the Reichstag dissolved by governmental decree? It was the latter which was the effective outcome of the hassle.

The new parliamentary elections in November brought more brawling and more confusion. The Nazis remained the strongest party in the Reichstag while dropping some of the seats they had won in July; the Communists and the Socialists could not get together in an effective political alliance, the doctrinaire vituperations of the former being matched in their contribution to futility by the injured self-righteousness and German patriotism of the latter. Even if they had got together, the two parties would have had at best a weak plurality, all the weaker because the alliance with the Communists would have alienated the liberal Center and thrown the illiberal Center into coalition with the Nazis.

So the turmoil persisted after November. In Hochburg, a long strike by relief workers aggravated the tension between the Communists and Socialists. The Communists were aggressive backers of the strike; the Socialists were not against the strikers and did not want to appear to be, but they saw wisdom in moderation. The strike was at once successful and unsuccessful enough to create bad feelings all around. On a higher level, General von Schleicher was made chancellor in December, but this attempt to exploit the national prestige of the army failed, and it was more of the same cross purposes and bickering during the transition from the wild year of 1932 to the fateful year of 1933.

It was hard enough for Sigmund to penetrate the confusion of events as they played themselves out in the microcosm of Hochburg; it was even harder to understand events nationwide. Where the miniature confusion around Hochburg was concerned, Sigmund was often involved in the judicial aftermath as participants were called to account before a more or less objective tribunal. He could hardly learn final truth, but the trials did permit some definition of the confusion. He could see pretty well how SA man Schultze got involved in the fight with Reichsbanner man Schmidt; how neither was a pacifist, and how each did his best to beat the hell out of the other. He could see the humanly understandable stupidities, the innocent malevolences, and the irrelevant motivations as they occurred among the political foot soldiers of *all* persuasions, as well as among the more respectable people who served in the courts as lawyers or judges or who read about the proceedings in the *Landeskurier* or the *Hessenblatt*.

Thus Sigmund was forced to go beyond the brawling and confusion in order to arrive at tenable judgments about what was taking place. He was forced to go to the assumptions about reality and the ideological goals within the framework of which the various parties were operating. Here Sigmund and others, deeply caught up in the events of the time, could find perspective, if at all, only after an arduous search.

It would hardly be denied that a change of regime is important, and this was almost as obvious in the German January of 1933 as it is in retrospect today. Chancellor von Schleicher, the socially minded general as he was called, radiated the undeniable prestige of the army but found that he could not govern with the parliament as it was then constituted. So he went to President von Hindenburg and said so. Von Hindenburg, however, decided that this was not the time to have another parliamentary election, and he accepted von Schleicher's resignation. A few days later, Adolf Hitler was chosen to take his place, with von Papen as deputy chancellor and high commissioner for Prussia. Within a week, von Hindenburg had been persuaded that it was indeed a time for new parliamentary elections. The old Reichstag was dissolved and the violent business of electioneering begun once again. The difference was that Hitler was now chancellor and Frick, a Nazi, minister of the interior and therefore top police official for the entire Reich. Goering was minister without portfolio but not, as events would prove, without ideas.

Like other voters, Sigmund Stein was not consulted in these decisive moves which were to make his vote a farce. He looked on Hitler's rise with real misgivings for himself, his family, and his fellow Jews. And yet his misgivings were lightened by his belief—shared by countless other Christians and Jews at the time—that the responsibilities of power would soon have the Nazis in trouble. Sigmund may even have thought that a short period of authoritarian rule might do some good. As a lawyer, he had had to familiarize himself with the piecemeal authoritarianism of a stream of emergency decrees which had been flowing out of Berlin since 1931. These were varied, complex, and in their final outcome insidious, but when these decrees were issued real alternatives must have seemed remote.

Three weeks after Hitler became chancellor, Goering told the police he "didn't believe it was necessary to emphasize" their duty to take decisive action against all disturbers of the public peace. The police would "naturally" recognize that patriotic groups like the SA and the SS were their allies in the national struggle against subversive and un-German elements. Sigmund, along with most people who were not out-and-out Nazis, did not like this, but he could comfort himself with the reflection that criticism was still possible, since the Goering proclamation was strongly attacked in the *Taegliches Hessenblatt*, the *Frankfurter Zeitung*, and other liberal papers.

It was even more discomfiting when, on the day following this proclamation, it was announced that in order to keep the peace during the coming election campaign special auxiliary police were to be deputized. These would "of course" have to be Germans of voting age, honorable and devoted to the National Idea. That is to say, SA men and—a neat play—members of the veterans' organization, the Stahlhelm. This measure was justified by citing the fact that the Weimar government had at an earlier period deputized Reichsbanner men in the same way.

This was certainly disconcerting, but it was hard to rally any real opposition after the "Iron Front" a week later held a demonstration in Hochburg which not only went off well but was also protected by the police with what even the *Hessenblatt* admitted was exemplary impartiality.

There was in fact a constant pulling and hauling from conclusion to counter-conclusion. True, the homes of Communists were constantly being entered and searched, and there was a constant flow of front-page news about the horrendous caches of propaganda and secret documents which were being found. Yet this was nothing new—it had preceded every free election for the last two years. Of course, the fact that this time the police were extending their searches to the homes of Social Democratic leaders gave food for thought. But it would have been more surprising had the Nazis let the Social Democrats alone, in view of the antagonism which had been shouted between the two parties for the preceding ten years.

The pace and direction of rationalizations changed on February 27, 1933, with the burning of the Reichstag building in Berlin, six days before the Germans were scheduled to go to the polls to elect new occupants. Not everyone believed the official story that the blaze had been set by the Communists. But *nearly* everyone did, Sigmund Stein included. What else could be expected? Ten years' harping on the evils of Communism had had their effect, years during which the antagonism between Communists and Social Democrats had often been aggravated by the fact that the latter had had the responsibilities of political power. There was a bitterness on the non-Communist left which made it only too eager to believe the worst of the Communists. And much Communist behavior gave substance to such belief. The Communists derived inspiration—and who knew how much else?—from a foreign power. The Social Democrats had gained a modicum of cherished respectability by their rejection of such inspiration. Yet the Social

Democrats had in their time conspired and maneuvered toward many of the same objectives as the Communists. Perhaps what they interpreted as the ruthless fanaticism of the Communists had the effect of a reproach. Among men who had been revolutionaries and conspirators themselves, there was special reason to believe that the burning of a major public building was a conceivable tactic.

The trouble was, the Communists did not do it. Perhaps the Nazis did.

Dr. Muehlenbach, dean emeritus of the Hochburg legal community, tells about the daring attempt of Hagen, Stein, and Mannheimer to attend the lawyers' ball. He comments on cases which Sigmund Stein had conducted. More surprising, however, is his willingness to talk about his divorce in 1932, since he had, according to others, "left his wife and five kids in the lurch," obtained a divorce, and promptly married the likewise newly divorced wife of a judge in the Hochburg district court. This had caused a tempest in the Hochburg legal teapot which had consequences for Hagen and Stein.

By his own account, Muehlenbach was already somewhat unpopular at the time the incident occurred. The "exclusive circle" of lawyers in Hochburg was no empty geometric, and its small compass contained professional jealousies and petty intrigues. Muehlenbach was the object of some of these because he was both successful and a Freemason. Not even the fact that the revered Frederick the Great of Prussia had been a Freemason had sufficed to make the lodges wholly respectable. Freemasonry occupied a place in the heart of Nazism similar to that occupied by Jewry. The lodges were not and could not be hated by the Nazis as the Jews were, for as "Aryans" the Freemasons were corrigible. Yet their feeble, somewhat bizarre internationalism and the fact that they formed a secret society earned them anathema.

Muehlenbach, with the divorce on top of everything else, was haled before a professional court in Kassel to show why his right to plead should not be transferred away from the Hochburg courts to avoid the indecorum of husband pleading before ex-husband. Kassel ruled in favor of Muehlenbach, however, arguing that since there was no question of any actual impropriety it would be unjust to transfer him. With this judgment, the agitation against Muehlenbach faded. It had not died out, however, and its re-kindling in March, 1933, became the occasion for an odd tribute to the standing of Hagen and Stein. They had had no part in the earlier agitation. Now, with the Reichstag arson having made a Nazi coup nearly certain, with the propaganda against the Jews increasing rapidly in both scope and violent effect, Hagen and Stein were approached by the anti-Muehlenbach forces with the request that the two men add their signatures to a petition demanding Muehlenbach's disbarment.

It is possible, however unlikely it may appear in retrospect, that the full gravity of Hagen and Stein's position was still unperceived by their colleagues, who thus sought their backing simply to have the entire legal community lined up against Muehlenbach. This is Muehlenbach's explanation. An element of blackmail could have been involved: Hagen and Stein could have been counted on to come through with their signatures in order to ingratiate themselves with their colleagues and thereby gain support which might very soon be necessary. To Sigmund and Werner, certainly, the situation at the ides of March in 1933 must have been painfully clear.

And yet, in spite of six weeks of Hitler as chancellor; in spite of the "purification" of the police nine months earlier and their more recent injection of Nazism; and, most of all, in spite of the open terror and repression during the week between the burning of the Reichstag and the March elections, the Nazis had failed to get an absolute majority of popular votes or parliamentary seats. With around 45 per cent of both, however, compared with less than 20 per cent for the next strongest party, the Social Democrats, the Nazis emerged as the most powerful group, parliamentary or otherwise, to appear on the German scene since the founding of the republic. With the Nazis in the seats of power and given the mood of the people, the Nazis' lack of a majority could be of but little concern to them and a feeble consolation to the opposition.

Still, Hagen and Stein refused to lend their signatures to the anti-Muehlenbach petition. The refusal may not have been heroism, but it called for a courageous decency.

The emergency decree which followed the burning of the Reichstag was drastic. On the basis of Article 48, paragraph 2 of the federal constitution, the following measures were decreed as "safeguards against acts of Communist subversion": freedom of the press; freedom of assembly; the privacy of the mails, telephone, and telegraph; the security of the home against search and seizure—these were all suspended. The Communist party was forbidden to function, and the Social Democratic party was put under close surveillance, although it was not banned. Neither party was removed from the ballot in the imminent election. How many men reassured themselves with this news?

There were other straws to cling to. Freedom of the press is nowhere absolute, and it had been even less absolute in the Germany of the twenties and early thirties. If liberty is defined as the right to do what one wishes so long as the similar rights of others are not infringed, then the whole complexion of liberty changes with population density and social complexity. Throughout the early thirties but especially after August 1, 1932, press bans had been frequent in Germany. Most often it was the Communist publications which had been banned, with those of the remaining left running a poor second.

Freedom of assembly had been infringed by at least one of the earlier decrees, and the security of the home had been invaded. The Communist party had not been previously banned, although raids on its offices and harassment of its functionaries had been a regular feature of pre-election periods in 1931 and 1932. The technical freedom of the elections themselves had come to be a sop thrown to anyone who began to have doubts about the freedom of the electioneering. Such a person was always able to say to himself, as the *Frankfurter Zeitung* said to its readers, "We'll get our innings at the ballot boxes." To have raised serious questions about the tangible restrictions on electioneering would have opened up the question of the intangible restrictions and inequities, such as the lack of financial power and the smearing of unpopular ideologies. If the Nazi coup had become inevitable by March, 1933, it was because the Germans had been unable or unwilling to face up to and answer such questions since the end of the World War.

It was a peculiar coup, this "seizure of power" by the Nazis.

After the elections of March 5, the change from the course which Germany had been following for the previous two years was one of speed rather than direction. It was an acceleration due to visible events, the knowledge of which influenced the feelings and judgments of the majority of people. The Germans did not know the way in which the Nazis were implicated in the Reichstag fire. The accusation against the Communists was overwhelmingly authoritative, and by serving as the immediate and convincing occasion of the measures which followed, the arson became the visible symbol of the peculiar coup.

The effects were quick in coming to Hochburg. One short week after the election, the *Taegliches Hessenblatt* was suppressed for a day. The town clerk, in a typewritten chronicle of events lifted mostly from the *Landeskurier,* explained the confiscation with an unintentional display of humor in the dark: the SA had occupied the editorial offices of the *Hessenblatt* because, the clerk originally wrote, "the paper had on its local page repeatedly cast unjustified slurs on the Reichschancellor, the NSDAP, and the Hochburg auxiliary police." Then, with obvious concern that "unjustified slurs" might be taken to imply the existence of slurs that were justified, the adjective was neatly crossed out.

It was to Konrad Muenschner's credit that the accusation of slurs had been true, but he is ill at ease in telling of the incident. Like Werner Hagen, he knew that the Nazis were loaded against him, and had he been a Jew he would have fled. But he was not a Jew. With all his Social Democratic liberalism and—for Hochburg —personal radicalism, his ties to the town and the surrounding countryside were more nearly like Sigmund Stein's. An amateur historian, Muenschner was proud of Germany and proud of Hochburg. He knew that the mere masthead of his paper stood for opposition, and he could not bring himself to say, "This is the end." That he was afraid is obvious. He would have been a fool if he had not been apprehensive. And so he gave his written word that no more such "slurs" would appear in the paper, which came out the next day with a labored and painful explanation of why it had not appeared the day before.

From this point until its final dissolution at the end of April, the general pages of the paper are a colorless repetition of the rest of the papers in Germany. The mats for these pages were delivered daily from what had once been the Social Democratic press service in Kassel. The dissolution of this organization had been announced in the first issue to appear after the early suspension; the physical plant remained to grind out pap. This parroting of Nazi sloganry did not afflict the local pages of the *Hessenblatt,* however. From these it is evident that Muenschner was not writing what and how he wanted to write; under the circumstances the visibility of the pressure is almost refreshing. Beyond this negative virtue there is the positive one that events not reported elsewhere are written up. While these are necessarily described without comment, their straightforward details plainly reveal the nature of the forces which were taking over.

There is also a reporting of the undramatic, day-to-day events which, in other papers, were being drowned either in flamboyant enthusiasm or brown and turgid seriousness. Thus, along with Muenschner's labored explanation of the suspension, there is an entirely usual story about Sigmund Stein's defense of a carpenter against a charge of perjury. This was in the second half of March. It was to be the last case which Sigmund handled as a fully qualified lawyer.

From the Hochburg pages of the *Hessenblatt* during these, its last, days; from the *Landeskurier*; and from the typewritten chronicle of the town clerk it is possible to get a picture of the way in which the Brown Wave broke over Hochburg, where the only event which approached the conventional notion of revolutionary turmoil was the replacement of the mayor. Mayor Remsbach was no Socialist, but he had made himself unpopular with the Nazis, particularly those among the student body at Hochburg University. As a career official concerned with public order and safety, he had frequently forbidden Nazi student demonstrations during "the years of struggle." Thus it was fitting—and had been so arranged—that the student, Landsmann, with the ex-student and *Kreisleiter*-to-be, Kleinwitz, whose father was the respected shepherd of a fundamentalist religious community in Hochburg, should be leaders of the delegation which visited Remsbach at the end of the month in order to inform him of something he well knew: that he was *persona non grata* to the new regime. Among the other members of the delegation was the Nazi lawyer, Kutscher, following his rising star.

Remsbach was told that he would have to get out. He did not comply at once but asked for and was given an hour to think it over. During this period he got in touch with the higher-ups in Kassel and was told that he should take an indefinite leave of absence. Since he was, so to speak, the meeting point of the revolutions from above and below, this could hardly have surprised him. He was not pleased, but the matter was in order and his hands were clean. He called back the delegation and told them as much. They were satisfied, and the administration of the town was turned over to the mayor's deputy, Herr Brecht. Brecht seems to have been a decent enough man, who eventually came to disappoint the confidence the Nazis placed in him. Casimir Dombrowski, the Jewish tailor who managed to survive the Nazi era in Hochburg, described Brecht as one of the few city officials who had never ceased to greet him when they met on the street.

Upon the mayor's abdication, the student Landsmann went out to announce the result of the negotiations to the crowd assembled in the Marktplatz in front of the town hall. The *Machter-greifung* (the seizure of power) had come to Hochburg, where an ironic aspect of this peculiar coup was the fact that the Nazis had obtained a better than two-thirds majority in the local election for the town council which had followed close on the national elections at the beginning of March. They were thus assured of getting their own mayor eventually in any case.

The revolution was real enough to its perpetrators and its victims. Like the Jews elsewhere in Germany, those in Hochburg were anxiously waiting out events. Their anxiety was punctuated by attempts at adjustment, the inadequacy of which would seem, in retrospect, to have been as pitiful as their inherent compromise was hopeless. At the time, of course, neither the inadequacy nor the hopelessness was obvious, and there is little reason why they should have been.

The boycott of Jewish enterprises which the triumphant Nazis planned for the first of April was many things in one. The general anti-Semitism of the Nazis had aroused protest in the world's press, and this protest had been strengthened by the reports of specific anti-Semitic agitation and violence during "the years of struggle." These reports had often enough been carried by the German press. During 1932 and early 1933, however, the German press and especially the press which was accused by the Nazis of being under Jewish control seems to have developed a tendency to evade the inanities and insanities of the Nazi racial policy. The observation is not clear-cut, but it was as though an effort were being made to tread lightly in this area in the belief that too great an emphasis on it could play into Nazi hands.

The result was that the prominence given to the anti-Semitic aspect of the Nazi movement in the foreign press contrasted with the subordinate place it occupied in the German press. To the German who read little or even much more than the headlines of his own papers, the agitation in the foreign press appeared exaggerated. After January, 1933, when Jews began to leave Germany in substantial numbers, the situation was intensified. More material became available to the foreign press and more reason for caution shaped the policy of the German opposition press. Thus, by March the Nazis were able to talk about the "hate-mongering" and "atrocity propaganda" of the foreign press, adduce this as proof of Jewish control, and threaten retaliation. All of this, as a result of the situation just described, had scattered glimpses of reality to many Germans, including many who were not in sympathy with Nazi anti-Semitism. A factor which would play an important part in Nazi propaganda and German reaction to this propaganda already appears here. This was the exploitation by the Nazis of the resentment which Germans—Jews and non-Jews alike—felt toward the Allied atrocity propaganda during World War I, so much of which had been proved false.

It is hard to believe that anyone seriously thought the boycott announced in the last week of March would have the effect of toning down comment in the foreign press, yet millions of Germans did believe just that. Many of these were not ill-disposed toward the Jews and hoped the boycott would have its intended effect because they were direct witnesses to the use which the Nazis were making of foreign criticism. Such hopefulness was mistaken not so much in its immediate logic but rather in a belittlement of Nazi anti-Semitism made possible only by the failure to appreciate the extent to which racism had infected Germany.

The picture of the boycott which comes out of Hochburg is typical of the all-German picture. It was officially to be a limited action against all *German*-Jewish businesses, "Jewish goods, Jewish physicians, and Jewish lawyers." It was to be orderly and disciplined, and foreigners, "regardless of confession, origin, or race," were not to be affected. But the SS who were assigned to go around town placarding Jewish businesses and the SA who were assigned to picketing those businesses, and to seeing that the placards were not removed, were ordinary people whose triumph had been one of narrow and resentful idealism sauced with gutter hatreds and brawling the good brawl. They sensed the métier of the movement and the temper of their leaders.

Consequently, there were incidents of one kind or another in and around Hochburg. For example, in Huehnerhausen, a small town lying about halfway between Hochburg and Bachdorf, a Jewish tradesman was forced to walk through the streets up to the gong that was used to signalize public announcements, strike it, and then declare to the assembled villagers his repentance for an insult which he was supposed to have directed against Adolf Hitler.

There were no recorded instances of violence in Hochburg itself. Casimir Dombrowski was technically a foreign national in 1933, actually a stateless person, since his passport had been validated by the defunct Kerensky government of Russia. He believed he had grounds for objecting to the labeling of his tailor shop as a Jewish business and sent his Christian wife to Kleinwitz, already the neighborhood Nazi leader, to see if the sign could not be removed. Kleinwitz, say the Dombrowskis, was not unpleasant. But the sign was not removed.

Simon Leopold, the heretofore respected proprietor of a clothing store, made a gesture which was duplicated many times throughout Germany that day. He dressed himself in formal clothes, pinned his Iron Cross, First Class, on his chest, and stood at attention outside his establishment. Others, like the Mannheimer brothers, placed their Iron Crosses, properly dignified in lined jewel boxes or chaste frames, on display in their shop windows.

Only too often such acts became the occasion for the already quoted comment, "Where'd they buy those things?"

By and large, however, the Jewish community in Hochburg lay low, waiting for the squall to pass. After telling of Leopold's attempt to shame the Nazis, the teacher Klingelmann adds that Sigmund Stein would never have done that. He explains that Sigmund was not afraid to do such a thing, but that it just was not in keeping with his personality. Similarly, Sigmund did not tell jokes which put the Jews in a ridiculous light and had refused to join the Jewish Korporation which slavishly imitated the dueling and other conventions of its non-Jewish counterparts. Thus he combined a deeply felt desire for assimilation with a dignity which refused to go beyond a certain point in the effort to attain it.

To be sure, a law office on the Bahnhofstrasse was neither as conspicuous nor as symbolically Jewish as a clothing store or dry-goods store in the Windstrasse. Werner Hagen's widow says that an SA man did stand outside the office on the day of the boycott, but since the boycott started on a Saturday morning at ten o'clock and ended the same evening, it is unlikely that either of the partners spent any amount of time in the office during the action.

Later on, Sigmund, too, made much of the fact that he had won the Iron Cross. He never did so publicly but, by that time, few Jews did anything publicly. In 1933, however, as March passed into April, the Hochburg Jewish community still felt that something was to be gained by a public appeal, a kind of figurative display of the Iron Cross. Several days after the boycott had been announced and two days before it was to take place, there appeared in both the *Landeskurier* and the *Taegliches Hessenblatt* the following declaration:

A STATEMENT BY THE HOCHBURG JEWISH COMMUNITY

The members of the Hochburg Jewish Community have learned to their great consternation that atrocity stories about the mistreatment of German Jews are being spread in foreign countries and are giving rise to agitation in favor of a boycott on German goods.

We dissociate ourselves completely from all these transparent lies. In justice to the truth and in response to our innermost desires we herewith declare that up to the present time not a single Jew in Hochburg has had so much as a hair on his head harmed. We request that this declaration be distributed and made use of wherever necessary.

The Hochburg Jews have felt themselves to be Germans and Hochburgers in both war and peace. They have participated actively in the athletic and organizational life of the town right up to the present day.

Students of the Jewish faith in both the Gymnasium and the vocational high school volunteered side by side with their Christian comrades in the World War. Many of them fell in action, even as early as the battle of Langemark, the national anthem on their lips. Many were the Jews of Hochburg who fought and bled at the front for the glory of Germany. The greatness of Germany and the recent upsurge in German strength are both near to our hearts. We are certain that the national government will see to it that justice is done to every upright person, and we protest with the government against any scorn for or belittlement of Germany.

By pointing to the "agitation in favor of a boycott on German goods," the declaration stresses a side of the April First action in Germany which was made much of in the German press—this is the designation of the action as an *anti*-boycott action. In his chronicle, the town clerk "made use of" the declaration by quoting the lines, "up to the present time not a single Jew in Hochburg has had so much as a hair of his head harmed." He made the passage of even greater use by omitting "up to the present time."

The next day brought more of the same in the form of an announcement in the *Hessenblatt* by the Mannheimer drygoods company under the headline:

AGAINST THE ATROCITY PROPAGANDA

We are informed by Mannheimer Bros., Inc., that, in order to combat the false and malicious rumors which are being spread abroad, they have sent Herr Herbert Mannheimer, who is currently in the United States, a telegram with the following contents: "Please quash USA horror stories about Germany. Exemplary order here."

The next day brought the boycott.

It is highly probable that Sigmund Stein participated in drawing up the community declaration. It was a tactical measure consciously designed as an adaptive response to the exigencies of the time. Yet Sigmund Stein had volunteered, and Jewish boys had died at the Battle of Langemark as in every other major battle of the World War. That they died with the national anthem on their lips is rhetoric, characteristic of all patriotic utterances. Yet the declaration had a deeper truth and a deeper sincerity, while to say that the patriotism and commitment to Germany of the German Jews were complicated by a variety of factors is merely to belabor what should be obvious.

Were the particular Hochburg Jews who drew up the declaration lying when they wrote that "up to the present time" not a single Jew in Hochburg had been harmed? Was the declaration perhaps extorted from these men, as a sop to throw to non-Jewish "sentimentalists" in Germany who might be concerned about what was happening? Again, the answer must be ambiguous. The statement was clearly extorted by the situation even if it was completely spontaneous. It was a sop to some, sentimentalists and others—it was good, from the Nazi point of view, to have such statements available. Actually, "up to this time" a good many people, Jews and non-Jews, Nazis and anti-Nazis, had had appreciably more than a hair on their heads harmed.

The writers of the declaration no doubt accepted the fact that a time of trial was ahead, and precisely in this realistic insight lay a particular reason to give whatever leverage they could to the moderates who they believed could be found in the Nazi party. At the very least, they may well have believed they would be fools to furnish the extreme anti-Semites with the leverage of their failure to speak out.

Such considerations may have been tortured and mistaken—they were not fantastic. They led to a total pattern of rationalization which was tragically convincing to those who were forced to rely on it, as were Sigmund Stein and the bulk of those Jews who remained in Germany. When people are accused of being un-German or un-American or un-anything, they rarely respond by asserting the irrelevance or negatives of the national concept, preferring instead to insist that they are in fact patriotic or that they are the true patriots.

Heinrich Preusser, a Hochburg Communist, responds vigorously to the topic of Sigmund Stein's patriotism and love for Germany. "We too," he says, "have a patriotic love for Germany," and there is no doubt that he means it.

Patriotism could lie behind affiliation with the Nazis. Robert Schmidt, who joined the party in 1932 and is scornful of the "March Violets," as the opportunists who jumped on the bandwagon in March, 1933, are called, claimed that he joined because of the party's strong affirmation of Germany and not because of its Jewish policy. His attitude toward the Jews seems a mixture of acceptance and rejection which lends credence to his claim.

The measures adopted by the Jews in 1933 and earlier were general human reactions to the specifics which characterized the Jewish situation. Yet the spring of 1933 in Germany was a waypoint on the road to a catastrophe unprecedented in the number of its victims, despite the fact that most of the ingredients of the catastrophe could be found in other times and places.

The pervasive difference between Sigmund Stein and Werner Hagen in reacting to the circumstances of 1933 revolves about aggressiveness of response. The difference appeared early, when both men were at the Gymnasium and at Jungmann's Boarding Home together prior to the World War. The original source of the difference is unknown, but it can be assumed to lie in a complex of personality and childhood experience. Only one major difference is clear: the fact that Hagen attended a Talmud-Torah school as a boy and was thus exposed to an intensity of dialectical training and an incisiveness of Jewish identification which were foreign to Sigmund's early years. Given this fact, the divergence of behavior between the two men in 1933 becomes more understandable.

In the maelstrom of German politics after 1918, both Hagen and Stein were all but inevitably committed to the support of the new republic, to liberalism, and to a general German patriotism. Consistent with his greater aggressiveness, however, was Hagen's tendency to go further than Sigmund. He ended up, politically, as a Social Democrat whom the exigencies of the time drove toward a non-ideological sympathy with the Communists. And he went further socially as well. Hagen's reputation for girl-chasing was certain to mark him for disaster in a Germany where even friendship with a Jew might "bastardize" Aryan blood.

Social ignorance, the absence of general knowledge about the details of an individual's behavior, will play an important part in the story of Sigmund Stein's relationships with the Hochburg Jewish community in the abnormal situation of the later Nazi years. In normal situations it plays a major role in gossip about sexual behavior. Both those who were "for" Werner Hagen and those who were "against" him speak of his many affairs with women. One woman admits peeping from her apartment into the Hagen's apartment which was just across the street. She clucks that she did not object to what a man did outside his home—a little diversion was natural enough now and then—but the least he could do was keep his own household clean. Just because his wife was away . . .

Hagen may simply have been a man for whom the moral conflict had ceased to be that between fidelity and infidelity and had become one between acceptance of his natural desires and the possible consequences of those desires. The German town, with its highly developed class and status lines, offers sexual opportunities of little consequence. Yet it is quite ready to give a man a reputation as a philanderer. Since the Nazis reveled in projecting the satyr-like Jew who lusted after pure Aryan girls, Hagen's reputation gave the Nazi antagonism to him a special and ominous spice.

For such reasons, Hagen's flight in April, 1933, does not presuppose excessive foresight on his part. His personality and style had created a situation where it was a clear case of self-preservation. Incidental to his personality and style was an insight into the society around him which was, no doubt, greater than Sigmund Stein's. And yet, it would be nonsense to conclude that Hagen foresaw what was to come in the late thirties and the forties. His widow says that when they left Germany they really did not have a good general picture of what was happening. They had to wait until they had been in France for some time before they were able to gain a true perspective. What Hagen did understand, however, and what Sigmund Stein may never have understood, was that the position he had won for himself in German society would not save him, that his Iron Cross would not save him, and that even what he knew to be the fundamental decency of many of his friends would not save him. When he left, he left for good. His wife returned a few months later in order to wind up their affairs, but Werner stayed on the other side of the Rhine.

In the second week of April, 1933, the law firm of Hagen and Stein was overwhelmed by the rush of events.

The ousting of the mayor had been followed by a series of measures designed to stress the loyalty of Hochburg to Germany and the new regime. Von Hindenburg and Hitler were made honorary citizens, and Hitler was further honored when the Heinrichplatz was renamed the Adolf Hitler Platz. As "the Victor of Tannenberg," von Hindenburg had long since been paid such homage: one of Hochburg's better residential streets as well as parks and buildings bore his name. Nazi bigwigs other than Hitler were also honored. Sigmund Stein had to see the Dietrichstrasse on which he lived become the Herman Goering Strasse. The Flachstrasse where Werner Hagen had his apartment became for half its length the Horst Wessel Strasse and for the other half the "Street of the SS."

The forerunners of National Socialism were commemorated, too. The Helenastrasse where the new Boarding Home for Jewish Students was located became the Wilhelm Marr Strasse, in honor of a nineteenth-century anti-Semitic pamphleteer. The Hospitallerstrasse where Sigmund and Werner once had their office became the Otto Boeckel Strasse, in belated recognition of the services to race and folk which this Hessian anti-Semite had rendered.

In other circumstances these name changes might have been looked upon as a bad joke. As it was, they were the petty reflections of more searing measures. The first of these bore directly on Hagen and Stein. This was the "Law for the Re-establishment of a Professional Civil Service." Included among its wide-ranging and not entirely malevolent provisions was the barbed paragraph: "Officials who are not of Aryan stock are to be retired; when the position of such officials is non-salaried, the function shall be considered dissolved."

The next paragraph seemed to save Hagen and Stein and was

welcomed by those who wanted to believe that there were moderate elements in the Nazi party:

> The preceding paragraph does not apply to officials who:
> a. have had official status since 1 August, 1914, or
> b. fought at the front in the World War for the German Reich or its allies, or
> c. whose fathers or sons fell in the World War.
> Further exceptions may be granted by the Minister of the Interior.

There followed, however, a provision which was to be a great catch-all for Jews and non-Jews alike: "Officials whose previous political activity does not give assurance of their unqualified loyalty to the National State can be dismissed. For three months after their dismissal they shall receive full pay. Thereafter . . . they shall receive three-quarters of the normal pension."

As veterans of the front in the First World War, both Hagen and Stein were permitted to retain their practice in the re-established civil service. The two men did not rejoice at the concession; it would have been foolish to assume that ambiguities in the law would be resolved in their favor. Two days after they had been told they would be allowed to continue their practice, a letter came from the Minister of Justice in Berlin. "As a result of Communistic activities," both men were henceforth to be barred from the representation of clients and from arguing before the courts.

Sigmund and Werner were puzzled at the specific nature of the charge, but Hagen, on checking through his files, found the probable source of it. This was a letter to the Communist legal aid organization, Rote Hilfe, in the form of a bill for services rendered. Hagen had dictated and signed the letter. In addition to rendering the bill, he had added a sentence or two expressing his general sympathy for the work which the Rote Hilfe was doing. This was an understandable (if perhaps incautious) statement in the atmosphere of late summer, 1932, when the letter was written. But such sentiments constituted an almost certain self-denunciation in mid-March, 1933, when the files of Rote Hilfe were seized by government agents.

Sigmund Stein may not even have known about the letter. But the fact that Sigmund had not signed the letter did not help him. Hagen had naturally used the firm's letterhead, on which Sigmund appeared as a full partner. Even if Sigmund had had reservations about Hagen's gratuitous comments in the letter, he would have written them off, at that time, as an expression of his partner's personal idiosyncrasies. In any event, with Hagen as the bull's-eye the Nazis were aiming at, Sigmund was well within the target area.

The case of Dr. Mordecai Mannheimer, the third Jewish lawyer in Hochburg, came close to proving that if one was a Jewish lawyer and for any reason unpopular, his fate was sealed, regardless of the provisions of the "Law for the Re-establishment of a Professional Civil Service." Mannheimer had been in the legal profession prior to August 1, 1914, and had an unsullied political record, even from the Nazi point of view, since he simply was not a political person. But he did have the reputation of being avaricious; he was said to keep his office open on Sundays for the express purpose of being able to charge premium fees to peasants who could not get there any other day.

Frau Zimmerman, the non-Jewish widow of the non-Jewish man who had been Mannheimer's office manager until 1932, agrees that the lawyer had been hard to get along with. "Hagen tried it, Stein tried it, my husband tried it. It just wasn't possible." But the stories about Mannheimer's working Sunday for premium fees were ridiculous, she asserted. Mannheimer did work on Sunday, and Herr Zimmerman had griped endlessly over this. But precisely because her husband had been so irritated, Frau Zimmerman is sure he would have thrown it up against Mannheimer if the lawyer had been taking premium fees. She thinks the Sunday work was an attempt to accommodate the peasants. Sunday was not so convenient that the peasants could not have come during the week if that had really been cheaper.

After the disbarment of Hagen and Stein, Mannheimer was the only Jewish lawyer left in Hochburg. Diabetic, with his condition aggravated by events, he had left town for a rest at a country resort. This may have been his undoing, because during his absence the Nazi lawyer, Kutscher, was able to get access to his records and obtain material on which to base several charges of malpractice. Typical of these charges in its pettiness was the accusation that Mannheimer had illegally pre-dated a document by three days in 1926! A warrant was sworn out, and Mannheimer voluntarily returned to Hochburg. Since he was sick, he was allowed to stay, under guard, in the medical clinic of the University hospital. This prompted his accuser to complain that Mannheimer was probably exploiting the visits of his wife to arrange for the destruction of additional, as yet uncovered, evidence of wrongdoing.

The whole set of charges was, in fact, such a ridiculous hodgepodge of trivialities and assiduously misinterpreted obscurities that they were all either thrown out by the court or disproved by Mannheimer. But the harassment, his sickness, and the general tenor of the times made practice impossible for him, and as soon as the legal proceedings were finished, Mannheimer and his family left for Holland, where he was able to take over the management of a small candy factory. His daughter believes that they did well to leave when they did, for a whole rat's nest of litigation was soon started against Mannheimer. If they had stayed they would have been impossibly entangled in it. From Holland, Mannheimer defended himself and finally, in 1938, cleared his name.

Both his success in getting a favorable judgment as late as 1938 and the fact that his daughter stressed the *inconvenience* they would have suffered had they remained in Germany are noteworthy. The legal victory was a satisfaction to Mannheimer—in 1938, to the Jews remaining in Hochburg, it was like a light in the general gloom.

Hagen and Stein were more popular than Mannheimer, but they were both politically tainted. When disbarment finally came for them in the second week of April, Hagen and his family left Germany immediately. Sigmund stayed on.

Why he stayed must be explained on the basis of everything which has been said about him. He did not want to leave, and unlike Hagen, he did not have to leave. Hagen loved Germany, but Sigmund was deeply *involved* in his love for Germany. Hagen had roots in the region around Hochburg, but these had been gradually loosening in the years from 1930 to 1933. Sigmund, on the other hand, reacted to the same set of circumstances by finding strength and self-justification in his identification with the history and land-scape of Hochburg and Hesse.

It is hard to determine the extent to which Sigmund was aware of his attachments. He could formulate all of them, but it is unlikely that he saw them as bonds which were preventing him from flight. He was shaken by the Nazi attainment of power, but his belief that they would stumble over the responsibilities of power was one which could be put to the test only if they attained it. Now that this had happened, the character of Sigmund's belief inevitably had to change from a more or less analytical conclusion to a desperate hope. Yet the hope was still disguised as a reasoned belief, and the belief implied that the Jews would once again find their place in Germany.

It was a storm which had to be weathered, and in his willing-ness to stick it out, Sigmund, the liberal Jew, found at least some strength in Jewish history and tradition. He found more support in plausible, even compelling rationalizations. Hagen's widow says that one reason Sigmund gave for staying was the necessity of taking care of his parents-in-law in Dreistadt. This was true, and his sense of responsibility was genuine, but surely this was an emotional rationalization.

Another rationalization has been mentioned earlier: how could he make use of his *German* legal training in another country? And then there were the simple, mechanical aspects of emigration. Of his feelings about those fellow Jews who emigrated from Hochburg, Casimir Dombrowski says, "How is one to say? They were lucky, they had the money or the connections, or maybe both." It was hard to face emigration if one did not have funds and foreign connections. Even if one did have these contacts in foreign countries, the fact was that most friends and relatives would still be left behind in Germany.

The chief rationalization of this kind was embodied in Sig-mund's father, Isaac, who still lived in Bachdorf. In his late sixties at the time, Isaac Stein was no candidate for emigration. Sigmund's roots were in Hesse and in Germany, but Isaac clung to the one tiny village of Bachdorf. He wanted to be buried in the lovely cemetery overlooking the Frieden River as it flowed past Weidenfeld, where his synagogue stood, past Bachdorf, where he had raised his children, and past Niederhausen, where he was born.

The peculiar yet characteristic thing about these "debating points" with which Sigmund was able to justify his refusal to emigrate is the fact that, when taken together, they have much the same shape as his emotional and personal commitments to Germany and his situation there. They illuminate, without essentially changing, the simple statement: Sigmund did not leave *his* Germany because he simply did not want to.

Hagen did not wish to leave either, nor did any of the Jews who fled in the first months of Nazi power. More than Sigmund they *had* to get out; more than he they had the opportunity to take up life again elsewhere. But the flight was a hurt which would never heal for them entirely, and the circumstantial necessity as well as the unequal opportunity were hard to admit. Thus, those who emigrated also had to have their rationalizations—among which a vaunted foresight was to grow tragically in importance—and the whole intellectual conflict between those who stayed and those who left was debated in terms which seldom penetrated to the determining issues.

Despite the greatly accelerated rate of Jewish emigration in the panic of the first months of Nazi power, the number of those who fled was but a small proportion of the entire German Jewish community. This general picture was reflected in Hochburg. For Sigmund, however, the situation was characterized less by numbers than it was by the fact that his partner was among these numbers, and that all over Germany men of his profession were especially hard hit. And near the end of April, a Jew whom he had admired and respected made his escape from Germany by another route—suicide.

In the last week of April the *Taegliches Hessenblatt* was still struggling against the inevitable; the muted resistance and resentment which Konrad Muenschner managed to get into the local page was inevitably being overwhelmed by the Nazi enthusiasm of the rest of the paper. The local page's last service to truth was a macabre one. The town chronicler reported for April 25, "A local resident committed suicide this morning by throwing himself in front of a Frankfurt-bound express train." The *Hessenblatt* for the next day reported this suicide in similar anonymous fashion, but in a separate item printed the report: "Yesterday morning Professor Doctor Heinz Mendelsohn, Director of the Near East Institute, departed this life at the age of 51 years."

On April 7, however, in what was to be the last issue of the *Hessenblatt*, there appeared a tribute to Professor Mendelsohn which unambiguously if implicitly referred to his suicide. It spoke of the esteem he had enjoyed in his field of study and how life became impossible for him when he was excluded from teaching and research. As a professor he was, like Sigmund, a member of the civil service and thus a victim of the decree relating to the "Re-establishment of the Professional Civil Service." Sigmund had always looked up to Professor Mendelsohn, and the relationship between the two men had been a warm one, in spite of the fact that Sigmund had always spoken of "Herr Professor" and Mendelsohn never of "Herr Doctor." Mendelsohn's death, like Hagen's flight, was only a beginning. For Sigmund, there would be many more forced sunderings of close and meaningful relationships.

Meanwhile, he had to make a living. He and his family were still well off. There were savings, and there was Esther's modest wealth, so they were in no immediate financial danger. But the loss of his legal practice and the income which went with it would eventually have been disastrous had not some substitute been found. In this connection it is surprising that Sigmund never seems to have appealed his disbarment. Although some witnesses say he protested it, there is no record of any formal action. The "Law for the Re-establishment of a Professional Civil Service" was designed specifically to be hard on Jewish lawyers and yet, one year after it was decreed, Jewish lawyers still constituted 19 per cent of all lawyers in Prussia. This was a precipitous drop from the 29 per cent of a year earlier, to be sure. And it was obvious that the drop would increase, but it was *not* obvious that Jews would disappear from the legal profession by the autumn of 1935. The 19 per cent remaining in 1934 was still almost twenty times the proportion of Jews in the total population. Sigmund pointed out, several years later, that, were it really necessary to do something about the Jews in Germany, the rigorous application of a *numerus clausus* to the various professions would at least have had the appearance of fairness. Thus he could hardly have been unaware that it was still possible for a Jew to practice law in 1934. Yet there are no traces of energetic attempts to regain his practice.

Within the murk of misfortune which had descended on him and other Jews, it was perhaps fortunate that necessity did not drive him so far. Reinstatement would have been difficult for Sigmund without a demeaning disavowal of his previous relationships and positions. Two main ways of making a living remained open to him, both of which were closely related to his earlier activities as a lawyer.

The one was entirely legal and above board. It involved the counseling of would-be Jewish emigrants in matters relating to their financial and legal status in general, and to the taking of funds out of Germany in particular. As the only Jew in Hochburg who had been a lawyer, and as a man, moreover, who still enjoyed much of the personal and professional respect which had been accorded to him by the entire community, Sigmund was sought out as an adviser on such matters by Jews from the whole area around Hochburg. He came to know the economic and general situation of these Jews as well as or better than anyone else. The responsibilities he assumed in this connection were to become a fateful tangle of additional ties to Hochburg.

The second course open to him was general legal counseling. Much, but not all, of such activity was permitted under the Nazis although, needless to say, real difficulties and hindrances in both kinds of activities constantly arose out of the underlying anti-Semitic tendency of the regime. This tendency was an overwhelming fact and lay behind the "Law for the Re-establishment of a Professional Civil Service" as it lay behind the proliferating system of racial laws which eventually followed.

Yet despite the widespread anti-Semitism, Hitler and his tacticians had not been deceived by the "revolutionary enthusiasm" which accompanied the seizure of power. They did not want to rule by parliamentary means, and they knew they could not. On the other hand, they wanted to preserve an illusion of constitutionality. Hence, the "revolutionary enthusiasm" was exploited in order to obtain a blanket enabling law from the new Reichstag at the end of

March. This law permitted the new regime to rule by decree under the emergency provisions of the Weimar constitution. In view of the reliance which had been placed on these provisions for the preceding three years, and in view of the majority by which the enabling law was passed, the step did not appear as radical as it otherwise would have. But it killed the ailing parliamentarianism of the German state.

Had such a measure as the "Law for the Re-establishment of a Professional Civil Service" been subjected to normal parliamentary discussion, it would have been delayed and changed, in spite of all the basic anti-Semitism which was there to smooth its way. The Nazis had, to a degree, been hypnotized by their own propaganda. They had continually portrayed Jewish officials as men who had sneaked into office during the "Jew Republic" of Weimar. They had also repeatedly accused the Jews of evading active service in the World War. Hence, they simply underestimated the number of Jews who by reason of service at the front or length of service as officials would be exempted from the provisions of the law. If the law had been discussed, these questions of fact would have caused difficulties, even for the honestly malevolent.

Yet this was not the only cause of the "mildness" of the law. After all, it would have been entirely in keeping with the racist beliefs of the Nazis to dismiss all Jewish civil servants. If this was not done, the moderation arose from considerations independent of Nazi theory and sometimes opposed to it. Had all Jewish civil servants been summarily dismissed, it would have created real problems of administration and social welfare; the impact on foreign opinion would have been greater than it was; and domestic opinion would have received a shock for which it was not ready.

The fact that such considerations were expedient was a godsend to all those who, in sincere or opportunistic agreement with parts of the Nazi program, had gone along with the Nazis in the spring of 1933. Most of these people were not pro-Jewish, but among them, among the general population, there were many who had no thoughts about a complete eradication of Jews from German life. And there were many who, vaguely anti-Semitic in general, had not yet renounced those among their best friends who were

Jews. In fact, there were those among the "March Violets" who, in broad agreement with the national aims of the Nazis, were not in sympathy with anti-Semitism. These were the people who came into Meyer's jewelry store in Hochburg to commiserate with old Meyer and his sons: "It's tough," and if the Fuehrer knew what was going on. . . ." These are the people who are characterized by their friendship for "a fine man like Meyer . . . practically a fellow-citizen." These are the people who said of Esther Stein that she was "a lovely woman, so dignified and respectable, only an expert could see the Jew in her." Among them were professors, teachers, judges, and bureaucrats.

But there were also thousands of little people, like Frau Baker Schmidt of the Stadtplatz, who was caught up in the enthusiasm for specific Nazi promises, but who also had close and good relationships with such men as Herr Solomon, who had canceled the interest on the money which she and her husband owed him. There was Herr Kornmann, a minor official in the Hochburg district court and a true-blue German nationalist who got himself in trouble several times by saying in front of the wrong people that it was a shame what they were doing to men who had fought for their country. There was Frau Mahler, one of the few practical nurses who was to remain on call to care for Jewish patients. She liked the Nazi policy on unwed mothers, but she tried to comfort Frau Goldberg by telling her that the SA was just a stupid mob and did not mean anything personal when they sang their murderously anti-Semitic marching songs. Frau Mahler was for Hitler until one of her three sons was killed in North Africa.

People like these were looked upon as the "moderates" within the Nazi milieu which had forced Sigmund Stein and other Jews from belief to hope. It is almost certain that the early anti-Jewish measures would have been less moderate if such people had not existed. They were continually and, in the end, devastatingly undercut—because their very sincerity held too much of the soil out of which the Nazi racial ideology had sprung. In the spring and summer of 1933 and for several years thereafter, they walked a tortuous path. They had to avoid using arguments which could be labeled as "misguided humanitarianism." Instead, they stressed expediencies, such as considering the impact on foreign opinion

This makes the question of motive behind such arguments difficult, since one man could use them as a thoroughly Nazi realist who wanted to see anti-Semitic measures introduced at a point where their ultimate stringency would not be jeopardized. On the other hand, the arguments could be used by a conscious opponent of the racial policy who viewed himself as fighting a delaying action against the racist radicals. He could see himself as working from within to reduce particular Nazi inanities for the purpose of preserving Germany's reputation in the eyes of the world.

Hypocrisy and fear sometimes took the form of the man who opposed the anti-Semitism of the regime but in public encounters with Jews affected a display of severe and unfriendly correctness. Herbert Durckheim was this kind of a man. Long a friend of Sigmund Stein's, he had fallen for some of the Nazi arguments at an early period. He was never entirely won over, but his indecision was such that he was not disturbed when he saw the Nazis capture the town administration, in which he was a minor official. He dates his inner break with the party from the murder of Roehm in the summer of 1934. Durckheim is not the hero type, but he is a gregarious, active man with a streak of stubborn egoism which leads him to go what he feels is his own way. The inner break grew into a violent and nervous antagonism which finally resulted in his drawing close to several members of the Hochburg Jewish community. His relationship with Sigmund Stein became the closest of these.

Durckheim was and remains something of a ham actor. He tells how he used to visit Sigmund in the evening, armed with some document which made his visit plausible in terms of his official duties. He would try to make his entrance into the Stein apartment unobtrusively but if, as sometimes happened, he was observed, he would make a great show of severity when Sigmund came to the door saying, for instance, "Doctor, I regret that I have to speak to you once again about one of your fellow Jews . . . the situation simply can't be allowed to go on . . ." and more in a like vein. Sigmund would answer meekly and respectfully, suggesting that Herr Durckheim come in to talk the matter over. Once inside, with the danger of observation passed, they would both laugh heartily and make a great joke of their acting.

Durckheim was no angel, and in 1940 when incidents like this had become commonplace—for several years after 1933 they had only occasionally been necessary—the motives in his relationship with Sigmund contained elements which, pure enough politically, were questionable economically. Given such mixed motives, the relationship between the two men was a genuine and apparently easy one, camouflaged by severity on the one side and humility on the other.

In a way, the existence of pockets of moderation within and around the Nazi regime was a curse as well as a blessing for the Jews who remained in Germany. Sigmund Stein lived out nine years of this regime on the crutch of the fact that there were numerous people in the town administration and populace who never ceased to call him "Herr Doctor" and continued to seek his opinions and advice. Impossible as life was to become, the hope of an eventual change was never extinguished. In the beginning, Sigmund's advice was sought openly, and it may be that a reason for Sigmund's failure successfully to contest his disbarment lay in the fact that his counseling of emigrants and his rendering of legal advice did not leave him time enough to handle the other matter with the singleness of purpose necessary for success.

One of the people who sought Sigmund's advice in the first year of the Nazi regime was Dr. LeMaitre, his friend of long standing. As a Social Democrat, LeMaitre was fair game for the Nazis. As an affluent and generally respected physician, however, he was not as easy a target as a Jew or an ordinary grass-roots Social Democrat. Thus the attack on him, planned or unplanned, opened from a quarter which was as respectable in degree and kind as he was. He was accused by a fellow physician of being a Communist. In Nazi Germany, such an accusation was clearly grounds for a libel suit, and LeMaitre did not hesitate. Engaging the services of the eminently respectable, respectably non-Nazi, and politically pure attorney, Winckelrod, LeMaitre counterattacked with the assertion of libel. The difficulty was that Winckelrod wanted to remain respectable and pure, so that he was exceedingly uncomfortable about representing a man who had been a prominent Social Democrat against a Nazi who had called that man a Communist. Consequently, LeMaitre felt he should have some kind of control over the adequacy of Winckelrod's handling of the case. With this in mind, he went to Sigmund Stein.

A procedure was evolved in which LeMaitre, with Sigmund's help, would lay out the general points of his case. These would then be written up by Sigmund with an eye to their strictly legal aspects, though with a minimum of technicalities. LeMaitre would then turn over the resulting statement to Winckelrod, with the comment that this was the way he thought the case should be handled. Winckelrod recognized that the approach was a good one—in all probability he also recognized its origin—and was covered by LeMaitre's claim that it was his own. LeMaitre won the case, Winckelrod was shielded, and Sigmund was kept busy.

The fees from this kind of legal service and the counseling of Jews who planned to emigrate were probably adequate to support Sigmund and his family; they did not move out of the Dietrichstrasse apartment until seven years later, and when they did, it was not for inability to pay the rent.

There are, however, hints of other reasons for Sigmund's continued disbarment. Frau Wolff-Foerster, daughter of the Jewish legal adviser, Heinrich Wolff, claims that Sigmund was held in Hochburg and kept under surveillance as a hostage for the good behavior of Werner Hagen. It will be recalled that she is down on Hagen because of her belief that he defrauded her father. She is well able to believe that Hagen had left unsettled matters in Hochburg for which Sigmund was held to account. Her opinion may relate to the widespread and unconfirmed report that Hagen spoke on French radio in a broadcast that was aimed at Germany. His widow, saying she had heard the story and thought it was possible, explains her not being sure by pointing out that she and her daughter had returned to Germany for a few weeks after the initial flight to France. During this period Werner Hagen was alone in Metz and, she says, might have become involved with the French radio.

In any event, if Hagen did make such a talk, and if this became known to the Nazis, the fact would have been damaging to Sigmund Stein. Regardless of what Hagen may or may not have said, a broadcast on the French radio in 1933 by a Jew who had just fled Germany was a potential source of real difficulties to the associates he had left behind. Such a broadcast on Hagen's part would certainly have added its weight to the other elements which entered into Sigmund's decision not to push for his own reinstatement as a lawyer.

Understandably, Sigmund had to give up the office on the popular corner of the Bahnhofstrasse and the Wiesenstrasse. He was also omitted from the group of lawyers in the classified section of the first issue of the Hochburg town directory to appear after the Nazi takeover. Nevertheless, in the alphabetical section of the directory he was still listed as "Sigmund Stein, Doctor of Jurisprudence" at his Dietrichstrasse home address. This was consistent with a problem which the "Law for the Re-establishment of a Professional Civil Service" had created and failed to solve. The fiction was supported by the decree itself and at various times explicitly voiced by spokesmen for the regime, that officials who had lost their positions as a result of the measure were "honorably discharged." The law clearly provided that, with certain limitations, they were to receive retirement pay. The problem was: were they to be allowed to retain their titles and attach to them the designation "in retirement" or "out of service" which are almost universally utilized by German officials who have left their professions honorably and in a recognized way? Such titular distinctions are not wholly honorific because, for example, the "Lawyer in Retirement" may be approached for paid legal advice, and with greater confidence than the person who has never been more than a legal adviser.

This was the rub in the case of the retired Jewish officials, for it meant that Jewish lawyers who had been released from service as a result of the decree would be placed in competition with both Jewish and non-Jewish legal advisers and would enjoy an advantage in this competition since the desire for competent advice often outweighed sound Germanic Folk feeling. Why should anyone with a legal problem bring it to a legal adviser when he could call on the services of an experienced and successful lawyer? The situation exemplified the contradictions arising out of the point of view—genuine in some of its proponents, feigned in others—that German racial policy was not anti-Semitic but merely imbued with a concern for racial purity. If the Jews were not per se bad, then they could not be dishonorably discharged from service. But this would have almost the consequences of an assumption that the Jews were per se good, since it put them in an advantageous position vis-á-vis non-Jewish legal advisers.

Prior to the Nuremberg Laws of 1935, there was no general regulation of this matter, and Hochburg does not appear to have been among those few communities where the discussion in the legal press led to local regulation. However, in the second address book to be published in Hochburg after the Nazi accession to power, Sigmund Stein appears simply as "Legal Adviser" without academic titles. But this directory dates from January, 1936, after the Nuremberg Laws, and is not informative for 1934 and 1935.

Another matter in which Sigmund gave legal advice is removed from any undercurrents of moderation which may have existed. Casimir Dombrowski was married to a Catholic woman. He and his wife, both having been deeply disturbed by the Nazi coup, were anxious to reduce the possible hardships their two sons might face. The sons had not yet been raised from the status of "Non-Aryan" to that of "Mongrel, First Degree." Despite the courage which Catholic priests sometimes showed in those days, the one to whom Dombrowski and his wife turned for advice was not helpful. "He was scared of getting mixed up with us," the Dombrowskis say. So, late in 1933, Casimir and his wife went to Sigmund. He advised them to separate their property, so that each of them would have independent control over a fixed portion of their previously common possessions. In this way, the portion assigned to Frau Dombrowski would stand a good chance of being unaffected by anything that might happen to her husband. Sigmund undertook to fill out the requisite forms and the process was successfully completed.

One event in particular must have diluted the effect of any signs of moderation that any Jew who was married to a Christian might see around him. In the *Town Chronicle*, under the date July 25, 1933, there appears the report: "Accompanied by the SA musicians of Sturm III, Troop 7, a Jew was led through the streets of Hochburg today. The Jew bore a sign with the inscription, 'I have besmirched a Christian girl' and the procession ended at the Market Place, where speeches were made." The man was not a member of the Hochburg Jewish community, but rather a university student whose home was in a small town about twenty miles distant.

An acquaintance of the girl involved blames her parents for failing to prevent the mistreatment of the young man. There had been a somewhat similar incident in Giessen, another university town to the east of Hochburg, where, according to the acquaintance, the father of the girl had put his foot down, telling the SA that if they made anything out of the matter he would write to friends in England and France about the incident. For, despite the pressure felt by Werner Hagen, it was in fact to be another two years before the Nazis felt strong enough to give comprehensive legal stature to their views on "interracial" marriage and sex relations. The threat of such measures was, of course, present from the moment the Nazis took over. But incidents like that in Hochburg, staged to promulgate Nazi views on the matter, could for some time be prevented by resolute and intelligent handling. Casimir and Sigmund were both aware of the prurient procession in Hochburg, and the whole tendency it represented made the property separation between Casimir and his wife a prudent precaution.

An additional event contributed to the bitter flavor of the days. Kurt von Schlegel, the son of old Professor von Schlegel and his Jewish wife, and himself a professor in Berlin, had been dismissed from his post in the first days of the Nazi revolution. His status, like that of Dombrowski's sons, was still indeterminate. He had married Lotti Kleppmeier, a Christian girl from one of Hochburg's better families. His professional situation, because of both ability and family connections, seemed promising. When he was dismissed, his desperation seemed less than that which had driven Professor Mendelsohn to suicide. Young von Schlegel immediately left Germany for Italy, in the hope of finding a position there. His wife remained with her family in Hochburg, prepared to follow him. This was not to be. A few days after his arrival in Italy, his death in a remote village was reported. The public explanation was "heart attack." The private explanation was and is suicide. His death was the more tragic because he was reinstated at Berlin on the day the news of his death arrived in Hochburg.

Casimir Dombrowski saw in this incident the fate of a "hybrid" like his sons; Sigmund Stein saw it as the fate of a completely Germanized individual who did not fit the Nazi racial demands. But the young Frau Professor von Schlegel was changed by her husband's death to a bitter and active opponent of National Socialism. Forced by circumstances to remain in Hochburg, neither she nor Sigmund Stein could foresee the fatal crossing of their paths in the years ahead.

There were victimizers as well as victims among the German academic intelligentsia. Professor Gottfried's wife was Jewish. Their daughter tells how, after the Nazi seizure of power, she was avoided by professors and instructors who had previously been only too glad to show a courtesy to the daughter of a well-known colleague. Explaining how such slights materialized out of the general atmosphere of the time, Fräulein Gottfried laughs, "Well, when you saw an eminently respectable and somewhat stuffy associate of your father quickly disappear into a ladies' lingerie shop as you approached, it was hard not to conclude that he was trying to avoid you." On the other hand, it was a convinced and enthusiastic Nazi professor who was instrumental in helping the sons of Jeweler Meyer get out of Germany in 1939.

The first months after the seizure of power by the Nazis were crucial in the life of Sigmund Stein. Nazi power was at full flood. Having survived this initial onslaught, Sigmund looked about him and saw the ebbing; saw the Jewish friends and relatives who remained; saw his professional activities undiminished despite his loss of professional status; saw the will-o'-the-wisps of moderation in the gloom—and was advised by well-meaning non-Jewish friends to stick it out, advice which he himself wanted to believe was sound. He found himself leading a busy life and gaining a stature in the affairs of the Jewish community that afforded at least some compensation for the stature he had lost in the community as a whole. He should have been aware that the incoming tide rises in successive waves.

[Ambivalences]

Epochs, periods, and phases—these units are oversimplifications torn out of the web of events. They are as necessary as they are dangerous, as helpful as they are misleading. So it is with an "epoch" in the life of Sigmund Stein and his fellow Jews in Germany. It is convenient to speak of the two years from mid-1933 to mid-1935 as a discernible "period." One storm of change had been ridden out. The German Jewish community had been battered physically and psychically. People had suffered. Even if the future had turned out to be an improvement, the experience of suffering would have remained. The "period" would be closed by a second storm: the passage of the Nuremberg Laws. Between the two was a relative calm which was nevertheless not free of disturbance.

For example, Sigmund Stein's neighbors in what had become the Hermann Goering Strasse were not Jewish. On the floor above the Steins were the Schlossers, who had moved to Hochburg in the early thirties as a consequence of Councillor Schlosser's transfer from the Berlin to the Hochburg courts. On the floor below lived the teacher Klingelmann, with his wife and son. All three families had associated with one another, and the relationship between the Steins and the Klingelmanns was especially close because their two children were the same age and good friends. Marion Stein also seemed to have brought her parents and the Schlossers together. Dorothea Schlosser, daughter of the councillor, was several years older than Marion, but says she found the younger girl a pleasant if rather serious little companion. The relationships among the families continued after the Nazis took over.

They did not remain the same, and it is inadequate to say merely that they became either better or worse. Councillor Schlosser died in February, 1935. Normally, with such close neighbors, Sigmund and Esther Stein would have gone upstairs to express their sympathy and offer assistance. The Klingelmanns make a great point of Sigmund's thoughtfulness in such matters, telling how he had always brought flowers when someone in the house was sick and how concerned he had been on one occasion when the cleaning lady was ill. Esther Stein was not a person to overlook the amenities either. Nevertheless, the Steins did not call upon Frau Schlosser at this time. Instead, Sigmund wrote a note to the family—a note which, according to Dorothea Schlosser, showed great sympathy, delicacy, and tact. It demonstrated these not least in the explanation given for the failure to make the customary visit: Sigmund did not want to embarrass the Schlossers at any time, and especially not at a time when their concerns were so great.

The response to this note came in the form of a visit to the Steins by Dorothea Schlosser and her mother who, as it happened, was a convinced Nazi supporter. The conversation during this visit was mainly an expression of appreciation for Sigmund's note. In the course of talking, however, there arose an occasion for the mother to use the word "Jew" or "Jewish." In an effort to be, as she thought, tactful, she used instead the term "non-Aryan" since, as her daughter says, "Jew" sounded so crass at the time. But Sigmund, recognizing the situation, smiled and interjected, *"Nen-*

nen uns doch ruhig Juden"—"Please don't hesitate to speak of us as Jews."

Meyer Rosenblum is well-informed about the famous Gosmarshausen brawl, because he had been a cattle dealer there for several years before the Nazis came to power. His house was next to that of a well-to-do peasant, and the two men were on good terms. One day in early summer of 1934, a car drove up the narrow street and stopped in front of the neighbor's house. Behind the car was an open trailer divided into four sections, in each of which was a pig. At this time Meyer was still carrying on a much reduced cattle business with the best of his old customers. On the present occasion, as too often, he had time on his hands. He dealt in cattle himself but naturally had an interest in all kinds of livestock. So he watched as the driver of the car proceeded to sell two of the pigs to the peasant.

As Meyer looked on from the window of his house, he saw the deal completed. The peasant went indoors to get the money. At this point, Meyer saw the dealer switch two of the pigs in such a way that the peasant ended up getting one pig he had actually chosen and one he only thought he had chosen.

Well, Meyer says, he did not want to run and tell the peasant. As the only one who had seen the switch, he would be offering his Jewish word against the word of a Folk-comrade. He would have been denounced as a Jewish meddler and liar, and it would all have been very unpleasant.

Not having said anything at the time, he could hardly say anything later and thereby bring down the peasant's wrath on his head for not speaking up when it might have done some good. But two or three weeks later he did remark to the peasant that he had noticed a couple of new pigs. How were they doing? The peasant replied that one of them was all right, but that the other was a damned runt if he ever saw one. And he added, in what was intended to be a friendly remark, "No Jew would ever have sold me such a creature."

Such dubious tributes to the Jews have become almost a part of the folklore of the Nazi years. The tribute was often dubious and often included the pejorative, "not *even* a Jew." But often, too, it was not dubious at all, as when the Jewish grain or livestock dealers were unreservedly praised in the damning of the men who replaced them.

The atmosphere of the years between 1933 and 1935 was in many respects a provisional one for the German Jews. It was by no means certain that those Jews who had been sturdy or weak enough, fortunate or unfortunate enough to hold on to Germany through the first Nazi onslaught would not be able to hold out against all that might be brought to bear on them. The problem for the Jews took shape less as the threat in the future—though such a threat was certainly felt in the form of insecurity—than as the pressing need to come to terms with the humiliations and difficulties of the present. German Jews had not been brought up to believe they were second-class citizens, and they had tacitly claimed every right which sometimes they had tactfully renounced. They were supported in this claim by the constitution of the German Republic, and if they yielded a point here and there, they did it to keep peace in a family to which they felt they belonged. Such concessions strengthened the sense of their right to belong.

In the relative calm which followed the Nazi accession to power, the Jews were faced with the naked assertion that they were different. The ranting malice of Julius Streicher's *Stuermer* had not yet become official policy. There were spokesmen for the regime who talked and acted in such a manner as to mislead the Jews into thinking the Nazis meant no malice. In the end the chief contribution of such spokesmen was a negative one. They gave the Jews hope. With their "equal but different" theories, these spokesmen for the regime created a situation where the Jews could continue to live and could, indeed, find comfort in a parallel with their former situation: where before 1933 the Jews had never claimed all the rights due them and had gained self-justification from their sacrifice, now once again they could find proof of their attachment to Germany in the fact that they continually put up with an abuse which the "equal but different" doctrine theoretically forbade.

The contradictions in the doctrine were merely a sputtering in the fuse. The equality which was thrown to the Jews as a sop for their exclusion from German racial honor was denied by the very nature of that honor. The petty sophistication behind the "equal but different" doctrine lay in the recognition of the infinity of human differences, but collapsed into an unsophisticated and fateful inconsequence when it imposed race as the equalizing and differentiating principle. It was the colossal *irrationality* of Nazi race doctrine—and the manner in which this irrationality acted as a sponge for all the different malices of the flesh—which made futile every German Jewish attempt to come to terms with it. It was not the *wickedness* of the Germans, nor even the *wickedness* of the Nazis.

By the same token, the Jewish attempt to come to terms with the Nazi regime was not a shameful dalliance with evil. The race ideology of National Socialism was monstrous and led to monstrous results. But the human situation in Germany, as *a* human situation, points up with tragic and terrible intensity many problematical aspects of *the* human situation. As late as 1939, there were still well over 300,000 Jews in Germany. They could nòt achieve a modus vivendi, but they had to try.

Inevitably, Sigmund Stein was to become embroiled in this attempt. That he could not escape was foreshadowed by his entire life: from his birth in Bachdorf through his childhood there and in Weidenfeld, where he responded to the scenic beauty and the human rhythms of the Hessian countryside; through his schooling in Hochburg, his experiences in the war, and especially through the academic career from which he emerged as a lawyer.

In the narrower sense, it was the fact that before 1933 he had been one of the three Jewish lawyers in Hochburg, and that after 1933 he alone of the three remained which led directly to his embroilment. The moment after the Nazis took power in 1933, when emigration probably appeared as a theoretical possibility, it soon was overgrown by the thicket of work at hand: the counseling of his fellow Jews about many ordinary legal problems as well as about all the special legal problems which Nazi rule had created for them; about emigration, with all its personal and financial complications.

"I am like the captain of a sinking ship and cannot leave until the entire crew is safe," he said later. "I cannot abandon my people." There is little doubt that these were public expressions of inner feelings which were less assured. Perhaps the declarations also covered feelings which were not always noble either. David Stein says, at least, that Sigmund once remarked, "I don't intend to leave until I see Kutscher pulled down the way I have been."

Ultimately, an attempt to weigh the meaning of such comments is beside the point. Sigmund really did help people to emigrate, really did aid them in steering a course through the dangers of the time, many of which he was in a position to see more clearly than they. The shadows cast on his behavior by the way life had to be lived at the time remain strikingly few, and the manner in which Sigmund Stein dealt with his tasks as well as the understanding of his position shown by Hochburgers who survived reflect credit on him as well as on the insight of the Hochburg Jewish community.

Sigmund's attempts to deal with some of the specific problems thrown up by the Nazi revolution establish his connection with the *Central Union News,* the weekly publication of the Central Union of German Citizens of Jewish Faith. His first contact with this intelligent, liberal, and assimilationist tendency in German Jewish affairs had come through his membership in the Korporation Minerva at the University of Augsburg. The Central Union was a natural refuge for Sigmund, embodying as it did the contradictions as well as the consistencies of his attitudes toward Germany and toward himself as a Jew in Germany.

The *Central Union News* had the largest circulation of any periodical for German Jews. Both before and after the Nazis came to power, it devoted much of its space to combating anti-Semitic myth and malice. At the same time—for it was a large newspaper—it reported at length on matters of general cultural and intellectual interest, usually highlighting their relevance for the Jewish community in Germany. During the first years of Nazi rule, it changed little in format and style. Later it did change considerably in content, since it tried to deal with the overall policies of the regime as well as with many of the specific problems which resulted from these policies. Much of this discussion seems more to the point and more penetrating than similar analyses in the issues before March, 1933. Understandably, during the Nazi years of its existence, the *News* left much unsaid in its references to the political and social structure of the regime, and said much by indirection. Also, a great deal of comment was clearly governed by the sure knowledge that the reader was only too painfully aware of what was going on. Such restraints nevertheless differed in degree rather than in kind from those which had prevailed in an earlier and friendlier era. Then tact and policy had dictated—in the *News* as in any other paper—how firmly established a fact had to be before it could be reported as fact.

After the Nazis took over, tact and policy acquired a unity of orientation much greater than before. In the earlier period the men and women who put out the paper may have known that the Jewish position was shakier than they could admit journalistically. After 1933, some of them may well have felt that it was about all up with the German Jewish community. Yet this community consisted of several hundred thousand people who could not simply be abandoned to despair. The result was, on the one hand, an intensification of concern for the whole problem of being a Jew, in general as well as in German society. In this concern, previous inhibitions, reticence, and any assumption that *this* problem had been resolved were cast aside to be replaced by an honesty and forthrightness which would have been refreshing had the price not been so high.

On the other hand, as such realism increased, the ability to comment on political and social developments decreased. Many of the paper's writers simply accepted the fact that German society had made its position on the Jews very clear. Too, there was the knowledge that the situation could become worse, that National Socialism harbored malice as yet unleashed, and that a false step could sever the frayed restraints by which this malice was held in check.

In pre-Nazi Germany, there were many Jewish leaders who had attained liberality of creed but who moved in cultural and intellectual circles where there was little pressure on them to abandon their Jewish identity. Such leaders were prominent in the Central Union and believed that the Jewish tradition was something which should not be sacrificed. For them, a major problem was to keep the little man, who had emulated their attainment of a liberal creed but who bore the scars of his Jewish identity on his back, from slipping away from Judaism. In part, the solution of this problem seems to have been the assertion that the Jews enjoyed more acceptance in German society than they actually did, and that anti-Semitism was further beyond the pale of respectability than it actually was. With the Nazi attainment of power, almost all such illusions disappeared.

Between 1933 and 1935, Sigmund Stein appears three times directly and once indirectly in the pages of the *Central Union News*. He is first mentioned in the issue of January 25, 1934, where he is described as having "prudently" chaired a meeting of the Hochburg chapter of the Central Union. The meeting had been announced in the preceding issue as a lecture and discussion on the topic, "German Jewish Goals in Life," with two speakers from the organization's regional office in Frankfurt. This meeting and others were held in the Cafe Altmann in the Bahnhofstrasse. (Herr Altmann, who had established his business in the early 1900's, was like Sigmund in his explicit refusal to leave Germany in 1933. It is also of some interest that the Zionists, whose enthusiasm for their own ideas gave them a rather penetrating alertness to the weaknesses of the Central Union position, held meetings in the Home for Jewish Crippled Children in the Helenastrasse, usually the scene of gatherings sponsored by the Hochburg Jewish community as such.)

At the meeting in the Cafe Altmann, according to a separate report on the youth page of the same issue of the *News*, a Hochburg unit of the Society of German Jewish Youth was organized. There is no reference to another meeting of the youth group in subsequent issues of the *News*, and only one reference to a later meeting of the Hochburg adult chapter. This was in the *News* for February 24, 1935, where no names at all are mentioned. This lack of information is in keeping with the obscurity which surrounds Sigmund's connection with the Hochburg activities of the Central Union. He is mentioned once, and there are some indications that he was connected with the organization earlier, but beyond this his connection with the group as well as the group's Hochburg activities are obscure. What evidence there is suggests that the movement failed to take hold in Hochburg in spite of the efforts made to plant it there.

Sigmund's training and experience made it inevitable, however, that he would be active in a general community sense during this period. One facet of this activity is seen in his two other appearances in the *Central Union News*. The first of these occurred in May, 1934, as an article, "The Protection Offered the Guarantor and Co-signer under the New Agricultural Debt Laws." Over and above its relevance to Sigmund Stein, this article is illuminating as an indication that once again the Nazis had been trumped by their own propaganda. Having claimed that the peasants' blood was being sucked by Jewish moneylenders, the Nazis instituted a procedure whereby a debt moratorium and reduction could be attained, and they socialized the borrowing procedure. The measures were not aimed explicitly at Jewish creditors, but it was believed that these would be affected more than they were.

The measures were actually needed because the peasants were deeply in debt. Because of the economic and social structure of the villages, the debt was more often to the local cattle or grain dealer than it was to the banks and other lending institutions. The fact that the debt was as great as it was pointed neither to the indolence of the peasants nor to the avarice of the traders, though it is in the nature of things that some peasants were indolent, just as some traders were gougers. Most German Jewish leaders recognized that too many of the traders were Jewish for the situation to be healthy. But the complexities of the situation were great, and the Nazi assumption that the Jew was the root of the difficulty repeated the mistake which had been made in the late nineteenth century when the *Raiffeisengesellschaften* (rural cooperatives) were formed, a meliorative action which did not touch the basic landholding structure and which, like the Nazi measures, was often seen as a means of saving the peasant from the "subservience to Jewish capital." In fact, the peasants frequently *preferred* to "go to the Jew," because the cooperatives were too public and too impersonal. The Jewish cattle dealer would keep his mouth shut about loans, and the peasant had to have dealings with him anyway in order to trade his cattle. But when the peasant went to the cooperative, it is said, everyone knew about it and why.

The problem to which Sigmund addressed himself in his article indicates both the slipperiness of half-measures and the fact that it was ordinarily the peasant's initiative and not the trader's greed which produced the debt. "Frequently," Sigmund writes:

> . . . a peasant needed money for repairs or for the purchase of livestock, but was not in position to get a loan from his bank. The cattle dealer or merchant, who had a regular and continuous relationship with a bank, could get a loan much more easily.
>
> In some cases the peasant was assisted in getting a loan by the fact that the cattle dealer or merchant was willing to become a guarantor. In other cases he made the loan himself, receiving the money through his regular account with the bank and assigning a mortgage or other property asset to the bank as security. In general, if the loan is not repaid, the peasant owes the dealer and the dealer owes the bank.

He points out that the trader was often unaware of the protections which the Agricultural Debt Laws offered him and the losses which the trader could avoid through such awareness.

Three months later, Sigmund followed this article with a related one in which he hinted that the courts and the debt reduction offices were expressing the spirit of the regime by adhering rigorously to the letter of the law. He warned co-signers and other mediate creditors that they must follow all prescribed procedures exactly, carry on all correspondence by registered mail, and thus, by implication, see to it that they did not leave themselves open to a chicanery which could be legalistically justified by their own negligence.

The indirect appearance of Sigmund Stein on the pages of the *Central Union News* occurs in the issue of September 13, 1934, and has a similarly prosaic ring. In the feature "Among Our Families," the seventieth birthday of "Isaac Stein, Elder of the Weidenfeld Synagogue Community" is announced.

It would be wrong to say that, when one reads the *Central Union News* for these first years after the advent of the Nazi regime, the impression is one of complete normality. It was normal, of course, for Jewish leaders (as reported by the *News* in May, 1934) to send Hitler a collective telegram of protest at the "Ritual Murder" issue of Julius Streicher's anti-Semitic sheet, *Der Stuer-*

mer. The issue included sensationally irrelevant pictures and the usual screeching text. The Jewish leaders, angered by the exhumation of this old and rotten chestnut, took the only course which seemed consistent with the mood of the times. They cited, almost in passing, the innumerable authorities from the Pope on down who had refuted the myth, and then went on to stress the fact that Germany itself had been made the object of similar lies during the World War. This seems to have been effective; at least the *News* was able to announce three weeks later that the objectionable issue of the *Stuermer* had been withdrawn from circulation. The withdrawal did not come, however, until two weeks after the protest, so one may wonder about the concession. This mixture of superficial normality with underlying doubt often characterizes the *News* in these years.

The paper did succeed, however, in maintaining a calm and serious tone. It showed concern and it betrayed repressed anger, but it never gave way to the panic which its readers and its staff must sometimes have felt. Objective trends in circulation, for example, must have been a constant concern. The number of copies printed fell from 64,000 in 1933 to 40,000 by October of 1935, a rate of decline appreciably higher than that of the Jewish population in the Reich. It is unlikely of course, that many readers knew about this, but a change in the physical make-up of the paper could hardly have gone unnoticed. This was the forced alteration of its masthead in March, 1935. The whole philosophy of the Central Union had been well summed up in the subtitle of the *News*: "Pages for Germanism and Judaism." With the issue for April 4, 1935, the symbolism was at an end, and the paper appeared as the *Central Union News*—"A General Newspaper for Judaism," the change being regretfully explained to the readers as one imposed by a decree of the German Literary and Journalistic Association. The staff and the readers could not know it, but the general appearance of the paper after mid-1935 came to be more and more that of the mutely eloquent herald of disaster, *The Jewish Newssheet*, which was to be the only and inadequate vehicle of intra-Jewish news during the years of dissolution after 1939.

As late as the beginning of 1936, a wanly flourishing Jewish literary and cultural press still existed. The *Central Union News* had the largest circulation, but there were several other periodicals which were important to specific sectors of the German Jewish community. One of these, *Der Morgen* (*The Dawn*), was the more scholarly and philosophical organ of the Central Union. Another, *Der Jüdische Rundschau* (*The Jewish Scene*), was the vehicle of the Zionists. Both before and after 1933, a dialogue, usually friendly, occasionally sharp, was carried on between these two periodicals. Still other periodicals, both national and local, continued to serve the needs of different sectors of the Jewish community.

In a general way, these sectors were all represented in Hochburg. More specifically, it is possible to discern a polarity in these early years of Nazi rule between Sigmund Stein, affiliated with the Central Union, and the banker Tannenbaum, who was the Hochburg representative of the Joint Distribution Committee, took a generally Zionist position in Jewish affairs, and urged emigration on his fellow Jews. Stein and Tannenbaum were friends, but the antagonism between them was substantial. In view of the fact that Sigmund advised prospective emigrants against leaving Germany, it seems reasonable to assume that the tension between the two men spread out in circles through the community as a whole. Tannenbaum did emigrate and subsequently died a natural death. His sister's statements are an excellent example of many which were made about Sigmund Stein by people who took a different view than he did of what the German Jews should have done. She expresses the belief that Sigmund was mistaken but nonetheless shows great understanding for the line he pursued. Her point of view shows the effects of having lived in the same impossible situation with Sigmund; she is aware that at the time there could be no certainty that one policy was wrong, another right. For the action which in retrospect turns out to have saved one Jew from destruction was subject to a different perspective in the early 1930's: flight meant abandoning one's home and everything he knew.

Some of the grounds for this general ambivalence are seen in two situations in Bachdorf in which Sigmund and his brother David (then a physician in the industrial city of Hoechst) became entangled. Whatever may have been the attitude of his neighbors toward Isaac Stein in 1935, it is clear that the Nazis had scored successes among the peasants of Bachdorf and the surrounding area. The "Jew-free" cattle and swine markets, reported in Hochburg and elsewhere at various times during these years, kept anti-Semitic feelings alive. But a remark which the lawyer, Muehlenbach, says was made to him in late 1933 by a Jewish cattle dealer seems to have proved true: "We'll be able to get along without the peasants," the dealer said, "but I don't see how they'll be able to get along without us." For in October, 1935, it was officially recorded that the Hochburg police took action against a group of SS men who were threatening the Jewish dealers in the Hochburg swine market.

In any event, Isaac Stein had continued in business and even found it necessary to employ a helper. One of those who occupied this position was a twenty-year-old Jewish boy from the town of Weidenberg. The young man was a good worker and is well spoken of in Bachdorf. But he also seems to have had the urges and initiatives common to his age and sex and through some combination of boldness, heedlessness, and the opportunities of village life proceeded to father a child with an attractive but retarded Bachdorf peasant girl. The child was born in the early fall of 1935 at about the time the Nuremberg Laws were decreed with their stringent provisions against sullying German blood. The tendency so formalized has already been seen in the case of the Jewish student in Hochburg who had "besmirched" a Christian girl. The Nazis delighted in exploiting the prurience to which "revelations" of this kind appealed.

The young man from Weidenberg could have gotten himself, his family, Isaac Stein, and the girl into serious difficulties. This did not happen because Sigmund took care of the matter, it is said, with great efficiency and discretion. The child was born in the Women's Hospital in Friedenberg, a town where Sigmund had excellent relationships with the juvenile courts. A settlement was arranged whereby the young man paid sixty marks a month to the family with whom the mother lived. Significantly, the couple with whom the mother and child found refuge were Trina Koehler and her husband. Trina, who had helped to rear Meta, David, and Sigmund Stein, eventually became the child's foster mother when both parents abandoned it. Frau Koehler speaks unself-consciously of having brought the little boy up as a "white child." The term has echoes of anti-Semitism at its worst. But the boy, now a strapping young peasant, is still with the family. He is the apple of Frau Koehler's eye.

The story emphasizes the skill with which Sigmund Stein handled the matter and the resulting lack of scandal, but implicit in it is all the bizarre mixture of humanity and inhumanity, traditional anti-Semitism and human contact which defined and flavored the normality of the time. Different ambiguities but much the same atmosphere of diffused ambivalence feature an incident of the same period involving David Stein.

Elisabeth Kohlhausen still lives across the brook in Bachdorf from the old Stein home. In 1935, her son, Fritz, was a member of the Hitler Youth. One day he came home sick after a hike with his group. In the course of a few days he became worse, and his mother grew disturbed about his condition. Then she happened to see David Stein, who was home from Hoechst to visit his father. Frau Kohlhausen knew, of course, that David was a physician, but she also knew that "they" did not want people to have anything to do with Jews any more. Still, she continued to think of herself as being on good terms with the family. And her son was ill. So she waited until she saw David come out of the house and then opened the window and called to him across the brook. David quickly said he had to go to the garden first but would slip in to see the Kohlhausen boy on the way back. After examining Fritz, David Stein was emphatic in saying that Elisabeth should get hold of the local doctor and keep the boy under his care.

Elisabeth Kohlhausen put a great deal of reliance on David's advice because, as she explains it, she knew that he had spent a long time in the children's clinic of a large Frankfurt hospital. She gives the impression, though, that this is a rationalization and that the important element in her confidence had been the familiarity with David and his family, and the fact that he called her "Betti" and she called him "David." Anyway, she followed his advice. As David had predicted, the boy first became worse, but then he recovered completely. Not long after his recovery, Elisabeth Kohlhausen spoke to Emma Stein, telling her how valuable David's advice had been. Emma was pleased and proceeded to tell how David had been more concerned about the boy's condition than he had felt able to tell Frau Kohlhausen. In fact, said Emma, David had written her from Hoechst and had remarked on how he had been watching the death notices in the local paper which his father regularly sent him from Bachdorf. Elisabeth Kohlhausen accepted this as sign of genuine concern.

A German woman mothering a half-Jewish child. And a Jewish doctor worrying about one of Hitler's youths. Is it not quite possible that these particular circumstances, observed in a rural Hessian context where birth and death are facts of life, must have shaped Sigmund Stein's perspective on the Nazis? It is almost certain that Sigmund never heard Trina Koehler use the term, "white child." And if he had heard her say it, well, he was used to such things. Was she not taking the child into her house? Seeing that child in that house, Sigmund may have felt that Adolf Hitler was very far away.

10

[Bloodlines]

The realities of life under the Nazis are to be found in various sources. Frau Kohlhausen remembers what things were like in Bachdorf. A series of typewritten reports, written by the mayor of Hochburg or his deputy and submitted to the provincial president in Kassel, suggests what things were like in Hochburg. These reports were secret and were demanded of the mayors in all the major towns of Germany, the original order for them being dated July 17, 1934. This was shortly after the murder of the SA Leader Ernst Roehm. The internal tensions in the Nazi party which became visible with Roehm's murder were probably among the reasons why such reports came to be thought necessary. According to the order, the reports were not to be "mere copies of the reports to *Stapo*," and they were to be "the unvarnished truth, without regard to personal or other factors."

As sources, these reports are not, of course, unimpeachable.

It is quite evident that political and local, if not personal, considerations influence the style and content. That the reports are fallible does not arise primarily from the fact that the person reporting was a Nazi; every political movement has areas of sophistication where the broad sloganry and propaganda are seen with the cold eye of the initiate, and the depth of commitment is revealed in the very objectivity with which events are viewed. The fallibility comes largely from another source: the way in which we know what we know. Neither the mayor nor his deputy had direct knowledge of most events reported; the picture they transmitted was colored by many and various people. But overall these reports are extremely valuable for their detail.

Brecht, the mayor, eventually came to betray the trust which the Nazis had put in him, the betrayal being foreshadowed by his less than radical adherence to the more radical Nazi aims. His reporting is conscientious, but his generally Nazi position does not hide the fact that his primary interest was the well-being of the town of Hochburg and a desire to draw as little unfavorable attention to it as possible. This is vividly seen in his reporting of the long, drawn out friction between the Nazis and the Korporation students in Hochburg University.

It is also obvious in his treatment of the Hochburg Jewish community under the heading, "Jews and Freemasons," which appeared in every report until October, 1935, when it was changed to "Jews" alone. His frequently repeated formula, "The local Jewish community has given no cause for concern and goes about its business quietly and unobtrusively," was no doubt true. This was, after all, the period in which Meyer Rosenblum refrained from telling his neighbor about the swindling pig dealer. It was the period in which Sigmund Stein declined to visit the bereaved Schlosser family, choosing instead the less obtrusive form of a letter of condolence.

The desire to project an image of the town as an example of quiet order is seen in the frequency with which Brecht went beyond the formula to stress the diligence of the Jewish community in reporting its group activities. Even more indicative is the tone of restraint and objectivity with which he reported the few incidents that marred the ambiguous tenor of the relationship between Jew and non-Jew.

The entire absence of such incidents in the series of reports for 1934 must not, of course, be taken to mean that a happy harmony prevailed between more fervent members of the Germanic Folk community of Hochburg and its Jewish "guests." It was simply that there were no events during the year which were disharmonious enough to be reported.

Sigmund Oppenheimer, for example, was a Jew, a humanist, and a non-doctrinaire Socialist. Like Casimir Dombrowski, he survived the Nazi era in Hochburg; like Dombrowski, he was married to a Christian woman. In 1933, Oppenheimer was living in Felsendorf, a village which had been absorbed by Hochburg but had retained its identity, substituting a festive local patriotism for independence. Officer Schumann also lived in Felsendorf at the time, and the two families had adjacent plots in the public garden area. A feature of almost all German towns, these garden areas are apportioned out to families who work their plots with devotion, trying to make them as attractive as possible. The usually well-kept and rustic little garden houses are pleasant places in front of which to smoke a pipe or drink a glass of wine on a summer evening.

In this way the Oppenheimers and the Schumanns had become acquainted, the two men talking with one another across the fence separating their plots. The Schumanns had another garden close to their house, and the acquaintance which began in the public gardens led to afternoons of knitting together by Frau Oppenheimer and Frau Schumann in the Schumann home garden.

All this continued for a while after 1933. The first sign of change was a reluctance on Schumann's part to talk across the fence with Oppenheimer when anyone else was around. The break was gradual, yet Oppenheimer's suspicion that something was behind it (a feeling which under other circumstances might have been paranoid) was confirmed when Schumann's reluctance turned into refusal. This breaking off of the talks was the more objectionable, Herr Oppenheimer feels, because there was no real danger. The relationship between the wives likewise cooled gradually and then ended.

Herr Oppenheimer contrasts Schumann's behavior with the more honest behavior of friends who took one aside and said, un-

comfortably and apologetically, "Sigmund, I hate to do this, but
. . . well, they're talking about how much I see you. . . . I have my job
and the family to think about . . . " Oppenheimer sees Schumann's
behavior as dishonest because the latter, when no one was around,
did continue for a while to converse across the garden fence just
as though there had been no change. Finally, hurt and vexed, Oppenheimer simply refused to answer. At that point, Oppenheimer
says wryly, the policeman gave all the appearance of a man whose
feelings had been hurt!

Mayor Brecht, of course, was never near the gardens. If he
heard about the silence between neighbors at all, he would not have
reported it. The disharmony of such events was muted, and their
melody, which may have been sad for some of the Germans involved, was a scratchy bowing on the spirits of the Jews.

Although he was no more religious than Oppenheimer, Sigmund Stein, more aware of his position and of his Jewishness,
appears himself to have taken the initiative in discretion, as he
did on the occasion of Councillor Schlosser's death. Stein's school-
mate, Hermann Hessner, says that it must have been terribly
hard for a man as sensitive as Sigmund to face the affronts and
rejections to which he was exposed. Yet Sigmund's tactic of falling
back upon his belief in the fundamental decency of the German
people may well have been successful in the first years of Nazi
rule. There is little doubt that the mayor was both honest and accurate in his failure to report major frictions between the citizens
and the "almost citizens" of Hochburg for 1934. One member of the
faculty at Hochburg University, a sociologist who was probably a
junior member of the Hitler Youth in 1934, says that until late
1935 it was possible for a Jew to live a fairly unharassed life if he
was clever and flexible enough. But the sister of the banker,
Tannenbaum, who did not leave Germany until 1939, says that the
restrictions on the Jews had only begun to become onerous at the
time she left.

Even the Freemasons got more attention from Mayor Brecht
in 1934 than the Jews did. As the reports point out, there was only
one lodge in Hochburg. With thirty members, "who belong to the
better situated merchant and professional class, most of them
being former members of the German National People's Party,"

there was little enough to worry about from this quarter, especially since, as a report of early 1935 put it, "the local chapter has not up to this time accepted Jews as members." Despite the fact that, as the lawyer Muehlenbach insists, the Freemasons taught tolerance, it can be taken for granted that they did not start accepting Jews as members thereafter.

Three major themes run through Mayor Brecht's reports during 1934: the damage which the Nazi campaign against the Korporations was doing to student morale and the financial hardships resulting from the consequent drop in attendance at the University; the Hochburg version of the general friction between the Evangelical Church and the regime; and the persistent economic difficulties of the town's few industries.

It has been shown that the Korporations were conservative, even reactionary. Even in Sigmund's university days, they were usually anti-Semitic. Accordingly, they seem at first glance to have been destined to have much in common with the Nazi movement. Yet their tradition had a definite relation to national freedom, and it was this tradition, along with the fact that they were centers for the actual lives of young men feeling their oats and impatient of restraint, which gave them their luster. Then as now, it was the generosity of the *Alte Herren* (alumni brothers) who were interested in successors with the proper social and ideological outlook that gave the Korporations their substance.

The *Student Prince* romanticism and the inculcation in members of a rather stodgy conservatism created friction between the Korporations and the Nazis. The interest of German finance and industry in both the Korporations and the party delayed—but could not ultimately prevent—the friction from producing flame. With national political power and the support of the "free" or unincorporated students, the Brownshirts were ultimately able to win the ensuing battle. But the victory took almost three years and was not easy. The result was, as Konrad Muenschner puts it, that all of the gay colors of the Korporations were mixed to produce a hateful brown. Muenschner is not precisely a sentimentalist for the Korporations, but he is somewhat nostalgic about historical Hochburg and has concern for the town's well-being. "Ask any of the cab drivers down there by the Bahnhof," he says, "when business is best for them, and they'll all say, 'During Korporation festivities.' "

This has always been a widely held view in Hochburg, and it was the view taken by the mayor in his first report when he blasted an analysis of the Korporations which had been sent to Gestapo headquarters in Kassel by an agent assigned to Hochburg. In view of the opposition to the Korporations among the Nazis, it is remarkable that this long communication, Gestapo to Gestapo, adds up to a blast against the party. To save himself trouble, the Gestapo agent had gone to the horse's mouth—the chairman of the Joint Korporation Committee in Hochburg. This chairman took the courage to say what he felt from the fact that Deputy Chancellor Franz von Papen, in a speech at Marburg University on June 17 that had rocked the Reich, had said what *he* felt, criticizing the continued dictatorship of the Nazi party from the standpoint of a nationalistic and Catholic conservatism.

For his part, the chairman of the Joint Korporation Committee complained that Korporation students were being kept from their traditional pursuits by SA service and indoctrination meetings; that they were being demoralized by Nazi criticism of the Korporations as groups which were out of place in the Germanic Folk Community; and finally that these same young men had worn the Brown Shirt before they put on the colors of the Korporations and resented being looked upon as second-rate Nazis. He continued by saying that the von Papen speech had created confusion among Korporation students. A minority of them had joined with the Nazi student leader, Gorlitzer, in his telegram of support to the Leader. But the majority refrained from doing so because—as a consequence of Goebbel's immediate banning of the text of the von Papen speech—they knew what the Deputy Chancellor had said only in part and by word of mouth. Of Gorlitzer himself, the chairman of the Joint Committee said that it was most unfortunate that an unincorporated student had been made leader of the Hochburg undergraduates, since he was unable to appreciate the reactions of those he was supposed to lead, so many of whom came to Hochburg precisely because of the Korporations.

Mayor Brecht's tactic in dealing with all this was clever and effective. He reported how he had gotten the Gestapo agent to admit that he had done no more than transcribe the views of the chairman of the Joint Committee, thereby neglecting the proper function of an agent—to get a sampling of opinion. The mayor noted that the ex-student, Kleinwitz, had read the agent's analysis and agreed that it was one-sided. Thereupon Mayor Brecht went on to give what he considered a proper view of the situation. This turned out to be more subtly and judiciously expressed, a repetition of the major complaints which the chairman of the Joint Committee had voiced.

Earlier references to the Nazi anti-Semitic propaganda of the late twenties and early thirties has suggested that, as a result of the social tradition into which it was injected, such propaganda often became a call to "follow your conscience." In the mayor's first report, the same approach can be seen at work on a more sophisticated level. For the mayor wrote:

> The Korporation student of today is not in a position to evaluate the worth of the Korporation and goes through a conflict of conscience as between it and the Party. . . . The leader elite among the students . . . is still too sparse . . . and some of the leaders are too one-sided. The result is a conflict of conscience among the students, and these conflicts are aggravated by something like the von Papen speech. . . . Students are mercurial, and any passing event can give rise to protest. For example, at the moment less is being said about the von Papen speech than about the fact that the Hitler Youth burned a Korporation cap and cummerbund in the Midsummer Eve Bonfire.

As Mayor Brecht was well aware, fundamental resistance to the Nazi regime was not to be expected from the Korporations. The conflict was more one among different levels of respectability within the regime and the people who supported its major goals. The Nazi student leader, Gorlitzer, was an SA hooligan type transplanted to the academic world. The economic well-being of Hochburg weighed little against his enthusiasm for the cause. Kreisleiter Kleinwitz, on the other hand, had been born and brought up in Hochburg and had a feeling for the town. He could be counted on to counsel moderation in relationships between party and Korporations, as in another context he could deplore attacks against the Jewish traders in the swine market.

The economic well-being of Hochburg was the mayor's prime concern. During the remainder of the 1934 summer semester at Hochburg University, there seem to have been no special difficulties between the party and the Korporations. The organizations still had powerful advocates in and out of the party. But the trend of events was clear, and the time had come to stand back and look at the Korporations. Was membership in them desirable enough to offset the disadvantages of tying oneself to a declining principle in the face of the party's ascendance? Some students thought so; others woke up to the ludicrousness of such ritual as removing one's cap before going to the toilet in order to prevent the Colors from being dishonored by the locale. In late 1934 it made sense to ask the question: Was all this really worthwhile? A negative answer was marred less by unreason than by the suspicion of cowardice.

For the Korporations were becoming unpopular. A 25 per cent decline in the number of students at Hochburg University from mid-1934 to mid-1935 was multiplied in its economic effect by the fact that most of those who stayed away were students who would normally be attracted by Hochburg's reputation as a center of Korporation activities—in other words, the wealthier students, the spenders. According to the mayor's reports, barbers, tavern keepers, tailors, and the purveyors of dueling equipment were especially hard hit. Loud complaints came also from families whose student rooms were empty, for not every Korporation had its own house and when one did, not all members lived there. Griping and grumbling in the town were the surface of a genuine discontent and hardship, so when the mayor used these successfully as levers with which to pry concessions from the regime, he provided an excellent illustration of the fact that even in a totalitarian state public sentiment is never inconsequential.

Eventually, early in 1936, the Korporations were closed or converted into "Houses of Comradeship." But surprisingly, in view of the Nazi reputation for the swift and cruel stroke, the process was marred by tactical blundering, false starts, and indecision. Thus, for instance, Sigmund Stein, well aware from his youth of the anti-Semitism of the Korporations, could have read in the *Central Union News* for September 21, 1934, that a chapter of Korporation "Bubenruthia," after having been kicked out of the all-German Fellowship of Korporations for its refusal to disavow a Jewish alumnus brother, had to be readmitted when the Reich Minister of Education ruled that an organization should not be punished for loyalty to its members.

Quintessential Nazis were against the Korporations. But they were a minority in the party and were opposed by another power, the nature of which is suggested by a comment at the end of the mayor's catalog of regrets at the manner in which the whole matter had been handled: "This . . . has had economic and political consequences which are not confined to Hochburg; through the innumerable alumni brothers they have radiated out into the entire country."

The decline in attendance at the University was a major problem for Hochburg, a minor one for Germany. Nationally, the major problems were unemployment and political unrest. The Korporation conflict in Hochburg was important because of its impact in both areas.

In addition to the University, the economic base of Hochburg consisted of a firm that fabricated small structural steel units, a carpet factory, a tobacco processing factory, and the regional agriculture. The well-being of the small industrial sector and the agricultural matrix in which it was embedded were carefully watched and reported on. In 1934, the picture was one of moderate activity in the factories, inflation in the uncontrolled weekly produce market due to the newly introduced retail price control for more formally organized outlets, and a general slackness in those service and retail trades which depended on the University and on activity in the other sectors.

The Nazis were unable to bestow any great surge of prosperity upon Hochburg, and the gradual advance which did take place started from so low a base that relief and emergency public works continued to be necessary there—and throughout Germany—until well into those years when rearmament brought its own ominous solution. The Nazi economic program was a mush of expedient promises and fairly intelligent policies. Its early moderate success lay in the way the Nazis had parlayed their dubious electoral mandate into a popular dictatorship which enabled them not only to project plans but to apply them. What magnified the proportions of the Nazi success and gave it meaning it might easily have lacked was the regime's ability to convince the people that something was being done and, more important, to persuade the people that they had or could have a part in doing it.

The ultimate poverty of the Nazi response to genuine needs was long obscured by press-agentry, by the saturation of the program with traditional prejudices, and by sheer power. The poverty is symbolized by the final response of the regime to the loss of students at Hochburg University: it was decided to garrison a reserve battalion of the recently revived Wehrmacht in the town. In his report which followed the announcement of this measure, Mayor Brecht was careful to praise the garrison's contribution to profits and patriotism. But a sour note slips in with his reminder that "the University represents an economic asset of fifteen million marks to the town, whereas the corresponding value of an infantry battalion must be estimated as, at the most, one million marks."

The superficial paradox of the conflict between the German-Folkish Nazis and the German-Folkish Korporations reappears in the attention which the mayor gives to the clashes between the Nazis and the Evangelical Church. The extent of this conflict cannot be detailed here, but a few of its specific manifestations will be dealt with in later chapters because of the manner in which they mesh with the Hochburg Jewish community and the life of Sigmund Stein.

It has been noted that in none of the mayor's reports for 1934 was there more than a stereotyped phrase about the docility and unobtrusiveness of the Hochburg Jewish community under the heading, "Jews and Freemasons." This pattern holds true until the report dated April, 1935, covering the events of March. Here the rubric suddenly comes to life, and from this point until April, 1936, when the last of the reports appeared, there is much valuable material about the Jewish community. There is neither direct nor indirect mention of Sigmund Stein, for individual members of the community are seldom named.

A more regrettable shortcoming of the reports is the fact that they are almost totally unconcerned with feelings and emotional reactions. This is due less to callousness on the part of the mayor than it is to the new status of Jews as people whose reactions were significant to the regime only as they had some calculable political consequences. As a matter of fact, it can be argued that Mayor Brecht's handling of the Jews in his reports betrays a desire to keep things from getting too rough for people, most of whom he knew and some of whom he liked. But the Nazi administrators cared only about reactions as *factors* in the domestic harmony or foreign relations.

The flamboyant anti-Semitism of Nazis like Julius Streicher has come to be thought of as characteristic of the party as a whole, and there is deep truth in the identification. But this truth does not lie in the fact that such flamboyance was evenly distributed throughout the party. It was not, and the danger in assuming that it was lies primarily in the consequence of finding out that by no means all Nazis were wild anti-Semites. This consequence is the impulse, exploited by changed political circumstances and hindsight, to revise the condemnation of Nazi ideology. For the deeper truth is that the madness of that ideology made decent people into responsible accomplices in mass murder and catastrophe.

The mayor's reports for August and October, 1935, contain several significant items. In August, Mayor Brecht wrote:

In July four *Stuermer* display boxes were put up in different parts of town. Shortly afterwards mimeographed lists of Hochburg businesses owned or operated by Jews were posted in them. The proprietors of these businesses complained to the local Retail Merchants' Authority which passed the complaint on to the regime in Kassel. From there it was returned to the local police who got in touch with the town's SA units and the lists were removed.

Three weeks later the lists appeared once again, but this time they were immediately removed by the police. . . .

A few days thereafter, the *Stuermer* boxes were used to display a mimeographed list of the names of people who traded in Jewish shops. This gave rise to a certain uneasiness and the lists were removed on the request of this office. . . .

Generally, the Jewish question has become acute again as a result of propaganda by the SA. . . .

The first of the lists mentioned, that of the Jewish businesses, includes Sigmund Stein, listed as "legal adviser" in the Bahnhofstrasse; Casimir Dombrowski, tailor; Meyer Rosenblum, the cattle dealer in Gosmarshausen; Heinrich Wolff as "legal counselor"; Meyer the jeweler; and others. One characteristic of the list stands out. Apparently in an effort to get across the idea that the town was still saturated with Jewish commercial activity, the list was blown up to its full length of sixty names by including all the members of a particular family who could possibly be considered as having a gainful occupation.

Three months later the mayor reported that:

> . . . the laws announced at the annual Party Celebration at Nuremberg were welcomed by the local populace. . . . The public has also welcomed the fact that the *Stuermer* is now to be seen in the display boxes, since every Folk-Comrade wants to be kept up to the minute on the Jewish Question. Be that as it may, there were a few pages of Nos. 34, 35, and 36 . . . which seemed quite unfit for young people, and they were removed on order of the local state police office. . . . In order henceforth to avoid making unsuitable material available to youngsters of school age, the local police and the SA have agreed that the latter will submit to the former every issue of the *Stuermer* which it contemplates displaying.

The Nuremberg Laws! Respectable apostles of Folk and Race were being pulled and lured ever further in the direction of the *Stuermer*. The whole of 1935 before the September announcement and, in particular, the SA propaganda which had "once again" made the Jewish question acute, must be seen as preparation for the codification of cruel absurdity which was the Nuremberg Laws. In July, Jewish businessmen had been able to protest the use being made of the *Stuermer* boxes. By October, the *Stuermer* was welcomed because it kept the Folk Comrades up to the minute on the Jewish question. And the ambiguities connected with both observations pale before the fact that in September the Nuremberg Laws were announced.

Mayor Brecht's report for June, 1935, has little to say about the Jews except to tell how two Zionist meetings, originally scheduled for May, had been held finally in June. Both gatherings were kept under surveillance and neither gave cause for intervention. In the report covering July, the details about the *Stuermer* display boxes appeared. Significantly, these details had not appeared under the heading "Jews and Freemasons" but rather under that in which the "General Picture" for the month was presented. Under "Jews and Freemasons" the July report merely presents this short but eloquent paragraph: "The Jews and their organizations have been very quiet during the last month and have held no meetings or other group activities. In general, a certain fear and reticence are manifest among them."

For the first time in several months the Freemasons are mentioned, with an account of the voluntary self-dissolution of the local "Frederick the Great" lodge. For the Freemasons as for the Korporations, the presence of obvious external pressure introduced cowardice as a possible factor in a decision which may have come quite rationally, in the process of reassessment.

In the report for September—the month when the Nuremberg Laws were announced at the annual Nazi conclave in that city— Mayor Brecht mentions the laws only in passing, as though not enough time had passed to permit any kind of a general commentary on their effect. In spite of the dissolution of the Hochburg Freemasons, the heading remains "Jews and Freemasons," and the section is devoted to another meeting of the Zionists, attendance at which is set at "about thirty." At this meeting a Berlin woman described her impressions as a traveler in Palestine and spoke of how the return to that land had become the heart's desire of every Jew. She spoke, the mayor reported, in an entirely objective and non-political manner, and there was no reason to interfere.

This meeting and the Zionist meetings which preceded and followed it illustrate the way in which Nazi assumptions had limited Jewish alternatives. Before 1933, the major tendency in German Jewry was toward assimilation. This varied from a consciously thought out policy to a kind of drifting with circumstance, and probably contained more contradictions and faced more problems than its proponents recognized. Christian society

in general and German society in particular had not reached out
to meet the Jews halfway. The harsh medievalism of the forced
conversion had been replaced by tolerance, but there is a real
sense in which tolerance tends to preserve the divisions among
men.

Believing in a Jewish homeland, in a "gathering in" of the
exiles, the Zionists in Nazi Germany found that the prevailing rejection of Jews confirmed Zionist theory. Extreme anti-Semitism
was indiscriminate, and its hatred strengthened the voice of the
Zionists vis-à-vis the assimilationists, to whom they could say,
"This, then, is your answer." Less extreme anti-Semitism, both in
and out of the Nazi party, could see in Zionism a secret solution of
its own moral dilemma. The Zionist alternative could, at one
and the same time, rid Germany of the Jews and the respectable
anti-Semites of the responsibility for violence they saw lurking in
the wings.

The result was something which might be called objective
agreement between the desires of the Zionists and those of a siz-
able group in the Nazi party. It would, of course, be unjust to turn
this into an accusation against the Zionists. It is no more reasonable to blame the Zionists for parallels between their positions
and those of the regime than to berate the assimilationists for
their love of, and loyalty to, Germany. What is important is to
register the fact that, for a brief period after 1933, Zionism was
one of the few alternatives open to the German Jews. Assimila-
tionism was no longer possible.

The mayor's report for October describes the way in which the
Nuremberg Laws were welcomed by the Hochburg populace. In
this same report is an account of the swine market incident—an
attempt by a group of SS men from outside Hochburg to interfere
with the Jewish traders in the Hochburg swine market. They were
thwarted by the Hochburg police as well as by the refusal of the
local SS to support them. The justification which both the police
and the local SS gave for their actions is of some importance, since
it will play a part in confusing the picture of coming events. The
Jewish problem, it was said—with sincerity on the part of the police
and a large dose of pious hypocrisy on the part of the SS—was not

to be solved by the sporadic action of individuals. Hence the harassment of the swine traders had been prohibited in the interests of order and the public peace.

The incident is reported under the "General Picture" heading. Under "Jews and Freemasons" there is merely the laconically revealing statement: "In the period covered by the report it could be observed that a lively interest in emigration was manifesting itself among the Jews."

A continued ferment in the Hochburg Jewish community is reflected in the report for November. Under the heading "Jews" the following statements appear:

> The general meeting of the Israelitic Social Service League which had been announced and reported to the appropriate authorities for the 20th of November and was to have been held in the Altmann restaurant, had to be forbidden on the basis of an order from the Kassel office of the State Police . . . since the named organization is not affiliated with the Jewish Cultural Organizations of Germany.
>
> There was a meeting of the Zionist Organization at which Dr. Eduard Tellerman of Breslau spoke on Jewish emigration. On Sunday the 17th of November . . . there was presented in the Home for Jewish Crippled Children a little exhibition of paintings and needlework by the students. Also in the exhibition were Jewish cultural objects and art objects from private collections. The course of the gathering was unobjectionable.
>
> In other respects the Jews have in no way drawn attention to themselves. Additional Jewish businesses have been given up or had to be given up because their proprietors plan to leave Germany.

The juxtaposition of the Zionist meeting and the banned meeting of the Israelitic Social Service League stands out. The Altmann restaurant, where the banned meeting was to have taken place, had of course been the scene of the meetings, conducted by Sigmund Stein, of that Hochburg chapter of the Central Union of German Citizens of Jewish Faith which now remained so curiously passive. The reason given for the banning is odd, for the League was a charitable and not a cultural organization. It is possible that the League had been formed as a general charity intended to serve the whole community. If this was true, an item in the *Central Union News* for May 9, 1935, hints at possible difficulties: under the headline, "No Contributions from Jews Desired," a Nazi District Leader from the Rhineland is quoted as having said, "I should like to point out to all departments the impropriety of accepting contributions from Jews while, at the same time, opposing the Jewish Race on the basis of folkish considerations."

In every way the German Jews were being thrown in upon themselves, being cut off from their neighbors and the society in which they had grown up. An exhibit for Jews of craftwork by Jewish children was unobjectionable, as was the propagation of a Jewish ideology such as Zionism. Such projects, as part of Jewish life at the time, were beset by difficulties from without and plagued by problems from within. Yet they were possible and their activities were not opposed to the guiding absurdities of Nazi racial policy. The attempt to knock down the walls and build bridges between Jew and non-Jew was anathema to that policy.

This isolation of the Jews was one jaw of the pincers which were crushing assimilationists like Sigmund Stein. The other jaw was the very acceptance by, and integration with, the German culture which men like Sigmund had striven for and to a large degree attained. In Hochburg, many non-Jews, official and unofficial, never stopped calling Sigmund Stein "Herr Doktor." On his part, Sigmund consciously tried to avoid embarrassing these friends, so that for them their behavior was a small price to pay for what they felt was a clear conscience. Too often, however, it was a substitute for more meaningful action.

Mayor Brecht's final report for the year 1935 casts some light on the whole complex of currents and counter-currents. Under the "General Picture" the mayor analyzes the relationship between the people of the town and the party. He writes that there has been no posting of "Jews Not Welcome Here" signs in the town, because those who had urged such measures were appeased by the explanation that this was no way in which to conduct a successful campaign against Jewry.

That was the mayor's view. The anonymous compiler of the *Town Chronicle*, which parallels Mayor Brecht's reports but is usually much less thorough, reveals a different view when, several weeks earlier, he writes:

> For about a week now there has been on the Hochburg slaughterhouse a sign which reads "Jews are forbidden to enter." With this, the slaughterhouse has at last become Jew-free, and this fulfills a long held wish of those among the local citizenry who give positive affirmation to their Germanness.

There is some indication that the mayor privately wished to spare the Jews difficulties—certainly he now believes that this was the case. Or he may have felt what he said at the time, that the struggle against Jewry should be waged in an effective manner—in terms of the public order, the international reputation of Germany, and the elimination of Jews from German life.

Several pages later in the same long year's end report, Mayor Brecht uses the section "Jews" to tell of the increasing number of them who were applying for passports. He also speaks of those who had already emigrated or who wanted to visit other countries for the purpose of investigating the possibilities of emigration. He comments on the number of Jewish businesses which had been given up because "they could no longer exist," as well as on the increasingly difficult position of those which remained. Anti-Jewish measures by individuals, continues the mayor, had not occurred. He attributes this to the educational programs which were pursued in the SA, the Hitler Youth, the National Socialist Women's League, and other branches of "the Movement."

The reports continue in 1936 until April, when they cease. But no account of 1935 can be closed without an examination of the event which was, for the Jews, the nadir of that year: the Nuremberg Racial Laws.

After the "Law for the Re-establishment of a Professional Civil Service," which had defrocked Sigmund Stein and driven Werner Hagen out of Germany, and before the Nuremberg decrees, racial laws had been a patchwork of ad hoc ordinances which implied without defining the position of the Jew in Germany. The implications had always been harsh and unmistakable, yet the very fact that the position of the Jews was not juridically defined added a dimension of uncertainty which could cut both ways. That the Jews could never relax under the old ordinances can be seen in a remark made by Heinrich Wolff to Johannes Kaiser, the shoemaker. Wolff, the legal counselor, whose Jewishness came as a surprise to Frau Hagen and who had little connection with the Hochburg Jewish community, was a good friend of Kaiser's. One day Wolff said to the shoemaker, "God, Johannes, why can't they just set aside a street for us here in Hochburg, and let us live in peace?" Johannes Kaiser says he almost wept to hear such despair from a fine man like Wolff.

Israel Stern of Dreistadt recalls another aspect of the uncertainty when he relates how the Czech Jews in the "Jewish Settlement," Theresienstadt, accused the German Jews of having voted for Hitler. Herr Stern comments that, of course, it was true in a way, but what could one do in the elections between March, 1933, and the withdrawal of voting rights from the Jews, when an SA or SS man was standing at your side? Until citizenship was withdrawn from Jews by the Nuremberg Laws, it was still the Jew's duty as a citizen to vote. But for what?

It is grotesque to think of the Jews voting in the first years of Nazi rule. Most Jews stayed away from the polls when they could, but it was occasionally the whim of the Nazis to extend their "Get Out the Vote" campaigns to the victims of their persecution. It was just this element of caprice which characterized so much of the pre-Nuremberg situation.

The populace of Hochburg may have "welcomed" the Nuremberg Laws. The Jews did not. The certainty the laws brought may have been in its way a relief, but the content of the certainty was devastating. Jews ceased to be citizens and became subjects. Only those "of German or related blood, who have demonstrated in behavior the will and the ability faithfully to serve the German Folk," could be citizens according to the first of the Laws, which defined citizenship.

The Second Law was for the Protection of German Blood and German Honor. It prohibited marriage as well as extra-marital intercourse between Jews and "subjects of German or related blood." The text of this law was a bizarre collection of paragraphs which would have been funny if their absurdity had not covered a chilling seriousness underneath. Jews were not permitted to have female citizens of German or related blood as house servants unless these ladies were forty-five years old or over. Jews were forbidden to display the national flag, but their right to display the Jewish colors was guaranteed. (The silly gesture to the Zionists is unmistakable.)

Most noteworthy about these laws is not any explicit stringency or barbarity, but the almost mad nonsense of the assumptions which lie behind them. Nothing is said about the Jews being bad —they are simply declared to be of other "blood" than the Germans and "hence" excluded from German society. Not Jews but "racial mixture" is what these laws assume to be bad; they assume that it is possible and desirable to strive for a "pure-blooded" society by the elimination of "alien blood." The Nazi theoreticians and legal experts who drew up the Nuremberg Laws were driven by ideology and situation to pursue their nonsense further than most of us are able to. They arrived at an obvious contradiction. They had to define "Jew" and did so by asserting that a "Jew is one who is descended from at least three *racially Jewish* grandparents." But what about the grandparents? "A grandparent is to be regarded without question as a full Jew if he was a member of the Jewish *religious* community." So much for the voice of the blood.

Less contradictory but fully as arbitrary is the contrast between the Nuremberg provisions and the corresponding provisions of the earlier "Law for the Re-establishment of a Professional Civil Service." The earlier law had defined "Non-Aryan" (i.e., Jew) as a person descended from only *one* non-Aryan grandparent. The effect of the Nuremberg provision was, of course, to reduce the number of Jews as compared to the number of "non-Aryans" created by the earlier law. The difference was made up by the application of the *Mischling,* or mongrel, concept. This was another attack on the internal cohesion of the Jewish community because a "mongrel" could, in certain circumstances, determine by his behavior whether or not he was to rate as a "Jew." If, for example, a person descended from two Jewish grandparents and therefore, according to the law, a "mongrel," were to marry a person rated as a Jew, then he himself would come to be classified as a Jew. Furthermore, a "mongrel" retained his citizenship, but citizenship in general was made contingent on the approval of the Minister of the Interior.

Also mischievous, if of lesser significance to the internal cohesion of the Jewish community, was the power granted to Adolf Hitler to free individuals from the definition of Jew. In other words, a Jew could be rated as a non-Jew if Hitler felt that this was, for any reason, desirable.

Once again, explicit malice, cruelty, and barbarity are absent. They are hidden not in the paragraphs of the law but in the assumptions behind it and in the opportunity for arbitrary interpretation which arose from the irrationality of those assumptions. The motives of the people who framed the laws could be either unreservedly malicious and include the desire for the ultimate destruction of the Jews, or they could be blindly innocent, old prejudices rolled up out of sight in a wrapping of "race purity," in benign ignorance of the consequences.

How these possible motivations were distributed in fact is difficult to say. The existence in some quarters of a pure and fearful malice must be seen not only for its own terrible meaning, but also for the way it points up the furtive gradualness of its legal expression. Much did happen and much had to happen before the malice of some unknown numbers of Germans found expression in the gas chambers of Auschwitz. The Nuremberg Laws stand or fall on their own terms and the assumptions about reality which lay behind them. Some of these assumptions maintain a respectable currency in situations where their tragic absurdity is still unfulfilled. Must German society, in which a complex pattern of events led to murderous fulfillment, be rejected while no guilt devolves upon other societies in which the fatal possibilities may not yet have been triggered by the appropriate combination of events? To reject people for their entanglement in the tragedies which have occurred in their vicinity is to deny the one real and consequential equality which defines the human being: his fateful nature as a living and innovating expression of the unique situation he finds himself in. This is what we share with the Germans, the living as well as the dead, the murderers as well as the murdered.

[Entrapment]

In September, 1936, after almost three and one-half years of Nazi rule and one year of the Nuremberg Laws; at a time when Sigmund Stein's emigration counseling was expanding because of the growing Jewish awareness that National Socialism was more than an ephemeral aberration; when *Der Stuermer* was shrieking its wild and salacious anti-Semitism without restraint and other more respectable journals were following suit in a milder manner—at such a time, one of these journals, the *Hessische Landeskurier* in Hochburg, printed the following obituary:

> Today at the age of 59, Hermione Stadtmaier, nee Rothschild, died of a heart attack. She was the widow of the world-renowned gerontologist, his excellency, Professor Wilhelm Stadtmaier. The deceased was for many years the president of the Patriotic Women's Society and a director of the Red

Cross. She was known and honored for her charities and her support of needy folk-comrades.

Any fool knew that, if the Frau Professor had died before 1933, an entire page of the paper would have been devoted to her obituary. Any fool also knew that before 1933 a distinction arising from "folk-comrade" would not have been made. But any fool did not know how to interpret this short but laudatory death notice of a Jewish woman in 1936. What did the word, "folk-comrade" actually mean in such a context? Was it high praise to point out that Frau Professor Stadtmaier had turned her charitable attentions to non-Jews? Was it a subtle attempt to emphasize the fact that she was Jewish? Or was it neither but merely, instead, the use of the prevailing jargon? It was impossible to say. Despite this semantic dilemma, it was obvious that the death of a Jewish woman in 1936 was not being ignored and was not being made the occasion for a frontal attack on the Jews. It was another bit of reassurance.

There was a disposition to clutch at the slightest signs of hope. In April of the same year Germany had sent her troops to reoccupy the Rhineland in defiance of the Versailles Treaty. There had been a great expectancy among the opponents of National Socialism. Now at last, they reassured themselves, Hitler had gone too far! Even the mayor, in his report for April, suggests that disaffection was visible. He describes the enthusiasm with which the occupation was greeted, the eager attention given to news broadcasts, and the proud display of the Reichsflag in front of private homes. But he appends to these comments the pointed observation that France's protest and partial mobilization had once more set the fainthearts and the mischief-makers to work.

"He's gone too far this time" seems to have become a slogan of the non-revolutionary opposition to Hitler and the Nazis. At any rate its feebleness is often cited in criticism of that opposition. Dr. Heinz Rupert recalls how he and Sigmund Stein would listen to Hitler's radio speeches together and how Sigmund himself used to employ variations on the "He's gone too far" theme. Sigmund and his fellow Jews had, of course, more reason to be wishful thinkers than the non-Jewish opposition. As long as he was not Jewish, the disappointed monarchist, the disgruntled member of the dissolved Stahlhelm, the bourgeois liberal, and even the Socialist or Communist could clutch at the scarcely conscious thought that if worse came to worst, a change of conviction was always possible.

The Jew could not change the convictions of his grandparents. He was trapped by the efficiency of the German bureaucracy. The Germans say, *"Von der Wiege bis zu Bahre geht's nicht ohne Formulare,"* which, freely translated, means, "Unless your life is certified with official stamp and seal, let me tell you, brother, it's a tough and dirty deal." For six generations preceding 1933, Jewish families, like all Germans, had left a trail of paper behind them. Every German town had a *Meldeamt,* an office where the citizens of the town are required by law to report their changes of residence. The master card for Sigmund Stein in the Hochburg Mealdeamt goes back to 1908 and shows all his moves to, from, and within Hochburg after that date. For the years before 1908, one is referred to the Meldeamt for the Bachdorf area, where one finds a similar card with similar information plus somewhat fuller data on his birth and parentage. The cards for Sigmund's parents carry things back even farther. Such material can get lost or destroyed, but the surprising thing is how much of it survives, an artificial and relentless memory, from which it was especially hard to eradicate the word *Israelit.*

The non-Jew, on the other hand, could escape the consequences of his past if he wanted to. Friedrich Michael, whom the Nazis had described as an "incurable blabbermouth" for his Social Democratic oratory during the years of struggle, was seen as a potentially valuable ally after 1933. They thereupon tried to get him to join up, attempting to make their goals acceptable to him. He was stubborn, and he says he told the Nazis that he would pay some attention to their arguments when they became International Socialists. The result was that, although he was finally released from the Hochburg jail where the conversion was attempted, he was blacklisted as far as his trade, die-making, was concerned and had to subsist hand-to-mouth on a series of poorly paid laboring jobs. And yet, he was still a Hochburger, still a folk-comrade.

In 1936, Herr Michael and his wife got a chance to make some extra money working for an evening as cloak room attendants at the big sanatorium-hotel on the Sonnenwiesen. It was some kind of

University celebration, and all the Hochburg party bigwigs were there. When the Kreisleiter and Landrat, Kleinwitz, came in with his new wife, he was affable to Michael, saying, "Well, Fritz, if you people had won, I guess you'd be where I am now and I'd be toting coats like you."

Michael comments with emotion on what Sigmund Stein must have suffered, remembering the fear and insecurity which he himself felt and reflecting on how much worse it must have been for the Jews. So it was. The affable condescension which men like Michael could expect, and the unquestioned prestige they could sometimes attain, were often humiliating, but these were different and better things than the sops to self-esteem which Sigmund could occasionally manage in the bitter knowledge that many Jews did not have even these small things. Even where it went far worse for a Socialist or Communist than it did for Friedrich Michael, suffering made its cruel sense. The radical knew why he was being hounded. As long as he bore up, each day's torment, every literal or figurative blow that he took, enhanced the ideal, dream, or conviction for which he took it. And always, if a man was driven beyond his limits, he could betray himself into a respite. Or he could die, knowing that he had not betrayed himself.

Conversion was not possible for the Jews, and in Hochburg they were far from being radicals. Whether or not the assertion by the Communist, Heinrich Preusser, that there were no Jewish Communists in Hochburg was accurate, it is obvious that any Hochburg Jew who was a Communist would have been a striking exception in the community. In 1932 and 1933, Werner Hagen had been an articulate Social Democrat, and he had gotten out immediately. There were many Jews who, like Sigmund, had been liberal democrats. But the tone of the community was bourgeois, conventional, and patriotic, even if Jewish emancipation had been too recent and the effort to assert this emancipation too real for the Jews not to be "tainted" with a certain liberalism. Not radical politically, many of them also had no fervent commitment to Judaism to fall back on. Their suffering and unhappiness did not make sense; worse, it often had visible or emotionally tangible origins in attitudes and beliefs which they shared with their tormentors.

Their main efforts, like Sigmund's, had been aimed at integrating themselves with the major features of the society in which they lived. They could not affect to be Hessian peasants or descendants of the craftsmen and handworkers who were the forebears of most Hochburgers. But they could be just as good and maybe even better Germans—until, finally, the German society with which they sought to identify was engulfed by the opinion that merely to be Jewish was a disqualification for membership. Then there was almost nothing left to the Jews except hope or hate, or more probably a despairing ambivalence of both. The need to go on living qualified and confused everything. Hope could always ferret out justifications from the detailed texture of life, and any blanket application of hate blotted out the pitifully few bright spots in that texture. Konrad Muenschner says it was surprising how few of his old friends let him down and adds that this was also true of the Jews to some degree. There was much dropping of Jewish friends, but as friends and acquaintances began to drop away, any act of common friendship loomed that much larger. Quality was exaggerated to offset the lessened quantity.

For instance, Karl Heinz Lessing had been a classmate and friend of the Jeweler Meyer's sons. In the summer of 1937, Karl Heinz was a lieutenant in the Luftwaffe and had not been living in Hochburg for several years. One day in July, Heinrich Meyer was walking along the Windstrasse when he saw his old friend approaching, resplendent in summer whites. Heinrich's first reaction was pleasure. But it was 1937, and his second reaction was to cross the street in an effort to avoid the embarrassment of a meeting. He tried to make himself inconspicuous, but Karl Heinz had seen him and he, too, crossed the street, came up to Heinrich, and greeted him warmly. Heinrich expressed his happiness and, in view of the way things were, his gratitude. He went on to say to Karl Heinz that he had no doubts about their friendship and felt that it would endure. Nevertheless, they were, after all, living under the Nazis, and Karl Heinz should be careful for his family's sake. At this, the young Luftwaffe lieutenant replied that if things were in such a way that he could not talk to his friends, then he did not want to live, did not want to stay in Germany. He was, in fact, killed in a crash about a year later. "The good die young," says Heinrich Meyer when recounting this incident.

Sigmund Oppenheimer, the Jewish humanist and non-doctrinaire Socialist, remarks that it was often hard for the Jews not to hate. Yet from what he and many others say it is apparent that it was equally hard to hate. This was not a rejection of hatred based on principle but rather on the desire to insulate oneself and preserve vestiges of emotional comfort in a nearly impossible situation.

The perceptive widow of Johannes Huss, and Frau Henrietta Korbmacher, whose association with the Stein family came chiefly at a much later date, are very different women. But they both remark on Sigmund's attitudes toward friends and former friends, Frau Huss saying that he was too trusting, and Frau Korbmacher describing him as having laid great weight on the fact that his friends and former clients had stuck by him. Many people say that Sigmund never hated and that he was never bitter. This is false, though it is clear that on several levels he could have given such an impression. What seems to have happened is that at first he directed his hostilities against the quintessential Nazis; thus, he saved his illusions about the German people and about men in general. This was a tactic which, at the beginning of the Second World War, the nations opposed to Germany relied on in their propaganda: the bad Nazis were separated from the good German people. The history of this line betrays its weaknesses. By the end of the war almost the whole German people were involved in monstrous acts; even the few remaining "good Germans" were afflicted by a fever of power lust here, a crippled conscience there. Sigmund Stein, of course, did not have the perspective of history.

His separation of the Nazis from the German people had the weakness of all such judgments. There is nothing surprising in the fact that he used this technique to preserve his illusions. It is easy to find flaws in Sigmund's love for Germany and the cheapest of intellectual accomplishments to analyze, from a new point of view in time, his attachment to Hochburg and the Hessian countryside into its shaky components. Yet what a victory for the patriotism urged upon him as it is urged upon the citizen everywhere!

Adolescence, first love, marriage, parenthood, and the approach of death are dominating and widespread patterns, no matter what the regime may be. In 1933, Isaac Stein was sixty-nine years old, and Sigmund was thirty-seven. Sigmund, we know, gave as one excuse for his refusal to emigrate at this time the health of his wife's parents in Dreistadt. It would be obviously unreasonable not to assume that he felt equally concerned about his own father. The announcement of the old man's seventieth birthday in the *Central Union News,* Sigmund's dextrous handling of the illegitimacy in Bachdorf, and the continued visits of both Sigmund and David with their father suggest that the old man in Bachdorf must have been on Sigmund's mind. The fact that Dela Stein had long since died added greatly to the symbolic finality which would characterize Isaac's death.

It came in June, 1937. The funeral and some of the circumstances surrounding it have already been described. Sigmund's disposal of the family property in Bachdorf symbolizes both the ending of an era for German Jewry and the beginning of one for Sigmund. The "ending" and the "beginning" of course were each painfully extended and tangled.

Between the Nazi accession to power and the Nuremberg Laws, there was still room for hope that some sort of a modus vivendi might be arrived at between Jews and non-Jews in Germany. Sigmund Oppenheimer—trapped into being a Jew by the trail of paper behind him, despite his having abandoned both the religion and the identification with the Hochburg Jewish community—was employed by the Hochburg tax office all during this period. Casimir Dombrowski had Christians working for him until early in 1939. Most of the Jewish-owned businesses and retail stores continued to operate, and, as we have seen, non-Jewish Hochburgers effectively resented attempts to keep them from patronizing these businesses. Sigmund Stein, even though he had been hit by the very first racial law of the regime, was able not only to maintain a gainful occupation closely related to his profession, but could also observe that many of his colleagues had retained their practices.

Mired as they were in the abnormal day-to-day life of the time, the German Jews could see the situation of the mid-thirties in the perspective of a greater earlier violence and the radically brutal thoroughness of the pre-1933 Nazi racial propaganda. The Nazis had obtained supreme power. Superficially, there was nothing to prevent them from putting their most radical policies into effect. Yet they had not done so, and the Jews, whose history includes total expulsion from Spain on a few weeks' notice, a four-century expulsion from England, sudden massacres and violence under governments which were not avowedly anti-Semitic—these Jews, without being either mad or foolish, could congratulate themselves on the course matters had taken after 1933.

With the appearance of the Nuremberg Laws in September, 1935, many hopes went out the window. Yet what seemed to be order took the place of what had often been seen as chaos. Sigmund Oppenheimer continued to be employed by the tax office; Casimir Dombrowski continued to employ non-Jewish help. Sigmund Stein's activities, precisely because of the new legal situation and the emigration which it encouraged, increased.

His functions as property administrator started to grow toward the importance they were ultimately to have. For understandably, when a Jew emigrated, he converted as much as possible of his property into readily negotiable assets—such as cash and jewelry. Even prior to 1935, there were certain general difficulties in the way of doing this, since the Nazi regime was concerned about the flight of capital from Germany and had introduced measures to diminish it. Nevertheless, it was not until 1938 that unique legal blocks were placed in the way of emigrating Jews. After all, the Nazis were supposed to be promoting the racial "cleansing" of Germany, and one decree of the Economic Ministry of 1933 even presented the appearance of encouraging the transfer of Jewish property to Palestine.

But the liquidation of property is an arduous task at best, and even in the normal course of events a house or a business cannot always be disposed of at the owner's convenience. Hence Sigmund was often made trustee for property which had not been disposed of by the time the owners left. What was happening and some of its many implications can be seen in Sigmund's sale of the Bachdorf property a few weeks after his father's death. There was no longer anyone from his family in the village. Emma, his aunt, who had been Isaac's housekeeper and companion since the death of Dela Stein in 1922, had gone to Kassel to live in a Jewish home for the aged. The Bachdorf property was therefore vacant and of little benefit to Sigmund, David, or Meta. If the times had not been what they were, there might have been point and profit in renting the house and Hof in order to keep it in the family for sentimental reasons.

It must be recalled that Isaac had come from Niederhausen and not from Bachdorf itself. The forty-five years of his adult life which he had spent in Bachdorf did not represent a familial tenure about which inordinate sentiment could be mustered. This is not to belittle the sentimental value which it undoubtedly did have. Nevertheless, the children, rising modestly in the world, had cut the decisive bonds of domicile and livelihood which bound them to the place. The anti-Semitic ranting about the rootlessness of the Jews is well illustrated here both in its absurdity and in the superficial meaning it could have. Isaac Stein had his roots in pre-emancipation Germany. If the four or five generations which his family had been in the Bachdorf-Niederhausen area were not as validating as the ten or more generations in the area which many of its families could claim, there were reasons for the difference which had nothing to do with any constitutional rootlessness of the Jews and a great deal to do with the fact that a Christian society had excelled in uprooting them.

Isaac's children, however, grew up in the wan flowering of German Jewry's emancipation. The inequities which had conditioned the character of the German Jewish community for preceding generations had been largely removed. Sigmund Stein was therefore able to become a lawyer and David a doctor. And the sentimentality with which Sigmund sometimes looked back at Bachdorf was free-floating and did not include the desire to continue in the ancestral ways. So he came back to Bachdorf after his father's death to sell house and Hof to the Sorges and the garden plot to the village. The sale was not as forced as many of the sales by Jewish families which came later. But it was certainly more forced than it would have been earlier. With few exceptions, and with a truth which finally became absolute, all liquidations of Jewish property between 1933 and 1945 were forced.

What about the purchasers? The prosperity of the business

after the first difficult post-war years and the generally increased security have blunted the edges of the Sorges' bitterness at the restitution payments which they had to make to David and Meta Stein. Yet it continues to linger, for they feel that they bought the property in good faith and had paid for it. It was the Nazi party and the Nazi government, they say, which persecuted the Jews. The Jews had a right to compensation, but why should it have been taken from the little people?

The greater the pressure on the Jews, the more crystalline their awareness of the necessity of leaving Germany, the greater could be the decency of the non-Jewish partner in a property liquidation transaction. More fateful for the eventual justice of the restitution program, however, was the fact that, as the pressure on the Jews increased, so likewise *both* decency and greed (or the profit motive) could enter such transactions. The Jew who felt that the time had come to emigrate, and who did not have enough money to do so unless he liquidated whatever property he had, did not go to the local Kreisleiter. Instead, he went to that one of his non-Jewish friends who seemed to display the best combination of decency and business connections. Or he went to another member of the Jewish community whose contacts were more extensive than his own.

In Hochburg, Sigmund Stein was sometimes called on to act as an intermediary of this kind. Early in 1938, for example, Meyer, the jeweler, came to him. As a respected merchant and craftsman, Meyer had been spared much but had finally had enough. Many of his customers had remained faithful to him, and even after it had become risky to be seen entering his store—in 1936 and 1937—they continued to trade with him privately, for which purpose he would call on them in the dark of evening.

At first, such indirection had seemed a way of keeping the business going, of holding on. At some point, however, the symbolism of the effort changed, and it came to stand for the impossibility of operating under Nazi circumstances. This is what led Meyer to Sigmund. Sigmund put him in touch with a Herr Heinicke. The latter was looking around for a business to invest in and to employ himself. The Meyer jewelry store had been prosperous; it could still claim a clientele which had not been wholly frightened away and which with any luck would be reactivated if the restraining fact of Jewish ownership were removed.

The Neisner jewelry store had long been Meyer's chief competitor, both by proximity and ideology. It was run by a brother of a man who had been Sigmund Stein's classmate in the Gymnasium, a lad of brilliance and promise who had rotated with Sigmund at the head of the class—and had been killed in the World War. The surviving brother, Karl, who then inherited the family business, had early shown the resentment-filled nationalism which the Nazis made their stock-in-trade. He was one of the anti-Semites among Meyer's competitors who are described as having kept their mouths shut until after the Nazis got in. In 1937, the Nazis had been in power four years, and Karl Neisner had long ceased to hide his disapproval that a leading Hochburg enterprise remained in Jewish hands. Nevertheless, he had not been able to exploit the political situation as completely as he had wanted to, so that his competition posed no serious problem to Herr Heinicke.

Heinicke dickered with Meyer after assessing these factors, and he offered what Meyer's sons insist was a fair price. Meyer accepted the offer, and a contract was drawn up. Before it could become final, however, it had to be approved by the economic ministry. Accordingly, two men from the Kassel office of the ministry came to Hochburg to check the property against the price which had been agreed on. Meyer's sons say that these two officials found that the contract was in order and the price right. They reported as much to their superiors. The higher officials, however, whether out of particular malice or in the framework of the petty regulations and ordinances by which the Nazi state expressed its general malice toward the Jews, decreed that the price was too high and that the sale would be approved only at a lower price. Since he wanted to get out of Germany, since time and effort had already gone into the deal, and since he was convinced of Heinicke's good faith, Meyer accepted this arrangement and the transaction was finally completed in the fall of 1938. Herr Meyer commended his successor to those of his customers he still saw. He was grateful to Sigmund and appreciative of Heinicke. But he was forced out of his business and out of Germany.

The liquidation of Jewish businesses in Hochburg as elsewhere in Germany was a gradual process from which any clear-cut ultimatum was missing. It tied in with the stereotype of the Jews as money men and commercial operators. Their concentration in these fields, though not as great as it was made out to be, was considered a bad situation which ought to be changed—and not only by the anti-Semites. The leadership of the German Jewish community itself, in the pages of the *Central Union News* and elsewhere, had long been advocating a professional and occupational restructuring of the Jewish community away from the manipulation of money to the manipulation and production of things. This concern of the Jewish leadership understandably was misused by the anti-Semites in their propagation of the stereotype.

Ex-Landrat, ex-Kreisleiter, Kleinwitz may or may not be entirely honest when he says that Sigmund Stein once told him that the difficulties in which the Jews found themselves were a punishment for their persistent concentration on trade. Sigmund may have said something like this, but he was too well informed not to know the responsibility of the Christian in the development of that concentration.

The German who sincerely believed in the racist arguments of the Nazis and who accepted the general proposition that the Jews were Germany's misery may well have been grateful, in the first few years of Nazi rule, for the "leniency" of Nazi policy, because it spared his particular Jewish friends. Such a person is unlikely to understand how he conspired in the murderous outcome of that general policy, and is likely to feel a grievance for having been condemned by a world in which many of those with a similar general commitment have fortuitously escaped its consequences.

Many of those who were decent and upright have been so embittered by the restitution that their statements have taken on the twists of protestation and have become nearly indistinguishable from the over-reactions of those whose consciences are guilty with more cause. This is true of the Krauses. Hannelore Kraus had long since ceased working for Isaac Stein. Years before, Dela Stein had dismissed Hannelore's pangs of conscience about going to a local Bachdorf festival with her betrothed at a time when Isaac Stein would be needing help. Dela's gesture found a harmonious consequence when shortly thereafter Hannelore and her betrothed were married. Isaac's suggestion that she and her husband both work for him was turned down with thanks.

Hannelore and her husband went to live in Friedenhausen, two villages away from Bachdorf. Here their two children, a son and a daughter, were born, and here they became close friends of the Jewish family, Stern. The friendship survived into the Nazi years, and the Krauses were labeled Jew-lovers. In 1938, Herr Stern offered to sell Hannelore's husband a meadow, in order to get cash for emigration. The price agreed on was 1,600 marks, of which 600 marks was over and above the officially approved price of 1,000 marks. Even at 1,600 marks, Hannelore and her husband were getting a bargain and one which was, objectively, a result of the pressures on Stern. Stern desperately needed cash; he had come to the Krauses out of friendship; and Herr Kraus had, so to speak, a genuine relationship to the meadow, since he had helped harvest it each year.

Shortly after the transaction and with the money from it, the three Stern children were sent out of the country. Their parents were never able to follow them and were finally deported. The Krauses' fortunes changed for the worse during the Second World War, when their son became disabled by arthritis and their daughter developed schizophrenia and was sterilized in accord with the Nazi eugenics program. After the war, Stern's son came back to Friedenhausen and began a restitution proceeding as a result of which repayment for the meadow was ordered. It is clear that the son was wholly within his rights, and just as clear that Hannelore and her husband have at the most an entirely abstract notion of what the son had been through. They are deeply bitter toward him. "He will surely get his just punishment for causing us all the sleepless nights he has," they say. They are so immersed in the traditional culture that it is hard to believe that the rancor toward the son will not, somehow, be generalized to all Jews. Yet one of its consequences has been to idealize the memory of the parents by contrast. In other cases, where the bitterness cannot be worked off against a single individual, the twisting may appear as a reactivation and whetting of many of the darker features of the traditional attitude toward the Jews.

When Sigmund sold the Bachdorf property in 1937, when he helped Meyer find a purchaser for the jewelry store, when he accepted property in trust from emigrating Jews, or when non-Jews with or without defensible motives bought Jewish property, all were bowing under the pressure of events, and by yielding this way, were abetting those pressures. Yet Sigmund and many of the others were acting as most men would have acted in parallel situations. Like most men, they drew the justifications for their actions from those provided by their human surroundings.

Sigmund did not know that he was writing the close to a chapter. By the end of 1938, however, he had probably begun to realize something which was to become the hallmark of his last years in Hochburg: that all his activity, all the efforts which seemed so necessary and—in the context of the situation—so desirable, were becoming bonds and fetters. Palliative activities always have something of this character, but it is not felt until the fate to which they tie us begins to show darkly over the horizon. In 1938, the contours of this fate were not clear to anyone, despite all the indications which hindsight insists should have been signs. Right up to the end such contours were, if visible at times, usually hidden behind the mists of hope or calculation, fear or the real confusion of facts. More and more the attachments, necessities, duties, and desires fell into place in the pattern of entrapment.

12

[The laws and two policemen]

In a long and detailed decree of April, 1938, the Nazis demanded that every Jew make an exhaustive official report of his real and personal property. (Of the latter, however, only that portion which was luxury property or destined for more than purely personal use had to be listed.) The Hochburg Jews had to have advice on how to interpret these provisions, and Sigmund's position in the community was such that it was natural for his fellow Jews to come to him for advice. For his part, while he was perfectly capable of reading a legal document, he could hardly read the Nazi mind. He still had both public and private relationships with various officials in the Hochburg administration and in the courts. He would have been foolish if he had not attempted to go beyond his reading of the law to a discreet investigation of the probabilities it presaged.

A feature of this and similar laws was the extent to which they enmeshed those who had anything to do with them. For such laws were never complete. Behind the original statement of each there stretched a long trail of administrative decrees. For example, the thirteenth administrative decree to the Nuremberg Laws did not appear until July, 1943. The characteristic was of course not peculiar to Nazi legislation; administrative law is a category of both the American and British legal systems. Such enmeshment is everywhere inconvenient, and only the content of the original law can say whether or not it will be fatal.

Sigmund Stein was too busy being a victim of this situation as it took shape in Nazi Germany, and too busy counseling other victims, to give it sustained and careful analysis. Yet it was precisely in Sigmund's rendering of advice to his fellows that the overriding Nazi assumptions about the Jews created moral problems for him. This had been true from the beginning, but at first the truth had been thin and counterbalanced by the fat necessity of his making a living for himself and his family and of helping tide his fellow Jews over a difficult and temporary period.

During the early months of the regime, Sigmund's arguments with Tannenbaum or the Zionists—his belief that the Jews should remain in Germany—could remain on an almost intellectual plane. Naturally, it was more than an intellectual argument, for Sigmund's adherence to Germany and to the idea of remaining in Germany was an expression of his whole being. It was still that in 1938, but as the years passed it had become ever harder to rationalize his refusal to leave Germany, and the refusal itself had produced its own entanglements.

Both omen and entanglement were repeatedly underscored throughout 1938. The proliferation of anti-Jewish laws and decrees brought forth such items as, in July, a change in German commercial regulations by which Jews and "Jewish corporations"—the latter being a concept given legal existence a few weeks earlier—were forbidden to carry on a variety of enterprises. They were excluded from being custodians, real estate agents or administrators, or matrimonial agents (except for marriages between "Jews or between a Jew and a mongrel of the first degree"). They were not allowed to be tourist guides. Finally, Sigmund's work was complicated by the fact that Jews were forbidden to convey information about property and personal matters on a professional basis.

A measure which followed in August, though in point of fact less significant than many others, in some ways indicates the depth of explicit meanness to which the Nazis could be brought by their theories. This was the second decree regulating the administration of the law on name changes. The law itself had appeared in January, 1938, as an apparently innocent measure by which name changes made before January 1, 1933, could be nullified if it turned out they were "undesirable." The change made by the second administrative decree went far enough to cause embarrassment and difficulties for the Jews, but not so far as to confuse the records. Thus, no change at all of either family or given name was demanded, although henceforth the given names of Jewish infants had to be picked from an approved list of presumably "Jewish" names. However, if the given name of an adult was other than one on the list, then the possessor of the name had to take on an additional one. For men, this had to be "Israel," for women, "Sara." Thus, Sigmund Stein became Sigmund Israel Stein, and his wife—a little surprisingly, perhaps, in view of the strong Old Testament flavor of Esther— Esther Sara Stein.

The Fifth Administrative Decree to the Nuremberg Laws, issued in September, 1938, was particularly relevant to Sigmund Stein, for it ended the legal profession for Jews in Germany. Not that there were many Jewish lawyers left. Certainly, there were none in Hochburg, and there had been none since April, 1933. The few Jewish lawyers who remained elsewhere in Germany could represent only Jews, and court appearances must have been unpleasant at best and impossible at worst. Since the beginning of the Nazi regime, Sigmund had been acting as a legal counselor to Hochburg's Jews, as well as, in a less open way, to some non-Jews. He rated as a lawyer in "honorable retirement," and by the exercise of discretion had avoided many of the pitfalls connected with the nature of the "honor."

As far as the Jewish trade went, he had no competition. In a town as small as Hochburg, it is understandable that Sigmund as a defrocked lawyer retained much of the technical prestige and respect that he had enjoyed previously. Within the limits set by the whole bizarre situation, his advice would be sought out. Even if there had been non-Jewish legal advisers in Hochburg during these years—and it appears that there were none—any Jewish clientele they had had would have vanished. After all, the von Schlegel's "Aryan" lawyer had gotten cold feet about representing a family of prominence and influence and had, so to speak, turned it over to Sigmund. A small-time legal adviser would hardly have been less timorous.

The only man who might have been competing with Sigmund was Heinrich Wolff. Sigmund had enjoyed prominence both inside and outside the Hochburg Jewish community. He was not insistently Jewish, but he was widely known as a Jew and never tried to deny it. In regard to Heinrich Wolff, the situation seems to have been more obscure. No one in the Hochburg Jewish community would ever have exclaimed about Sigmund as they have about Heinrich Wolff, "Oh, was *he* a Jew?" Even before 1933, Wolff's situation as a legal adviser had some spots on it. This, plus the fact that after 1933 he was thrown back on a Jewish community with which he was out of phase and sympathy, combined with Sigmund's greater prominence and respectability to produce a decline in Heinrich Wolff's fortunes which culminated in a tragedy.

Frau Wolff-Foerster, his daughter, is full of bitterness about the fact that her father was taken into custody as an idler in the summer of 1938. She is aware that there had been difficulties between her father and the police as early as 1933, and explains that he had been resented by "respectable" lawyers—from which judgment, however, she excluded Hagen and Stein, despite her accusation that Hagen had defrauded her father. She names the Nazi lawyer, Kutscher, as one who instituted proceedings against Heinrich Wolff before 1933, at which time the procedure had been unsuccessful. After April, 1933, with Kutscher riding high on the Nazi wave, his success in any such endeavor was almost assured.

Frau Wolff-Foerster has a virulent opinion of Officer Schultheiss' role in the 1938 arrest of her father—and in general. Schultheiss, she says, was *the* Gestapo in Hochburg. In contrast, she extols the character and behavior of Officer Schumann, who had been her father's regimental comrade in the World War. Schultheiss ordered Schumann to take Wolff into custody. This turned out to mean Schumann's accompanying Wolff on the train from

Hochburg to Kassel, where he was turned over to other authorities to be sent to the Buchenwald concentration camp. According to Frau Wolff-Foerster, Schumann's decency is signalized by his behavior when he parted from her father. He was supposed to relieve Wolff of his money and other possessions, and this he did. But, his duty having been done, Schumann then gave Wolff some of his own money and a package of his own cigarettes—there being nothing in the regulations against such an action!

Ordinarily Heinrich Wolff might have gone to jail for a day or so for the "crime" of being an idler. Schultheiss claims he was arrested on the complaints of his neighbors because he had been getting into fights—he who had refused to defend himself against an SA man in the last days of the Republic. As it was, he was sent to Buchenwald, and Buchenwald killed him. According to his daughter, he was assigned to the work gang called "Column 4711," in ironical reference to the famous German cologne. This crew, which consisted solely of Jews, had the job of cleaning the latrines. The men were not given adequate clothing or equipment. Heinrich Wolff already had rheumatism and his condition was so aggravated by the dampness, chill, and misery of the work that he finally was unable to keep it up and was allowed to starve. His daughter had been trying to have him released and had been told that the most likely way to succeed in this was to arrange for his emigration as soon as he got out. With great trouble she was able to get a passport and find a destination for him. The day the passport came through, she was notified of his death. She believes, indeed, that he was dead when the passport was issued. It is easy to comprehend her feeling that this was done on purpose.

Heinrich Wolff had never really competed for the position in the Hochburg Jewish community which Sigmund Stein occupied. Now, unknown to Sigmund, unknown to the community, and unknown to himself, he became the early herald of the future.

Both officers, Schultheiss and Schumann, came eventually to have critical relationships with Sigmund Stein. Frau Wolff-Foerster's hatred of Schultheiss and her tolerance of Schumann show the manner in which one person's inevitably unique relationship with another determines the entire complexion of that relationship. Both Schultheiss and Schumann show the effects of lives spent as "good policemen" in a land where the disorders of history have set a premium on order and on the role of those who maintain it. Both men look back with nostalgia to the Wilhelminian era and both have fundamental reservations about the Weimar Republic, while obviously believing that they had done their duty toward the republic and were right in doing it. Both admit the evil of the Nazi regime and the tragedy which it brought to the Jews. More important, both recognize that they had a part in the working out of this tragedy. Their nostalgia for the order which the Nazis brought was both explicit and implicit. This was, of course, an order according to their own lights. But the same lights illuminated the scene for thousands of other Germans and contrasted with the dark disorder of the Weimar Republic's last years.

Naturally there are differences between the two men. Schumann seems by far the more personable. He started his adult life as a wood-carver and carpenter, but a debilitating allergy to wood dust forced him to abandon this craft and to enter the civil service as a career policeman. As a consequence of the value traditionally placed on occupational stability in Germany, this change is of great significance in Schumann's life, a significance which can be summarized in the respect and friendship he felt for those people who, as he puts it, do what they have to do. This is patently related to the attitudes toward duty which characterize the German civil service.

Schumann, like many men, is a combination of naiveté and sophistication. He had a Hessian country boyhood which, with its setting amidst castle ruins and village peace, evokes an idealization of the "good old days" which is understandable but at the same time prevents Schumann's seeing certain things clearly. Yet he makes a reasonable analysis of the authority structure of his youthful surroundings, speaking with considerable insight about how, among the Jewish families of the area, an earlier exclusion from such occupations as farming and crafts had forced them into commercial and financial pursuits. He says that when one's father and grandfather had been in such occupations and one's own opportunities were limited, it was natural for a son to acquire the skills of the father and eventually take over the father's role. Thus, Schumann concludes that it was not necessary to assume peculiar racial characteristics to account for the financial "taint" of Jewish occupations.

Yet he shares most of the traditional attitudes toward the Jews. In this and other respects he has a striking ability to hold beliefs which seem mutually exclusive of one another. Yet when these contradictions are pressed on him, he is neither embarrassed nor unable to find a route between them, however circuitous the path may be. An example is the contradiction between his decent and understanding view of the Jews as human beings and his express belief that he had been right in participating in the deportations of Jews. True, he says, the Jews are human beings like the rest of us; true, it was Christian society which forced them into finance and commerce. But there they were, and this occupational concentration was an unhealthy state of affairs as even the Jews admitted. The war made necessary many measures which would not ordinarily have been considered. Schumann did not like the human effects of the measures which had previously been taken to drive the Jews out of the economic life of Germany. He agreed in part with the objective but disapproved of acts of violence against the Jews—and was supported in this disapproval by the directives of the regime. As a policeman, he had always had to carry out many orders the human effects of which he did not like. This, he says, is part of being a policeman and always was.

When the orders came through for the deportation of the Jews, Schumann and his colleagues were told that the Jews were being sent east to do agricultural labor, road work, and similar jobs. While he felt that it was bad to send people away from their homes —people who had, as individuals, done nothing wrong—nevertheless, it was understandable that in view of the measures already taken against them, the Jews should not have been eager supporters of the German war effort. He also felt that the Jews would benefit from the experience of working with their hands. All these beliefs permitted him to feel that the deportations were not essentially different from many of the other unpleasant tasks which had fallen to his lot during nearly thirty years on the force.

Eventually, Officer Schumann heard rumors that terrible things were happening in the East. He also knew the content of the enemy radio broadcasts which were being beamed into Germany. It was natural that he should connect the two. He had served in World War I and resented the falsity of the atrocity propaganda which had been spread at that time by the Allies. He felt that it would be senseless and disloyal to believe, let alone spread, all the rumors which one heard in wartime. In a general way it was obvious that terrible things happen in wartime, and it was obvious that each side tries to exploit them in its propaganda.

Schumann admits that he was wrong on many points, but he sees no contradictions between his beliefs and his actions greater than those which are common in the human condition. His regrets are genuine, but he does not have a guilty conscience. His rationalizations appear to be efforts to preserve his idealized childhood picture of the Germany in which he had to make his living as an adult. There were holes in his decency and intelligence, just as there were holes in his stern sense of duty. What gives him his special character is the fact that in his view of himself and his actions there is no admission that perhaps his basic premises were wrong or inadequate.

The same fixity in basic premises is also characteristic of Schumann's former colleague, Schultheiss. Their common adherence to a similar set of basic premises is the principal reason that attitudes toward them are so strongly determined by more or less fortuitous features of particular individual relationships with them. Frau Wolff-Foerster's detestation of Schultheiss and her regard for Schumann made Schultheiss out to be *the* Gestapo in Hochburg, with Schumann a well-meaning but powerless subordinate. Schumann himself modifies this picture by saying that, although Schultheiss had seniority, both men had the same rank, and neither had the power of command over the other. The fact that each man had his own area of competence sometimes led to the appearance of one's working for the other. It was possible to be arrested by Schumann in a situation where he could say he knew nothing about the matter since it had been processed by his colleague. And vice versa.

Schumann does not like Schultheiss, and says he found him hard to work with. Both had the same relationship to the Gestapo.

They were not members, but each could be commissioned to attend to Gestapo matters and each might make arrests ordered by the Gestapo.

To Konrad Muenschner of the *Taegliches Hessenblatt*, Schumann's colleague, Schultheiss, was a decent enough, if unimaginative, minion of the law. To the "mongrel" daughter of Professor Gottfried and his Jewish wife, Schultheiss is a man with whom a joke was possible on one occasion when he had had to question her. To Casimir Dombrowski, Schultheiss was a roaring anti-Semite and Schumann a decent and considerate man. People did and still do react to these two men not in terms of some final judgment about virtue and vice, but rather in terms of particular situations and the particular definitions brought to these situations. Perhaps this is because Schumann and Schultheiss related in the same way to the victims of their policemen's duty.

13

[Spared for a darker fate]

The cornerstone of the synagogue in the Landgraf Heinrich Strasse was laid in the year of Sigmund Stein's birth, 1896. Speeches made in honor of the occasion, together with related essays, were printed in a thin book published about a year later at the time the synagogue was opened for worship. The introduction describes the synagogue as "late Romanesque with certain Byzantine features." It was built of red sandstone and included, aside from the synagogue proper, a schoolroom and office for the rabbi as well as a ritual bath and a caretaker's apartment. Photographs show that the synagogue was an imposing building, standing in proud disharmony with its surroundings. Imposing, too, is the fact that it stood there not for a congregation but for a total Jewish community of four hundred. The seeming disproportion between the structure and those it served was typical of the area, where tiny synagogues sometimes met the needs of three of four families in a village.

215

Heinrich Martin, a Christian, was the last caretaker to occupy the apartment in the basement of the synagogue. In his retirement he is a gravedigger, yet he does not seem to belong in a cemetery. Gravedigging and synagogue-tending were not his chosen occupations. In 1933, he was dismissed from his position as fireman on the state railways because he would not give the Hitler salute. By 1936, it was getting hard to live on the odd jobs which had been the only kind of work open to him after his dismissal. When his friend Siebert, an old Social Democrat comrade, announced that he was giving up his job as caretaker of the synagogue to take both a new wife and a new job, Heinrich Martin saw this as a real, if not exactly golden, opportunity.

Martin was eager for the job, although he was fully aware that the problems involved had been increasing. Martin had inherited a house in the Enggasse, not far from the synagogue, and he thought that by taking the job he would be able to live at the synagogue and rent his house. So he went to see Koppel Herzog who was prayer leader of the congregation and major domo of the synagogue at the time. Like any job applicant, Heinrich Martin had to be interviewed. He says that there were almost a hundred others looking for the job; this jibes in an interesting way with the mayor's reports for the period which tell of the unemployment among the caretakers of the now closed Korporation houses. Through his friendship with Siebert, however, Heinrich Martin had an inside track, and Koppel Herzog, after making sure that Martin was not a Communist, agreed to let him have the position.

During the rest of 1936 and early 1937, things were not too bad for Martin and his family. Hochburg was, after all, a seasonal tourist attraction, and the synagogue's location in the Landgraf Heinrich Strasse was so prominent that the visiting busloads of foreign tourists could hardly see all the sights of romantic old Hochburg without coming face to face with the synagogue. Since the German government was officially dealing with the Jews fairly and without persecution, albeit within the framework of a racial theory of the state, it might have given the wrong impression to the visitors if windows, broken by vandals, were left unrepaired. Hence, all during the time that Heinrich Martin was caretaker, the police laid much weight on the prompt repair of any damage.

So he spent an increasingly large proportion of his time in 1937 and 1938 replacing broken window panes, removing litter, and cleaning walls which had been scrawled with "Death to the Jews" and similar sentiments. Heinrich Martin speaks of these tasks in a matter-of-fact way and tells with definite pleasure of his personal contacts with the more orthodox Jewish families for whom he lit fires and did other errands on the Sabbath.

With the same matter-of-factness, however, he tells how the pressure on him and his family finally became too great. His large, flamboyant ears, his bald head, and his gaunt figure suggest a man to whom teasing by brats is familiar, and he did not mind too much being called "Jews' slavey" in 1937 and 1938. But such epithets were the least of his difficulties. On occasion, he had been stoned in the streets, and his apartment in the synagogue was not exempt from the punishment the rest of the building took. His daughter, who had been a clerk in a Hochburg insurance office, was finally let go because her co-workers—"Little Hitlers, all of them," the old man says—made it too hard for her. In the early summer of 1938 he moved himself and his family out of the synagogue, although he kept on working there—until the end.

Asked about the burning of the synagogue in 1938, a Hochburger may respond with a straightforward story of the events of the ninth of November as he saw them or heard about them. Or he may betray a deeper involvement by a more elusive story. In either event, however, it is probable that at some point he will mention the general shock felt at this attack on a house of God. He may date the beginning of his final disillusionment with the regime from this, the *Kristallnacht*, the night of broken glass.

The people of Hochburg are neither more nor less religious than people in similar towns elsewhere in Germany. Both Lutheranism and Catholicism are traditional in the area. Hochburg itself has one Catholic and two Protestant churches, in addition to several small Protestant chapels. The Ursula Church is, of course, the most important of the larger edifices. For nearly three hundred years it was Catholic; for four hundred years it has been Protestant. On Saturday evening the bells of these churches dominate the town; on Sunday mornings the bright costumes of the Catholic villagers who have come to Hochburg for mass contrast with the sombre yet attractive costumes of their Protestant counterparts. The contrasts among the villagers are muted by the variegated uniformity of the Hochburg residents themselves, who simply wear their Sunday best and look much like church-goers in America. Not all villagers come to Hochburg to church; when they remain in the villages, there is little mixture of Catholic and Protestant, for the villages tend to be either the one or the other.

There is little point in wondering how deeply and truly religious the villagers or the Hochburgers are. On the whole, the church is very much a part of their lives, and there is little question but that in most villages the minister, together with the teacher, are still the two people to whom respect is automatically due. In Bachdorf, Elisabeth Kohlhausen wears the Protestant costume and speaks of a drought as God's punishment for their sins. In Hochburg, the locomotive engineer, Ehrhardt, is a deeply sincere Catholic who joined the Reichsbanner because it supported the Republic and who stuck to his colors after 1933. He does not think much about his soul, because he is confident that it will be taken care of according to the rules.

On a far more ethereal level, the theological school of Hochburg University is known throughout Germany and beyond as a center of Protestant scholarship. Its early association with the Reformation lingers as a certain academic mustiness. The zealous reformers of the past have been replaced by erudite scholars.

It is difficult to say how these various religious attitudes hold up when projected back to 1938. By that time, the open conflict between the Nazi regime and the Evangelical Church had considerably subsided. Though nominally a compromise, the settlement which had been reached was in effect a defeat for the church. Not only was the party as party strengthened, but the nationalistic and conservative trends within the church were set off against the oppositionists. In Hochburg, the grocer Keller, a pillar of the local Nazi party who had been seriously implicated in the Goldmann shoe store riot, was also a pillar of the Evangelical Church. His position was far from exceptional; probably most Nazis in the town were "good church people." The Kreisleiter and Landrat, Kleinwitz, as we have seen, was the son of a well-known fundamentalist minister.

Like the Soviet government, the Nazi regime in its relationship to the church could be looked upon as making certain astute concessions to a deeply-rooted tradition, the complete extirpation of which was neither necessary nor desirable. Unlike the Soviet government, however, the Nazis were not avowedly or even, to any significant degree, covertly atheistic. The party supported and was supported by one or more sects which presented a grotesque mixture of traditional Christianity and Nordic mythologizing. Chief among these were the "German-Christians."

Without doubt, Hochburgers were shocked when the synagogue went up in flames. But such shock proves nothing and is consistent with a basic consent to the policies which produce the shocking event. To argue that an action cannot be popular because of the shock which people feel at the burning of a "house of God" overlooks the fact that it has been precisely the burning of churches, synagogues, idols, and people which has so often characterized movements of great popular feeling.

It is because the Nazis exploited all such consideration that the events of the Kristallnacht are hard to assess. Hochburgers and other Germans often point to the fact that the synagogue burnings and riots of November 9 were organized from above. Yet this can be true of movements which attain genuine popular character. Indeed, in one sense it is always true, and differences in mass actions lie in the level from which manipulation emerges and from the purposes behind it, rather than from the presence or absence of manipulation. Manipulation goes with leadership, and leadership is necessary because separate individuals need a common intellectual and emotional definition of the situation if they are to act in concert—to burn a synagogue or to defend the Warsaw Ghetto.

It is hard to say when the manipulation of popular feeling becomes crass manufacture and provocation. The Nazi campaign against the Jews, both the legal measures and the concomitant anti-Semitic propaganda, was magnified in 1938. In October came the first attempt at mass deportation: sixty thousand Jews with Polish passports, many of whom had long been resident in Germany, many of them refugees from the more popular if less official anti-Semitism of Poland, were the victims. In anticipation of a German attempt to deport these people, the Polish regime de-

creed that unless they renewed their passports through a procedure which required a visit to Poland, they would be shorn of
their Polish citizenship and become stateless persons. The deadline was set for October 29. The German authorities, in order to
beat this deadline, rounded up fifteen thousand Polish Jews and
sent them to the border on October 28. But the border was closed,
and they were allowed to return home. The deportees of a few
days later were not so lucky. The border was still closed, but they
were simply turned out into the fields through which it ran and
forced over it.

Among this latter group were the parents of Herschel
Grynszpan. Whether because of this mistreatment of his parents,
or for more obscure and less relevant reasons, Grynszpan, at the
time a refugee in Paris, attempted to assassinate the German
Ambassador to France and succeeded in murdering the third
secretary of the embassy, Ernst vom Rath. Details of both the
act and the motives behind it remain unknown; thus it is interesting that a man prominent in the postwar administration of
Hochburg, a Social Democrat both intelligent and well meaning,
attributes the murder to deterioration in a homosexual relationship between the two men. The view is not groundless but is
based on a letter of doubtful authenticity which was later brought
to light. This letter, with the unsavory revelation about the
"martyred" vom Rath, was used as an indirect means of keeping
Grynszpan from public trial after the fall of France.

At the beginning of November, 1938, however, vom Rath was
a hero, struck down in dastardly fashion by the long arm of International Jewry. The German papers were full of the case, calling
for vengeance pure and simple, or for just and measured retribution. People were upset, the faithful Nazis for obvious reasons,
the waverers because the facts as presented demanded an act of
faith to be rejected. Nobody could know exactly what had happened, and anyone could wonder what it meant for his own immediate future. The opponents of the Nazis were not to be taken
in by the exploitation of such incidents; on the other hand, their
effective strength and their power of persuasion were at a low
ebb as a result of the series of Nazi successes in foreign and domestic policy. To cap the matter, the shooting had taken place on

November 7, and the annual celebration of the Nazis' Beer Hall Putsch of 1923, a rousing party occasion, was scheduled for the evening of the ninth in Munich and other cities.

Kristallnacht was indisputably planned. Just as indisputably, it was planned on the spur of the moment. Given the trend of Nazi policy and the shape of preceding events, the shooting of a German diplomat by a Jew was too favorable an opportunity to be missed. In the end, the question remains unanswered: were popular feelings the result of planning, or was the plan made because of an upsurge of exploitable popular feeling?

It is clear that in Hochburg the events of the Kristallnacht were the culmination of incidents which had begun almost as soon as the news of the Paris murder became known. The Hochburg synagogue was in a very conspicuous location, and many hundreds of people, going home by tram on the evening of November 7 could look up from their papers and see it standing there. A consequence was that Heinrich Martin and Koppel Herzog went to the police on the morning of the eighth to report that windows had been broken during the night and that a crude attempt had been made to fire the synagogue. The police records show that an investigation was made and that the evidence was consistent with the report.

Heinrich Martin says that there was more rock-throwing on the eighth, and during the day of Kristallnacht itself there was a lot of trouble with Hitler Youth who not only broke windows but also managed to enter the schoolroom on the first floor of the synagogue and throw some furniture out of the window.

At ten o'clock that night (November 9), the city auditorium disgorged crowds of SA, SS, and ordinary men who had just listened to speeches, poems, and songs in honor of the heroes of the Beer Hall Putsch—inflammatory oratory, filled with folkish sentimentality and malicious anti-Semitism, yet devoid of direct incitement. Many of these men went home to bed, but many headed for the various bars and coffee houses in the neighborhood. And all must have looked across the street to the synagogue, for the city auditorium is only about fifty yards from the synagogue site, on the other side of the Landgraf Heinrich Strasse.

Some of the gatherings after the ceremony had been planned

previously as comradely get-togethers of old Nazi fighters. In particular, the meeting of Storm Troop VI had been so planned. And the coffee house where this group usually met was the *"Engelsglueck,"* directly across from the synagogue. It is at this point that the appearance of a plan, of higher orders, begins to develop—not clearly, but with some confusion, nervousness, and irresolution. Even in those overall aspects of the situation where a plan is most evident—in the sluggishness of the police and fire departments, in the fact that the latter carefully doused the surrounding houses without drenching the fire itself—there is ambiguity. After five years of anti-Semitic policy, of libel and hatred aimed at the Jews, and after two days of an extreme intensification of these tendencies as a result of the vom Rath slaying, it would not have been surprising if a certain laggardliness had shown itself in the police and fire department even without incitement from above. Nor would it have been surprising if the crowd which quickly gathered to watch the fire—now with Storm Troop VI maintaining order—had produced such expressions as "It serves them right," and the like. The next day the *Landeskurier* wrote of "the wrath of an outraged people against the cowardly Jewish assassin" and of "the expressions of this wrath which were heard among the large crowd which gathered around the scene of the—relatively minor—retribution."

This is exaggeration and distortion, with obvious design. It contrasts markedly with the shock which people today report they felt at the spectacle of a house of God going up in flames. Neither description is proved true by the falsity of the other. The same person who tells of the widespread shock at the action against the house of God ten minutes later describes the delight of a friend who brought home a large fragment of a map of Jerusalem found at the synagogue site.

In the early morning hours of November 10, 1938, it was impossible to know what was going on in the minds of all the individuals who stood around watching the Hochburg synagogue burn. Any one of them could assume that the fire had been set by the Nazis, although the postwar court which came to this conclusion could not create a clarity about its details, for in the process of demonstrating the general conclusion such clarity was shown to have been lacking.

Not long after the fire had died and the crowd had dispersed, a roundup of Jewish men began. This lasted until noon of November 10, and later in some cases. These men were being taken into custody "for their own protection." According to Casimir Dombrowski, all men between the ages of sixteen and sixty-five were to be taken, with men over sixty-five being substituted if the younger men in their households were unavailable. The quasi-official list made out at the time shows that thirty-one Hochburg men were taken.

All but two were between the age limits mentioned by Dombrowski, who tells of one of the exceptions. Heinz Bernstein was seventy years old and lived with the family of his son, Moses, two floors above the Dombrowskis in the Landgraf Heinrich Strasse. Moses was sick, and old Heinz was taken in his stead. The other exception was the well-known and formerly respected merchant, Willi Schoenbaum. Since he was childless and there is no record of any younger man's having resided with him and his wife, his inclusion could not have been as a substitute and remains unexplained.

The roundup was conducted mainly by the SA. School inspector Wiegand, who is knowledgeable about Sigmund and the town's politics, was a teacher in Gymnasium. In November, 1938, on the morning of the tenth, he was walking to school when he saw a truck—"like those in which cattle are transported"—pull up in front of Treitschkestrasse 5, just off the Flachstrasse. Treitschkestrasse 5 was generally known as a "Jewish house" even though Henrietta Korbmacher and her family, along with one other non-Jewish family, shared the building with its Jewish owner, Herr Rosenstein; the teacher in the Jewish school, Rabenstein; and Rabbi Roth.

Wiegand tells how he saw the SA men taking Rabenstein and Roth to the truck. Rabenstein, he says, looked terribly desolate. The Treitschkestrasse, a short street, had been cordoned off by the police, several of whom stood around doing absolutely nothing: to the Jews, to the SA men, or to a crowd of about one hundred boys who were throwing stones at the windows of the house and insulting and spitting at the Jews in the truck.

Wiegand says little about the attitudes he might be expected to have felt in the circumstances, although he makes a great deal of the offense to his pedagogical sensibilities caused by the behavior of the boys, and he tells of intervening firmly against *them*. When he reported this to his supervisor after arriving at the Gymnasium, the supervisor, a strong Nazi, was aghast. But Wiegand stuck to his guns saying that as long as he was a teacher he was not going to stand for his charges' misbehaving as those boys were. In spite of his politics, the supervisor came around to Wiegand's view that such behavior was a poor omen for the future of the boys. The censure of his action which Wiegand expected from the party never materialized, however. The tempest was brewing in something other than a teapot at the time.

The men taken in this roundup were held temporarily in the city hall jail, as well as in an old workhouse across the Marktplatz from the city hall. During the afternoon and evening of the tenth, they were joined by a few victims who had been missed or by-passed in the initial action. One of these latecomers was Casimir Dombrowski. There had been some confusion and indecision about his nationality, and when it was finally decided that he should be included, Officer Schumann was sent after him late in the evening. Dombrowski had remained in his apartment all during the day of the tenth, thoroughly frightened by the rumors and reports his Christian employees were bringing to him. He knew that the synagogue had burned, since he could almost see it from his apartment, but he had not dared to do more than peek through his curtains at the time. Hence, it was only upon the arrival of his workers that he learned the details of what had happened.

Officer Schumann says, in telling about the arrest of some other "undesirables," the gypsies, that a policeman often has to do things which are unpleasant and the only way to somehow mitigate this fact is to do them decently, with courtesy and a certain compassion. They still, of course, had to be done. That Dombrowski appreciated this approach is evident.

Schumann came to the door, informed Dombrowski that it

was his unpleasant duty to arrest him, told him to take his time getting ready, and permitted Dombrowski's son to accompany his father part way to the city hall jail. Here Dombrowski was put into a cell with the banker, Tannenbaum. The tailor was honored by this and insisted that Tannenbaum sleep on the one cot; he, Dombrowski, would sleep on the bench. This need not, however, have been undue respect. The banker was, at sixty-one, thirteen years older than the tailor.

On the morning of November 11, the thirty-one men who had been taken on the preceding day were sent by bus to Kassel. From there, after being subjected for a night to the whims of the SA, they were sent by train to Weimar, city of Goethe, the German Republic, and the Buchenwald concentration camp. After another period in the Weimar railroad station, during which the SA played brutal games with them, the men were sent by truck to the camp, where the games turned into two months of killing reality.

Sigmund Stein was not sent to Buchenwald. There is no immediately apparent reason why this was so. In 1938, Sigmund was almost exactly halfway between the ages of sixteen and sixty-five. Moses Bernstein, who also fell between these age limits, was not taken, but he was sick, so his father was taken in his stead. Sigmund Oppenheimer was not taken. One or two others may have escaped, as an acquaintance of Sigmund Stein's from a nearby town did, by taking to their cars and spending a perilous few days at the wheel. Apparently Sigmund expected to be taken. Frau Klingelmann, who lived below the Steins in the Goeringstrasse apartment, went upstairs in the early morning hours after hearing a commotion in the streets and seeing what she describes as an "oxcart" full of Jews in front of the building. She wanted to warn Sigmund to get warmly dressed. She found the family already awake and much disturbed and apprehensive. Esther Stein was barely able to control herself, and the fourteen-year-old Marion was not able to do so at all. She was crying and saying over and over again, "They mustn't take you away! No, no!"

In the end the "oxcart" moved on, and Sigmund was not taken. Officer Schultheiss, who directed the roundup of the Jews on this occasion, says that Sigmund was purposely excluded. This was done on Schultheiss' initiative after consultation with his superiors. It was felt that Sigmund was "needed" in Hochburg because he knew the situation of the Jewish community so well, and because his previous experience in counseling his fellow Jews about emigration made him invaluable at a time when the purpose of the regime was to force emigration by providing a large number of Jews with a taste of concentration camp.

The net around Sigmund thus grew tighter, and its strands began to cut into his flesh. For this was the first occasion when it could be said that Sigmund was spared the fate of his fellow Jews. It was not his doing, and it was based not on concession but on the convenience of the state. In terms of this convenience it was logical, and the logic related to all of Sigmund's earlier activity. Morally and ethically, Sigmund was not compromised. But morality and ethics mean nothing except a vagueness of good intentions in a situation the determinants of which have escaped comprehension. Sigmund was trapped.

There are paradoxes in the information about Sigmund Stein and the Hochburg Jewish community between 1938 and the scourge of endings which, beginning gradually in the early forties, merged into finality for the German Jews. On the one hand, there are many accounts of isolated events; on the other, there is little material from which an idea of the Hochburg community's internal continuity can be obtained.

Yet the problem of sources is by no means hopeless. The abundance of information stemming from these years is such that comparisons among the accounts become more than a mere checking of their truth. The patterns take shape as the following constellations of events. Sigmund Stein becomes *Obmann,* or spokesman, for the Hochburg Jewish community in its relationships with the Nazi administration of the town. This includes his status as property administrator but goes far beyond it to the misery and tragedy of his relationship to the deportations. Much of this pattern will be explored now. Another cluster of events is centered around Sigmund's increasingly ambivalent concern with emigration for himself and his family. This began as a tension in his determination to remain in Germany, and was to end in a desperate attempt to flee the country. A third pattern involves Sigmund's relationships to his fellow Jews and to non-Jewish Hochburg residents, these to be seen as particular cases of the general problem of relationships among the Jews and between Jew and non-Jew in this period. A final pattern is of Sigmund as a human being, as a husband and father in a time when all of his personal relationships were being subjected to pressures and strains which had been totally unforeseen in the years when these relationships were established.

It is apparent that each of these patterns covers a great deal of day-by-day living. It is also obvious that none of them is independent of the others.

Sigmund Stein's position in the Hochburg Jewish community had changed, as we have seen, from his being a successful and respected lawyer prior to the Nazi coup to his being a man who, because of his special knowledge of the Jewish community and his usefulness to the Hochburg authorities, was not sent to Buchenwald after the Kristallnacht—spared, despite the fact that he should have been taken according to the rules by which the victims were selected.

Other men, such as Rabbi Roth and the teacher, Rabenstein, whose roles in the Jewish community were greater, were sent to Buchenwald. So, too, was the banker, Tannenbaum. Similar to Sigmund in the esteem he had once enjoyed throughout Hochburg, and the object, in the Jewish community, of a respect symbolized by Casimir Dombrowski's deference to him in the city hall jail, Tannenbaum was still not spared the ordeal of his fellow Jews. Finally, Simon Goldberg, a man whose stature was such that, in a still obscure situation, he was later to contest the "leadership" of the Jewish community with Sigmund, was among those taken into custody.

But none of these men was a lawyer. Long afterward one of them was to say that Sigmund *should* have been taken. Yet his point in saying this was not any kind of a reproach; instead, it was by way of explaining Sigmund's failure to emigrate—had Sigmund seen and experienced what happened in Buchenwald, there would have been no doubt in his mind that he had to get himself and his family out of Germany.

Officer Schultheiss, who arranged for Sigmund's exclusion

from the roundup of Jews after the Kristallnacht on the grounds that he was needed in Hochburg, rather inconsistently uses the exclusion as an example of how "humanely" the Jews in Hochburg were treated. The inconsistency betrays a familiar blindness on Schultheiss' part, and yet, as a man lives and feels, Sigmund probably was grateful for being passed over, probably felt guilt because of it, and probably tried to assuage this guilt by doing all he could for his fellow Jews—thereby becoming more deeply involved in his role as mediator with the Nazi authorities.

In one sense it is surely ridiculous to talk about his guilt for the exemption. In another sense, however, in view of the enormous difference it made between his physical comfort on the one hand, and on the other the filth and brutality which were the lot of those taken; and in view of his failure to insist that he be included—in these respects his guilt had meaning. Only he had the right to condemn himself, but it is hard to believe that he did not exercise that right. The source of his guilt narrowed the alternatives for atonement and left him little room to do other than what he did. By his mediation, by exploiting the respect which was still given him in many non-Jewish quarters, he sought to ameliorate the lot of his fellow Jews.

The month or so during which the "protective custody" in Buchenwald lasted was a busy period for Sigmund. On the day after the synagogue was burned, the remaining walls were dynamited, because, according to the *Landeskurier*, they presented a danger to the life and limb of passersby. Heinrich Martin tells a different story. Not only were the walls still standing, but the building as a whole was not structurally damaged, since the thick stone walls and generally solid construction had withstood the flames. With some difficulty, Heinrich had gotten permission to go into what had been his apartment on the ground floor. He had stopped living there some months previously but still stored his tools and various other articles in the rooms. As he went in, he met an SA man coming out carrying Heinrich's tool chest and other loot. Heinrich asserted his ownership but got nowhere. There were other SA men in the gutted structure, none of them fearing for life and limb. Later on, Heinrich watched the dynamiting of the synagogue from the cover of a doorway on the other side of the Landgraf Heinrich Strasse.

The ultimate fate of the remains of the synagogue and the parcel of land on which it stood represented a further involvement of Sigmund Stein. Some of this involvement was not to crystallize until much later, but the sale of the synagogue property to Hochburg University, although it did not become final until July of 1939, relates intimately to the destruction of the building and to Sigmund's now rapidly accelerating entrapment.

Once before, in 1914, there had been a dispute between the Hochburg Jewish community and the University over the synagogue property. Herr Ehrhardt, the locomotive engineer who combined devotion to Catholicism with devotion to the Republic, had been office boy at the time to the venerable Dr. Hirschberg, who had conducted the case for the Jewish community. The point at issue was one of abutment rights between the University property and the synagogue site immediately adjacent to it. Ehrhardt remembers well the dignity with which Hirschberg had conducted the case, because, as a consequence of Hirschberg's blindness, Ehrhardt had had to be with him more than an office boy would ordinarily have been. Ehrhardt speaks of the friendliness with which the whole matter had finally been adjusted and contrasts this harmony with the malice which came later.

The people who tell about the 1939 transaction between the Hochburg Jewish community and the University also speak of it as a harmonious one, but they are largely unconscious of the way in which the few tatters of harmony that appeared were magnified out of all proportion by the contrasting context of coercion and persecution. Indeed, even the traces of harmony could be deceptive. The eminently fair price which the University paid for the property, for instance, was not what it seemed to be, because the University, as an institution of the German state, was credited with a large percentage of the purchase price—the restitution by all the Jews of Germany for the harm *they* had done, a grotesquely unjust billion-mark fine.

This was the device by which the Jews were made to pay for the Nazi depredations of the Kristallnacht. "For assuming an attitude of enmity toward the German people and the German state, an attitude which did not shrink before committing a cowardly murder," the Jews were to take much of the load off the German insurance companies which would have been sorely pressed to pay the insurance on the property, buildings, and plate glass windows which had been destroyed by the Nazis. The billion-mark fine was assessed on the whole German Jewish community as a percentage confiscation of its property. Thus, in July, 1939, the Hochburg Jewish community "owed" the state a substantial portion of the value of the synagogue property.

It is obvious that the Hochburg authorities needed the help of Sigmund Stein in the application of the billion-mark fine to the Hochburg Jews. Indeed, various people refer to him as the "administrator" of the fine. The assessment of the fine was a complex and agonizing process. It demanded the accurate and legally proper filling out of forms, and as always with such procedures, the difference between technical competence and technical naiveté could be reflected in the difference between minimum and maximum loss.

Sigmund's participation can be seen in another perspective. In retrospect, the billion-mark fine was a weird and contemptible demand that the Jews pay for their own persecution. Neither Sigmund, his fellow Jews, nor most Germans were able to see it as such at the time. The Jews knew what it was, but to them, as to the non-Jewish Germans, the official organization of the Kristallnacht pogroms was neither as clear nor as obvious in its implications as it appears in retrospect. It could hardly be assumed that the German people were not genuinely aroused over the vom Rath murder. To be sure, statements about a nation's anger or grief or joy are incitement, exhortation, ritual. Yet their status as such does not mean that they can be disregarded.

The whole history of German society and the infection of that society by the Nazi movement were such that the exhortation, incitement, and ritual occasioned by the vom Rath slaying had points of contact with genuine popular feelings. Violent action preceded, paralleled, and followed the incitement. When the billion-mark fine was announced on November 12, rioting was still going on in some areas. The announcement of the official "punishment" of the Jews coincided with the end of the unofficial actions against them. For the victims of threatened lynch justice, the transition to an official and orderly justice, however perverted its foundations, must always come as a relief. The Hochburg Jewish community recognized most of the inevitabilities of Sigmund's position and could see his connection with the fine as little more than a congealing of those inescapable forces. The relief the Jews felt at the cessation of violence which was signaled by the fine may well have been occasioned also by the knowledge that Sigmund Stein would be able to guide and temper the administration of the fine.

When the contract with the University for the sale of the synagogue property was finally signed, the signature of the University officials was matched not only by the signature of the free-thinker, Sigmund *Israel* Stein, but also by that of the pious and orthodox prayer leader of the community, Koppel Herzog. Koppel Herzog says that, of course, it was a forced sale, that he had been released from Buchenwald in order to sign, and that he had not been permitted to consult the community on the sale. Yet the contract itself, as it appears today in Hochburg's registry of deeds, has all the appearances of a conventional legal instrument drawn up under normal conditions. What makes it part and parcel of mass murder is something invisible: the fact that a small, common, pestilential germ—the myth of racial superiority—had invaded a body which could offer it no resistance.

Sigmund Stein himself may or may or may not have recognized the legal inanity of the situation, but he was careful to comply with the rules. On November 27, he wrote to the recorder of vital statistics in Niederhausen—who had jurisdiction for Sigmund's birthplace, Bachdorf—on stationery with the letterhead, "Sigmund Stein, Rechtsanwalt," from which the "Rechtsanwalt" ("Lawyer") was carefully crossed out:

To: the Standesbeamter
Niederhausen. | Frieden
Re: The given names of Jews
I, the undersigned, was born in Bachdorf/Frieden on the 16th of September, 1896. I was given the name SIGMUND.
I herewith give notice of the fact that, from the 1st of January 1939 I will bear the additional name ISRAEL.
If possible, I would appreciate the immediate notation of this change in the Birth Registry and the dispatch to me of two copies of the Birth Certificate as so changed.

If the change cannot be made until after the 1st of January, 1939, I would request your written confirmation of the fact that I have made this present notification of the addition to my name of ISRAEL. Any costs may be billed to me by mail.

Sigmund Stein

A few days later, Sigmund wrote to the same official, this time as the guardian of a young Jewish girl in Hochburg. The purpose was the same, to register the addition of "Sara" to her name. Now, however, he was writing as an official representative of a Hochburg Jew. He did not use his old stationery but wrote instead on plain white paper, typing in the letterhead:

Dr. Jur. Sigmund STEIN
Financial and Foreign Exchange Adviser
For Jewish Emigrants
Hochburg.|Felsen

The law on Jewish name changes had been announced in August, 1938. It is not necessarily correct to assume that Sigmund was prompted by the events of the Kristallnacht into taking action he had hitherto avoided.

Koppel Herzog cites his own experience with the name law as evidence of the fact that some Nazis could be decent. On his release from Buchenwald in order to sign the synagogue property contract, Koppel Herzog was only too eager to get out of Germany and finally arranged to emigrate, obtaining a departure date a few weeks after the property transaction. Somehow he had managed to avoid registering an additional name as, despite the Jewish character of the name he already bore, he was legally obliged to do. But he tells how the Nazi official, when approached in connection with the emigration, spontaneously suggested that no change be registered in Koppel's name, saying that he was leaving so soon that it was not really necessary under the circumstances.

Koppel Herzog, as a matter of fact, is surprisingly charitable in his comments on Hochburg. He tells how, in his last days there, his neighbors brought food to him and his family; how decent Officer Schumann had been to him, and how helpful his landlady had been despite her devotion to Hitler. Hochburg, Herzog says, was never Nazi at heart. Where and how it *was* Nazi he avoids saying; he is certainly articulate enough on the fear and suspicion which he and his fellow Jews felt toward the small world which held them in its grip.

Herzog supplies what might be considered the other side of the picture given by those Jews who complain of the company they had been forced by the Nazis to keep. Of those upper-class Jews who resented sharing a common jail with moneylenders and cattle dealers he says, after wondering out loud whether or not such people had ever switched their allegiance, that they—and he includes Sigmund Stein—may never have been really good democrats. After all, they were very wealthy men, but he doubts that they ever became Nazis! The world of the Hochburg Jewish community in 1939 must have had its strange and bitter facets.

It must be stressed that, whatever Koppel Herzog's feelings about these things were in 1939, he speaks of them today with neither spite nor anger. He accepts the tragedy and inevitability of Sigmund Stein's position, pointing out how Sigmund was the only one who, after 1933, was both willing and able to give legal assistance to the Jews. He has much to say in connection with Sigmund's attitudes toward emigration and the problems which it created for Stein. One comment has relevance here, however, for rather in passing Herzog says that, after Sigmund had been *appointed* by the Nazis, it became impossible for him to leave.

The only evidence which bears on such an appointment is ambiguous. The teacher, Klingelmann, and Konrad Muenschner, when speaking of the years after 1939, both mention that Sigmund occasionally made a kind of bitter joke of the fact that he was safe because his identification papers bore that magic sign, the swastika. This is more than likely. The identification card which all Germans had to carry bore, for Jews, a large "J" on its face. This had been required since October, 1938. For validity, the card also had to bear an official stamp, which included the swastika. Sigmund may have carried more than this one card. As a legal counselor and adviser to Jews, his activities were increasingly controlled, and it is probable that he had to be able on occasion to show documentary evidence that he had the permission of the authorities to pursue these activities. In such circumstances, it is almost certain that the pertinent document would have borne the swastika.

These accounts by Herzog, Klingelmann, and Muenschner illustrate one of the most terrible aspects of a persecution such as that to which the Nazis subjected the Jews. This is the manner in which it charges with fear and distrust the normal ignorance about the details of people's lives. It is mainly this negative aspect of social ignorance which is seen in the case of Sigmund Stein. Frau Wolff-Foerster, Heinrich Wolff's daughter, came eventually to look upon Sigmund as a tool of the regime—however unwillingly —with close relationships to the Gestapo. She, along with the anti-Fascist Johannes Korbmacher, who shares this view, is neither uncharitable nor condemning in her judgment of Sigmund, but she includes in that judgment beliefs which raise a strong question about her attitude toward him in the late thirties and early forties.

Her interpretation is not unreasonable, however mistaken it may be. In September, 1933, the *Reichsvertretung der deutschen Juden* (The National Representation of German Jews) had been formed. This was a spontaneous response to the new situation, and the soul of the new organization lay in that spontaneity and in its representativeness. The Central Union of German Citizens of Jewish Faith loomed large in it, but so did the Zionists, as did the Orthodox groups. The Reichsvertretung was not free of government supervision, of course, but it was not a government organ, and it did possess an autonomy and initiative of its own. Sigmund Stein's connection with the Central Union, his legal activities, and his responsibilities all led naturally enough to his awareness of and affiliation with Reichsvertretung.

In July, 1939, by the usual fiat, this organization became subordinate to the Ministry of the Interior, with legal responsibility for those Jewish community functions such as welfare, schooling, and emigration (the promotion of which was declared to be the guiding purpose of the organization) toward which it had previously exercised merely a guiding concern. As so modified, the Reichsvertretung became an organization within the framework of the Nazi state, and its activities became ultimately subservient to the aims of that state.

Yet the only obvious change was the fact that the Reichsvertretung now became, officially, *Die Reichsvereinigung der Juden in Deutschland* (The National Union of Jews in Germany). No longer were there German Jews—just "Jews in Germany." In personnel and day-to-day function, however, there was no change at all immediately, and no marked change subsequently. The needs which the Reichsvertretung had met before July, 1939, continued to be met by the Reichsvereinigung after that date. These needs were pressing; often enough their fulfillment meant the difference between life and death.

For all the lack of a marked change during the years from 1939 on, there were gradual changes which eventually made the Reichsvereinigung an unwilling and tragic creature of the Nazis. Yet even in the face of such developments, the rationale which kept decent and honorable men from resigning their positions in July, 1939—the conviction that anything was better than exposing the Jews to the direct malice of the regime—this rationale retained what validity it had, just as it bore within itself a fallacy which only the event could prove. For it was to some unknown extent the existence of the Reichsvereinigung which enabled the later deportations to be carried out with a minimum of screaming.

The functionaries of the organization would, of course, have been less than human if they had not to some degree been influenced by their surmise that resignation in protest would have jeopardized their personal safety and put an end to the activities which the organization demanded. This was not fear of a final catastrophe which they could not see, nor was it anything as cataclysmic as annihilation from which they hoped to save their fellows and themselves.

Their position was similar to Sigmund Stein's. In 1933, it had been completely fitting that most of these men should assume leadership in the Reichsvertretung. By 1939, the experience gained had trapped them, making their presence as a buffer between Germans and Jews of value to both. Like Sigmund Stein, many of these men had resolutely rejected opportunities for emigration, however mixed the motives behind this rejection may have been.

This parallel between Sigmund Stein and the leaders of the Reichsvereinigung is not mere rhetoric. Sigmund was the Hochburg representative of the organization, and it is even possible that the bitter joke about the identification card with the swastika on it was the result of this connection. Frau Wolff-Foerster claims that the word went around among the Hochburg Jews to be cautious in relationships with any representative of the Reichsvereinigung, because "the Gestapo would be sitting behind him." Johannes Korbmacher says that Sigmund worked against his own people. Neither was in a position to have any clear idea about the Reichsvereinigung or Sigmund's place in it. They knew as little as Frau Huss, who demonstrates that social ignorance can be beneficial within the limits of a specific situation when she asserts that Sigmund had nothing to do with the deportations of the early forties and would have been betraying his people had such been the case.

Frau Wolff-Foerster and Johannes Korbmacher know enough to come to an unfavorable conclusion about Sigmund, but not enough to appreciate the actual situation. Despite their specific conclusions on this one point, Frau Wolff-Foerster was not bitter toward Sigmund, and Johannes Korbmacher had extensive and friendly associations with him. Frau Huss, on the other hand, knew too little of his activities to draw the unfavorable conclusions which she would have drawn had she known more.

Even before the Reichsvereinigung was formed, Sigmund had been delegated a task like those for which the organization would later be responsible. In May, 1939, there was a general census in Germany, and in connection with it, Sigmund carried out a census of the Hochburg Jewish community. Officer Schultheiss had formal responsibility for this project, and his delegation of the Jewish census to Sigmund was a mark of confidence, for the records in the Meldeamt were not sufficient to provide a complete check on Sigmund's accuracy. Schultheiss' confidence was probably justified, despite an understandable reluctance on the part of some Jews to cooperate with the enterprise. Professor Gottfried's daughter, for example, says that her parents were reluctant to give the required information because her brothers, taking advantage of the relative freedom granted to Mischlinge, had moved to another city and were maintaining little or no contact with the parents. The Gottfrieds gave the information, however, and nothing untoward happened to the brothers. The daughter is another person who believes that

Sigmund worked with the Gestapo, and the same irony appears here as elsewhere, for she does not hold the assumed activity against him.

Social ignorance, being the greater where it fulfills a need, is not neutral. This is especially true of that social ignorance which prevailed between Germans and Jews during the later years of the Nazi regime. How great it was may be measured by the extremes between which knowledge of Sigmund Stein's existence fluctuates. Dr. LeMaitre, who had friendly contact with Sigmund both before and after Kristallnacht, is surprised to learn that Sigmund was not sent to Buchenwald. A prominent Hochburg lawyer believes that Sigmund emigrated in 1937. An official of the Hochburg tax office, who had some business with Sigmund after 1939, believes that he was in Hochburg "until 1944 or early 1945."

Even Konrad Muenschner places Sigmund and his family in the Treitschkestrasse "Jewish house" four years before they moved there in 1940. It is likely that this error is at least in part simple forgetting, for Muenschner had had the courage to visit Sigmund at the Treitschkestrasse address. Nevertheless, it is clear that he actually was ignorant of much that was going on in the Jewish community at the time. His disposition toward it remained friendly, but his own position as ex-editor of the Social Democratic *Taegliches Hessenblatt* was exposed and precarious, and he seems to have retreated into the shell of his interest in local history while eking out a modest independent income by taking whatever occasional and innocuous printing jobs he could get.

Sigmund Stein did not move from the Hermann Goering Strasse to the Treitschkestrasse until 1940. But the whole matter of the domicile of the Jews was a chief form taken by his involvement with the Hochburg authorities from April, 1939, on. In that month the "Law Concerning the Status of Jews in Rental and Lease Arrangements" appeared. Like other racial legislation it was long, involved, and required the knowledge of a lawyer for its interpretation and "fair" application. In effect, however, it made all Jewish renters tenants-at-will if the landlord was non-Jewish. Jewish property owners were required to rent to Jews, and Jewish tenants were required to sublet to Jews. Some protection was offered to the Jews. Eviction by non-Jewish landlords was made conditional on the availability of space for the evicted, and eviction could be postponed if it could be shown that hardship would result directly from it.

The law did result, and was supposed to result, in a consolidation of Jewish domicile. Certain houses, owned by Jews, became "Jewish houses" even when, as was the situation with Henrietta Korbmacher and her family in the Treitschkestrasse, non-Jewish families continued to live there. Since there was occasionally, and to a degree varying from town to town, a concentration of Jewish ownership in particular streets or areas, something vaguely resembling a ghetto could develop. But the Nazis were not interested in creating ghettos. In the first years after 1933, there was perhaps some justification for the German-Jewish speculation that their place in the Nazi state might crystallize as a form of ghetto life. The prospect was not without its appeal in the context of things as they were and the hope that the Nazis would not last forever. By the beginning of 1939, however, it had become clear that the Nazis were aiming at the elimination of Jews from Germany, an aim given clear statement when it was made the all-embracing purpose of the Reichsvereinigung in July.

Officer Schultheiss was in charge of the practical details connected with the enforcement of this domicile law in Hochburg, and he delegated the actual determination of the available space to Sigmund Stein. It was up to Sigmund to find the space and inform the Jewish owner that he would have to take in more tenants. Sigmund having done this, Schultheiss would accompany him on an inspection trip in order, as he says, to make sure that the space came up to minimum standards.

Within the framework of the anti-Semitic policy of the regime, the law was probably necessary. The period from 1933 to 1939 had seen a movement of the Jews away from the villages and the rural areas to the more populated centers where they felt more secure. This movement was especially noticeable in the area around Hochburg, where Jews had traditionally lived in groups of a few families in the Hessian villages. But the ideological climate made non-Jews reluctant to rent to Jews, and it made the Jews themselves prefer to have one of their own as landlord. Like all property owners, however, the Jewish landlord was sometimes less than eager to have his building as full as the law allowed. Even when he was willing, he had to deal with people who were already his tenants. The result could be hardship for Jewish families moving into town unless legal or persuasive pressure, or both, could be brought to bear on Jewish property owners.

As noted earlier, the law did not *require* the eviction of Jewish tenants by non-Jewish landlords, and Sigmund Stein was not the only Jew in Hochburg who continued to live, comparatively undisturbed, in his "Aryan"-owned apartment. There were many landlords, it seems, who were willing to speak out against the Jews but were happy enough to collect rent from them.

It is clear that in these later years Sigmund Stein's activities automatically and without change in the essential quality of his behavior became more and more officialized. Moreover, the number of things he had to do increased to such an extent that he was left with little time to reflect on the moral issues involved, despite the fact that they were becoming increasingly acute.

The "protective custody" into which so many Jews had been thrown after the Kristallnacht had acted, as it was intended to act, as a spur to emigration. Those who could get out, did, but it was impossible to leave without money and a place to go, both problems being multiplied if one had a family. This was the period of the forced sale *sans phrase*, even though now as previously, the process could still be seen as an accommodation to the seller by the buyer. This situation, too, was one which increased Sigmund's usefulness to the Jewish community and the amount of work he had to do in order to be useful.

At no time during the Nazi era had a visit to officialdom been a pleasant prospect for a Jew. In the early years, however, the existence of hope and the possibility that the particular official would not be inexorably Nazi took some of the edges off the contemplation of such a visit. After the beginning of 1939, when the policy of the regime had been revealed as one which all but forbade the Jews to hope, such visits became more painful. Nazi success in the field of foreign policy had given the regime internal prestige, but had so aggravated the international situation as to make it point toward war. Increased reason for loyalty was thus supplemented by an increased demand for loyalty, neither of which was relevant to the Jews, and contact with officialdom became more unpleasant than it had been, the result being that in Hochburg Sigmund Stein was more and more pressed into service as an intermediary.

As a lawyer before 1933 and as a man who, after that date, had been in continual contact with Hochburg officials, Sigmund could see them as antagonists, as friendly or unfriendly opponents. He could guess which of them were secret allies, and knowing something of their ambitions and their places in the hierarchy, he could gauge the leverage which might be brought to bear on them. He was not a manipulator, and part of his ability to maintain good relationships with officialdom seems to have come from the conviction, shared by many, that Sigmund was not an "operator." He is explicitly contrasted with his former partner, Werner Hagen, in this respect, though the only thing that Werner was operating at this time was a small book shop in the illusory security of Paris. Sigmund was in fact a relatively simple and direct man, but he had had a great deal of instructive experience in dealing with the men who made up the local bureaucracy, and this made him invaluable to the Jewish community.

14

[Emigration]

Sigmund Stein made four attempts to leave Germany. Of the three legal attempts, one was made before the outbreak of the war and two afterward. Thus, during the three years, 1939, 1940, and 1941, when Sigmund's insistence on remaining in Germany impressed many people as heroic, he was looking for a means of escape and was three times on the verge of finding it. The antithesis between his expressed attitudes and his actions is striking when summed up in so many words. The unresolved contradictions underneath were what Sigmund had to live with.

Johannes Korbmacher, anti-Fascist and friend of Sigmund, chides him for what Korbmacher thinks was a foolhardy desire to remain. It was brave of Sigmund, Korbmacher says, but even if he wanted to be a hero, why did he have to expose his wife and daughter to the risk? No one gives the impression that Sigmund would have been blamed for trying to leave. Some people, like

Korbmacher, blame Sigmund for staying as *long* as he did. Sigmund himself apparently felt guilty about steps he did take to emigrate and said little about them. Few people know that he had made one attempt; no one knows he made three. As late as March, 1938, when his brother David came to Hochburg to urge a joint departure, Sigmund insisted that they both remain in Germany.

Eleven months later, David, now in America and burdened by the problems of adjustment and livelihood, made preliminary arrangements for Sigmund and his family to follow him. Sigmund cooperated, but circumstances did not. Arrangements had not gotten as far as the actual booking of passage when David received a letter from Sigmund saying that he had taken the initiative by booking passage with North German Lloyd through the Hess Travel Agency in Hochburg. Sigmund had made partial payment but stressed that David would have to pay the balance in dollars.

At this point the tenor of the times, David's own experiences, and circumstances conspired against the two men. David had left Germany legally. Like other Jews who did so, he had every reason to carry away with him an abiding distrust of all things German. Having left the scene, he was no longer in a position to observe the beneficent contradictions which now and then appeared in the texture of German treatment of the Jews. In short, he suspected that the ease with which Sigmund had been able to book passage was a trick. David was also in touch with the Joint Distribution Committee which was actively arranging for the transportation of Jewish refugees from Germany. He felt that it would be safer for Sigmund to arrange his passage through the JDC and so wrote his brother.

There was of course a deadline on the payment of the balance of the passage money to North German Lloyd, and David realized that, until he heard from Sigmund in regard to the JDC, he would have to pursue both lines at once. He managed to get the money and was about to send it to North German Lloyd when, two days before the deadline for payment, he received a cable from Sigmund agreeing to arrange passage through the JDC. Hence the deadline was allowed to pass without action. The Joint Distribution Committee was, however, overburdened at the time. Because the Jews who approached it felt they were dealing with sympathetic friends, more people came to rely on it than it could find space for. The spring of 1939 passed into summer, and Sigmund was still waiting. And he was waiting yet when Germany invaded Poland on the first of September. The situation now had changed radically. Jewish emigration was not completely cut off, but difficulties were raised which are summarized in David Stein's bleak statement that the arrangements with the JDC fell through and came to nothing.

That they did must have been Sigmund's fault, to some degree. With the coming of the war and even in the weeks before the beginning of September when war was looming on the horizon, the desperate situation of the German Jews was becoming more obvious and with it the obligation of Jewish leaders not to leave their people in distress. Through his connection with the Reichsvereinigung and all the activities which had led up to it, Sigmund was a personification of that leadership in Hochburg. His faltering in connection with emigration is consistent with the picture of a man on the horns of a moral dilemma: to save himself and his family, or to stick by his people. Each course of action involved both selfish and selfless considerations, and his wavering may well show how strongly affected he was by the important realities of both alternatives.

And Sigmund continued to waver. David and his sister—for Meta Stein had also managed to get out of Germany—did not give up hope of getting Sigmund out even after the war began. Two more attempts were made, and Sigmund seems to have cooperated in both. Early in 1940, David was able to arrange and pay passage for Sigmund and his family by way of Russia and Japan to America. How complete these arrangements were is not clear, but David is definite in his statement that they fell through because the American consul in Stuttgart did not accept the affidavits David had submitted.

The second attempt Sigmund made to emigrate after the beginning of the war is both obscure and in many ways informative. It occurred sometime in the first six months of 1941, after Sigmund and his family had moved from their fine apartment in the Hermann Goering Strasse to a much less comfortable and adequate one in the house at Treitschkestrasse 5—the "Jewish house" where the non-Jewish Henrietta Korbmacher lived and still lives. This move reveals a changed human situation which is an important part of the framework within which the 1941 emigration attempt took place.

It has already been noted that there were in Hochburg Jewish families which were never evicted until the day of their final deportation, or who left a home of long standing in order to emigrate. These were Jewish property owners or their tenants, and they were by and large better off than those members of the community who were forced to move. The latter crowded in on those who did not have to move but did have to take them. Everyone suffered from the crowding, but the property owners and their original tenants were at least spared the total disruptions which the others had to endure. In any event, the fact that Sigmund Stein remained as long as he did in the Hermann Goering Strasse was not a complete anomaly in Hochburg.

Before 1933 and even for a time afterwards, the comfort of the apartment and the pleasant respectability of its surroundings formed a proper frame for the solidity and prosperity of the Stein family. As the years went by, however, the frame began to become more and more incongruous with the fact that the Steins were Jewish. Speaking of 1939 and 1940, Friedrich Michael gives an inkling of how great this incongruity had by then become when he tells how Sigmund could sometimes be met, walking with studied inconspicuousness, in the out of the way streets of the Sumpfviertel, avoiding the more frequented streets because of the insecurity and embarrassment of meeting people. The ex-Reichsbanner leader adds that Sigmund's anxiety was understandable, since Michael himself had often felt threatened and isolated on a crowded street and he, after all, was not a Jew.

When Sigmund had moved into the then Dietrichstrasse in 1930, he had been an up-and-coming young man; in 1939 and 1940 the Landrat and Kreisleiter Kleinwitz was in the same position. Franz Wilhelm, who describes Sigmund as "a peasant with schooling" and who was to remain his friend until the end, was also on surreptitious good terms with Kleinwitz. Wilhelm comes from an old Hochburg family and was accepted both in the small world of the University and in the general society of the town. He was not a

Nazi and was in fact involved in one of those circles whose intellectual rejection of the Nazi program was to turn into abortive conspiracy against it. He thus had reasons to look for relationships which might be useful to him. One of these was with Kleinwitz. Wilhelm could and did help this fundamentalist pastor's son to gain an entrée into University society which his background and his earlier failure as a student had denied him.

One summer evening in 1939, Wilhelm went to his coffee house, *"Die Schlaue Katze,"* and, while drinking his grog, eavesdropped on a group of SA men sitting at the next table. What he overheard prompted him to action: it was gossip to the effect that "the redhead," as Kleinwitz was familiarly called, was going to kick "the Yid" out of the Goering Strasse apartment in order to take the place for himself. The next day Wilhelm sought out Kleinwitz to check on the truth of what he had overheard and to try to do something about it. "The redhead" disclaimed any such intentions, saying that the action had been urged upon him by party colleagues, but that he had turned it down. As Landrat, he worked with Sigmund on matters pertaining to the Jews in the villages around Hochburg. He told Wilhelm that he valued Sigmund, agreeing that underneath, Sigmund was as much of a peasant as anyone, and as long as he, Kleinwitz, was Landrat, Sigmund and his family would not be forced out of their apartment. As Landrat he had no jurisdiction over Hochburg, but as Kreisleiter of the party he did not need jurisdiction.

The Steins were left in the apartment for more than a year thereafter. It is unlikely, however, that after the beginning of 1939 Sigmund had any hope of being able to stay there. Thus, it is significant that when Jakob Mendel, his wife Veronika, and their unhappy spinster daughter, Rosa, moved from Dreistadt to Hochburg in June, 1939, they did not go to live with their daughter Esther and her husband Sigmund in the roomy Goering Strasse apartment, but instead moved into an apartment of the Rosenstein House, the "Jewish House," in the Treitschkestrasse. Here they had comparative security from eviction and a small community of their own. Whether or not Sigmund wanted to take in his in-laws, the fact that he did not was surely due in part to his own insecurity of tenure.

After 1935, their non-Jewish landlord could probably have forced the Steins to move at any time he really wanted to. But not until after 1939 does this failure to do so merit comment. Without doubt he liked their money, and without doubt he was aware of the feeble yet long, meaningful pressures which Sigmund could bring to bear against eviction. What happened to bring about the Steins' move to the Treitschkestrasse in November of 1940 is unknown, but it is clear that after the beginning of the war practical complications over and above the general sharpening of the Nazi ideology began to make themselves felt. Following the national pattern, for example, were various local ordinances which made it incumbent on a landlord to provide separate air raid shelters for Jews and non-Jews if he had both as tenants. The surprising thing is that the Steins stayed in the apartment as long as they did, and when the move came it had many of the characteristics of a normal one.

Prospective tenants came to look at the apartment. The first of these was the senior teacher, Michelheim. In late 1940, he was on leave from the Wehrmacht and using this leave for house-hunting. Michelheim was a Nazi through necessity, conviction, and opportunism, and his activities in the League of National Socialist Teachers had smoothed his advancement. Accordingly, in 1940 he was in a position to look for more suitable quarters. In discussing the apartment with Sigmund Stein, he does not seem to have had a picture of himself as one who was taking advantage of another's distress.

His wife is less certain. Her preliminary discussions with Esther Stein while Herr Michelheim was still in the field convinced her that Esther was reconciled to the fact that the move would "have to" take place. But the talks left Frau Michelheim uncomfortable enough to lose her enthusiasm for taking the Stein apartment, if for no other reason than that Esther Stein was a woman near the end of her rope. The eventual decision not to take the apartment may or may not have been related to sympathy for the Steins.

Michelheim may well have been the "colleague" from whom the teacher, Karl Grün, learned about the availability of the Stein apartment. Grün was also in the Wehrmacht in 1940. His wife was pregnant at the time, and he gives this as the chief reason for wanting to move. Both Grün and his wife talked with the Steins, and the conversation was undoubtedly made easier by the fact that Karl Grün was a man with an anti-Nazi record, with good family connections in Hochburg; a man who prior to 1933 had been, like Sigmund, a member of the Democratic party and who after 1933 had suffered for his known sentiments. At the time, he was a man who had consciously and thoughtfully knuckled under in 1937 when he joined the Nazi party out of despair that he would never become more than a village school teacher unless he did so. Having made this decision, he had to face up to its consequences. Thus, when he was asked to conduct party "schooling evenings" in his specialty, geography, he felt that this was a test which he could not refuse.

Yet all during his career as a nominal Nazi he tried in ways which his compromise left open to him to express his basic opposition. He discussed forbidden authors in his classes; protested against the synagogue arson; assisted the son of Franz Wilhelm when the boy got into a political scrape; and befriended old Professor von Schlegel's "mongrel" grandsons whose father had committed suicide in the early days of the Nazi regime. These were genuinely oppositional acts, yet they were freighted with the ambiguities of Karl Grün's major compromise, and he does not readily mention the fact that the boys' mother, Frau Kleppmeier-Schlegel, widow of the old professor's son, was his first cousin, or that the boys themselves were heartbroken when a change in the rule decreed that "mongrels" of their degree could no longer be members of the Hitler Youth.

These things are not said in order to incriminate Karl Grün. There were, after all, full Jewish children who were heartbroken because they could not join the Hitler Youth. The point is merely to suggest that the conversations between the Steins and the Grüns were amicable in part because both men knew the conflict associated with compromise. The Grüns took the apartment, and in an agreement which was satisfactory to both parties they purchased most of the furniture and furnishings.

The Steins had no place to go except to a second-floor apartment in the "Jewish House" on the Treitschkestrasse, where the Rosensteins lived on the ground floor, the Mendels on the second, the Korbmachers on the third, and the Rabbi on the fourth. The Treitschkestrasse address was not exactly a slum. Frau Mahler, who visited the Steins there, tells how Sigmund fixed up one room as a combined consultation room and office, even though, as a dubiously recognized Konsulent for Jewish emigrants he had a tiny office in the Bahnhofstrasse. In both places he had a telephone, permitted him only in his capacity as Konsulent, since the telephones of all Jews without officially recognized positions had been removed two months before the Steins moved.

It was in these surroundings that Sigmund's second attempt to emigrate after the beginning of the war occurred. It is obscure because so little reliable information about it is available, and confused because so much of rumor and half-remembrance persists. Only two features of the incident seem clear: it occurred in the spring of 1941, and the Kleins in America were associated with it. Hermann Klein's wife, Lisbeth, was a sister of Rosa Mendel and Esther Mendel Stein. Certain characteristics of the obscurity also have a definite outline. One of these is the amount of feeling connected with the matter; the other is the despairing irritation which was directed toward Hermann Klein and his wife.

Frau Henrietta Korbmacher is not well recommended. Frau Huss speaks of her as being of the Hochburg "demimonde," and other obviously respectable Hochburgers display related attitudes. Yet all that this seems to reflect is the fact that Frau Korbmacher is poor, husbandless, and has a granddaughter whose father may have been an American soldier. Her information, for all its gossipy flavor, is reliable. Living above the Steins and the Mendels as she did, knowing and feeling something of what it meant to be an outcast, concerned chiefly with the impact of ideologies on a personal level, she seems to have come close to the inner life of the Stein family. She phrases her descriptions in terms of what a "lousy" time the family had and how "rottenly" the Jews were treated—not in terms of high tragedy and drama. But she is very aware of how "things like that" disturbed and disrupted human relations. She is still as impressed by Sigmund Stein's respectability as by his father-in-law's wealth, and, like many others, she is certain that had Sigmund returned from the East he would have been made mayor of Hochburg. These were, after all, people from another social and economic level. She would never have known them as she had but for the disaster which had come upon them. Thus, she was especially aware of the family tensions she observed.

Chief of these was Frau Mendel's dissatisfaction with her daughter in New York, Lisbeth Klein. Frau Mendel felt that Lisbeth had abandoned them all to their fates. She was resentful and her resentment was flavored with guilt and made the more unhappy by her awareness of the difficulties which Lisbeth Klein and her husband, as recent immigrants, had to face in their efforts to help relatives who had been left behind. She felt that the Kleins were concerned about what she and her husband, as elderly people, would do in America, where Herr Mendel's experience as a dealer in certified cattle would scarcely be of much help.

As far as the Steins were concerned, the problem would have been not age but professional adjustment. Hermann Klein was very aware of this problem, because he, too, had been a lawyer before leaving Germany in 1934. Adjustment had been difficult and had carried him away from the profession in which he had spent half a lifetime establishing himself. Of course, Sigmund and his family were not the primary concern of the Kleins, for not only was Sigmund's brother David trying to help, but also the age of the Mendels made their escape from the German situation especially desirable, however much it may have complicated the problem of what to do with them in America.

It must be emphasized that, despite the emotional situation on both sides of the Atlantic at the time, despite the moments of bitterness, there is no evidence to show that either the Steins or the Mendels failed to emigrate in 1941 because of any omission or commission on the Kleins' part. Frau Mendel's feeling that they had not done enough could relate to the simple fact that things had come to a point where nothing was enough and to the human tendency to blame this somehow on those involved in the attempts to do something.

Just why the Steins as well as the Mendels were unable to emigrate in 1941 is unknown. It may well be that Sigmund was more vulnerable in this respect than the Kleins. Frau Korbmacher is not alone in speaking of a growing alienation between

Sigmund and his in-laws during this period. By the spring of 1941, Sigmund's emotional ambiguity on emigration had vanished. He was ready now to flee. But ambiguous personal feelings had been replaced by ambiguous circumstances. These underscored the desirability of leaving, but at the same time they threw into sharp relief the consequences for those whom Sigmund would be abandoning. Large-scale deportations of Jews had not yet started in the spring of 1941, and for months after they did start in October of that year their ultimately fatal character would be shrouded. Nevertheless, all the reasons which spoke for emigration could be phrased in terms of what the Jews were suffering in Germany and what they were being abandoned to by any nominal leaders who left. In a year, the unarguable demands of self-preservation would move Sigmund and his family to attempt a flight, the inherent peril of which could act as an emotional counterweight for the abandonment of his fellow Jews. In the spring of 1941 a sense of duty still created indecision.

It would be presumptuous to assert flatly that Sigmund definitely felt and reasoned thus. Yet certain features of the situation argue for such an interpretation. Chief among these, perhaps, is the desperate desire of Esther Stein to leave. Franz Wilhelm and the daughter of Professor Mendelsohn both report how Esther Stein often remarked that she would rather be a washerwoman in America than the wife of the most respected lawyer in Germany. The Durckheim brothers comment from an early date on her fearfulness, at a time when Sigmund himself had no thought of leaving. It is clear that her impulse to get out of Germany long anticipated Sigmund's. It is also clear that her desire to leave grew during the time when Sigmund's feelings were changing from the determination not to leave to an unresolved conflict between his need to do so and the Hochburg community's increasing need of his presence. After the move to the Treitschkestrasse, it is impossible that the Mendels should not have backed Esther in her desire to leave. At the same time, the two older people—and, because of her sickness, the spinster daughter, Rosa—became Sigmund's responsibility and factors in his ambivalence.

His failure to resolve these conflicts is reflected in the two faces which Sigmund, without guile or dishonesty, was compelled to show to the two different worlds with which he came in contact. To his family he had to be a man seriously applying himself to the problem of emigration. To the hundred-odd members of the Hochburg Jewish community who had not emigrated by 1941, he had to present the appearance of a man not about to abandon them. The latter role was genuinely felt. Emotionally, he did not want to leave Germany. Nevertheless, his love for his wife and daughter created in him an equally emotional need to calm their growing panic; and he lived constantly exposed to the pressures of his family. Only sporadically and less intimately was he confronted by the questions which the community might have asked him. Inevitably, the world outside his family became an escape from his family, and to the duplicity of his role was added the guilt engendered by his awareness that his activities outside his family had precisely this coloring of escape.

From the beginning of the war until "the final solution" was offered by the cruelty of the Nazi deportations, Sigmund could only have been a torn and troubled man. Emigration and the problems connected with it loomed large among his troubles. But the nature of Sigmund's entire development meant that conflict would also be found elsewhere, as persistent features of all his relationships with people.

15

[The man who did not have to work in the streets]

It was natural and understandable that Sigmund Stein became the recognized leader of the Jewish community in Hochburg in the late thirties and early forties. The process was surprisingly harmonious in view of all that was at stake for Sigmund and the community. Had less been at stake, however, the disharmonies might seem larger. Opportunity for rancor arose out of the relationships in which Sigmund was involved. As representative of the Jewish community to the town authorities, he had to maintain a working relationship with both—with the people who did not agree with him among the Jews, and with the convinced Nazis among the officials. As a man who had to attempt emigration for the sake of his family and who had to avoid it for what it would mean to the community, he was caught in the demands of each. And penetrating every aspect of these interdependent tensions were the attitudes and behavior directed toward Sigmund as a result of his developing role in the elimination of Jews from Hochburg. These three patterns of relationship will be dealt with separately, yet their details will reveal the way in which they are interlocked.

The Schmidt bakery faces on the lower level of Hochburg's many-tiered Stadtplatz. At a higher level, where the Dominikanerstrasse opens into the little square, stood the Goldberg grocery store. Before and after 1933, Frau Baker Schmidt and Frau Goldberg were friends, as were their husbands, and if Frau Mahler was naive when she tried to comfort Frau Goldberg's agitation over the vicious anti-Semitism of the SA's marching songs, Frau Baker Schmidt is not naive in her observations about the muted, miniature, and unhappy "struggle for power" between Herr Goldberg and Sigmund Stein in 1939 and 1940.

Simon Goldberg was by all accounts a fine man, successful in business, intelligent, and well informed. Frau Baker Schmidt thinks that the Goldberg family was not very Orthodox, saying that they ate pork sausage and did not hesitate to build a fire on the Sabbath. But others recall Herr Goldberg's general sobriety and active affiliation with the synagogue and make it appear as though Herr Goldberg's relationship to his religion was less problematical than Sigmund Stein's. The grocer is indeed a sympathetic figure, perhaps the more so because his nature was so unassuming as to be called "too meek" by Frau Mahler. Just as Werner Hagen's aggressiveness and sharp humor strike a favorable note in contrast to the solidity of Sigmund Stein, so too Herr Goldberg's "meekness" provides a certain relief in comparison with Sigmund's importance and activities. Yet Sigmund was what he was because this was the sombre shape his life had taken, and Simon Goldberg's belief that Sigmund had "usurped" the position of leadership in the community was a misreading of the whole situation.

Since Simon Goldberg was a good man and an intelligent man, it is possible that many members of the Hochburg Jewish community would have preferred him as their representative and "leader." His awareness of these things must have let him project the position of respect and trust he actually enjoyed to the status of a moral leadership which had ceased to have practical meaning. Even as a grocer he could have had knowledge of the Jewish community, of the laws which, after 1935, began to squeeze it, and of the officials who administered these laws. But his qualifications in these respects were not equal to Sigmund Stein's. This was not because Sigmund was a better man, but rather because in the early years of the twentieth century, conditioned by idiosyncrasies of personality, family, and situation, Sigmund made choices which took him into the law and into the complex association with and view of human beings which this career demands. Simon Goldberg went into the grocery business as a consequence of his choices. This business makes genuine demands on understanding and judgment, but it could not prepare Herr Goldberg for the ambiguous and tragic leadership ultimately to be contested with Sigmund.

Frau Goldberg's character may have had something to do with the position taken by her husband. The fact that she reacted to the SA songs as though they were aimed at her personally shows both insight and, perhaps, a greater than normal tendency to relate general happenings to herself and her family. In the presence of such a tendency, it is probable that the steady rise in Sigmund Stein's importance during the years after 1933 would have been felt by Frau Goldberg as a challenge to the prominence and prestige of her husband. In any event, the earlier friendship between the Steins and the Goldbergs was broken off sometime in 1939 or 1940, in a situation the obscurity of which is broken only by Herr Goldberg's accusation that Sigmund had behaved "unfairly" and by the prevailing image of the break as one in which Sigmund "took over" the leadership of the community from Simon Goldberg.

These difficulties with Simon Goldberg foreshadow the general problems which were to arise from the fact that Sigmund, as everything he was and had become, could move about more, engage in more varied activities, and live more comfortably than the majority of his fellow Jews in Hochburg.

It is hard to get a picture of how the Jews in Hochburg made their living after 1939 and before their deportation. Decrees on the use of Jewish forced labor did not appear until 1941, although there is evidence that such labor was used earlier elsewhere and, specifically, that it was used in Hochburg as early as July, 1940. What seems to have happened is that, after the Kristallnacht and the temporary detention of thousands of Jews in Buchenwald, the liquidation of Jewish enterprises accelerated greatly, often in anticipation of the proprietors' emigration. Those who liquidated their businesses but stayed on—voluntarily or otherwise—still had to feed themselves and their families. With the war coming on, and after it started, there were shortages of labor, particularly in those lower-level occupations which did not exempt one from military service. In this pinch, Jews were hired, usually by the municipal administrations. Technically, they were not forced laborers except in the sense that they accepted unwanted jobs in order to provide for selves and families. The "Law for the Elimination of Jews from German Economic Life" had, as of January 1, 1939, drastically curtailed the number of gainful activities open to Jews.

In Hochburg, as throughout Germany, the Jewish population at this time was made up of a disproportionate number of old people, the younger ones having been favored for emigration. Many of these older people had lived on pensions which had often been reduced by the anti-Jewish legislation. Hardship cases were the responsibility of the Reichsvereinigung; in theory, needy Jews could also get minimal help from public relief. Others lived off investments, rents, and such sources of income as were still open to them. Some continued to pursue an occupation surreptitiously and sporadically until they emigrated, were deported, or —rarely—until the war ended.

Casimir Dombrowski is one Jew who held out that long. The "Law for the Elimination of Jews from German Economic Life" had forced him to sell his tailoring business shortly after his return from Buchenwald early in 1939. But he was a tailor of acknowledged skill, and so people came to him with work which he was willing to risk doing at night, in a constant fear of discovery which was lessened somewhat when he began to get commissions from the Kreisleiter and Landrat himself, Kleinwitz.

Sigmund Oppenheimer, the non-doctrinaire Socialist, is another example. In October, after four years' unemployment, sporadic odd jobs, and work with the municipal street gang, he went to Koerner's carpentry shop. He knew that Herr Koerner was a sympathetic person and also knew that there were minor jobs he could do around the shop. Surprisingly, he was able to get permission from the local labor office to take such work on condition that it be manual and menial. Thus he became a handyman around the shop and remained there all through the war.

Both Dombrowski and Oppenheimer were married to Christian women; each of them had two sons who were, therefore, "mongrels of the first degree" and were caught up in the net of confused and changing regulations which governed this status. The two sons of Oppenheimer and the older son of Dombrowski were conscripted at an early date. In April, 1940, in accordance with a general decree, Oppenheimer's sons were transferred from the army to the labor battalions of the *Organization Todt*. For whatever reason, Dombrowski's son escaped this transfer and actually became a pilot in the Luftwaffe. His death in action over England put a tragic end to the grotesque situation where, during his leaves, he had been able to visit his parents—who were very proud of him —only under cover of ridiculous excuses.

Marion Stein, Netti Goldberg, and Elisabeth Rosenblum were not "mongrels," and so their fates were Jewish ones. In the early forties, they were among the few young people left in the Hochburg Jewish community. Shortly after the Kristallnacht, Jewish children were forbidden to attend German schools. Prior to that time they had attended them under increasing difficulties. Schoolmates and teachers were not always unfriendly and sometimes made special efforts to ease their lot. But the whole context of the regime was such as to encourage and reward any show of meanness toward the Jews. Laws might forbid, as they did forbid, individual attempts to deal with the "Jewish problem." But the total rejection of the Jews was too clear and anti-Semitism too definitely in the seats of power for meanness not to know that it could inflict its cruelties without serious fear of punishment.

When the Reichsvereinigung was formed, it was given responsibility for the education of Jewish children. In Hochburg, Sigmund Stein recruited a "mongrel," the daughter of Professor Mendelsohn, as a teacher. But Fräulein Mendelsohn was able to emigrate in the fall of 1940, and no one could be found to take her place.

Thus Marion Stein, Netti Goldberg, and Elisabeth Rosenblum, along with a few other Jewish girls from Hochburg and nearby villages, went to work at Hof Hessler. It is Frau Hessler, the proprietress of this large truck garden and nursery, who tells of her stall in the Mainzerstrasse marketplace, near the Stein's apartment, where Esther Stein had often shopped. It is not hard to believe that when Netti Goldberg was threatened with work in an armaments factory after she had been working for some months at Hof Hessler, her family went to considerable trouble to keep her on the farm.

Frau Hessler is basically a decent woman who got along well with "her" Jewish girls and valued the labor they provided. She has nevertheless absorbed much of the traditional picture of the Jews and comes close to saying that, in contrast to the lovely Jewish families of Hochburg, like the Steins and the Goldbergs, some of the swindlers, like the one who palmed off a scrawny and diseased cow on her father, deserved everything that happened to them. She is amused at the suggestion that the Jewish girls might have worked separately from the other help, pointing out that any such an arrangement would have been a great bother and was never thought of. The Jewish girls worked hard and got along well with the peasant girls from the nearby villages, who felt sorry for them, as did she herself. Frau Hessler speaks of Marion Stein and Netti Goldberg as especially "refined" girls, adding, however, that they had not felt superior to the other Jewish girls because of it, or, if they had, their very refinement kept them from showing it. There was no indication whatever that these two girls were aware of any falling out between their respective families.

Work at Hof Hessler does not seem to have been part of any special arrangement with the Reichsvereinigung. In the larger cities, however, where many young people still remained, greater efforts had to be made by the organization to provide education, occupation, and training for them. One of the ways in which this was done was a continuation of the "occupational readjustment" program which had been undertaken earlier by the predecessor organization, the Reichsvertretung. Young Jewish men and women were trained in "manual" occupations at several work camps; this was done with the explicit idea of preparing them for life in Palestine or South America. Often too, however, it was done with the idea that even if emigration should turn out to be unnecessary, as many hoped, the future of the Jews in Germany demanded a complete reorientation in occupational outlook toward the "healthier" and "more fundamental" horizons of agriculture and other "work with the hands."

Such a reorientation was jarringly present in the change which began in Hochburg in the middle of 1940. This was the use of Jewish labor by local municipal administration, a practice which then became national policy in the spring of 1941. Sigmund Stein was involved in this change.

The first municipal body in Hochburg to use Jewish labor seems to have been the gasworks. The war had forced postponement of a planned general overhaul of the Hochburg gas distribution system, but it was felt that a certain amount of preliminary work, such as the replacement of the worst sections, other general maintenance, and the installation of some of the most needed new mains, could be done during the war. Whether or not the presence of a Jewish labor pool was an incentive for starting on these preliminary operations is unknown, but it is clear that the existence of such a labor pool was opportune.

Much of the work was digging ditches, "manual" enough to fit the Nazi conception of the kind of work the Jews ought to do. Thus, in the late spring of 1940 a work gang was organized with twelve Jews and two non-Jews as laborers and with Johannes Demut as foreman. Demut had been a long-time employee of the gasworks who had retired to his farm near Hugeldorf but was drawn back into service because of the labor shortage. There are men in the Hochburg gasworks today who show traces of having been surprised at the diligence and technical intelligence of the Jewish workers, particularly at the speed with which the son of Meyer Rosenblum, the Gosmarshausen cattle dealer, became a skilled welder. Jewish blood, after all, was supposed to be of an exclusively commercial type.

Johannes Demut for his part shows no traces of having been thus surprised at the capabilities of "his" men. They, on the other hand, may have had occasion to be a little surprised at him, for he claims that one of the things he liked about working with them was the fact that in their hearing he was able to express his resentments at the war and the party—resentments arising chiefly from the fact that his son had been kicked out of the party for nonpayment of dues. Knocking the party in the presence of the Jews, though not wholly without risk, was a cheap way of getting a load off your chest, although, things being what they were, the Jewish labor crew probably did enjoy working under Demut. In prison, a near coziness can spring up between a moderately decent and casually human guard and the work detail he supervises, and the demands of the work at hand can come to take precedence over the formal requirements of the prison situation. This seems to have happened in Hochburg in 1940–1942 because the crew, which at first worked as a unit, doing nothing but pick-and-shovel jobs, eventually began to be broken up into smaller units for other work side by side with non-Jewish employees. This was true of the welder, Hans Rosenblum, and it was also true of the Jewish workers who occasionally took over necessary on-the-spot surveying.

Sigmund Stein was not required to work with the ditchdigging crew. His erstwhile rival, Simon Goldberg, was. The very real compulsion which lay behind the work was not iron, and the men were paid. Johannes Demut says that a man could stay away from work if he were sick or for some other special reason; he lost his pay for the time missed but was not otherwise penalized. One of Sigmund Stein's connections with the work of the crew was notifying Demut when a man was to be absent for such reasons. He also made "under-the-table" arrangements for the absence of the whole crew on the Jewish holidays, at least the major holidays.

This picture, derived in the main from the accounts of non-Jewish participants, is probably accurate as far as it goes. Compulsory labor for the Jews was not to be formally introduced until March, 1941, and it was not until October of that year that the Jewish worker lost the protection of the German labor laws. Even under the malicious terms of the "Decree on the Employment of Jews" which removed them from such protection, most of the alleviations mentioned would have been possible. What is not spoken of today is the extent to which the Jewish worker, regardless of rules and regulations, was exposed to the moods and the varying good nature of his supervisors. Johannes Demut may have been a decent enough sort, and his crew may have considered themselves lucky. They were not, and could not have been expected to be, happy.

One of the forms taken by their unhappiness was the relationship between the crew and Sigmund Stein. By the summer of 1940, the reasons for Sigmund's not having to work in the streets must have been obvious to everyone who remained in the Hochburg Jewish community. They knew he was acting in several ways as a spokesman for the community, taking care of property which had been left behind, and seeing to it that those evicted from one house found living quarters in another. How many knew that in these tasks Sigmund had to work with the police as well as with other town authorities is impossible to say, but if they thought about it, they could hardly have avoided concluding that he *would* be dealing with the regime. Sigmund had taken the census of the Jews early in 1939. A year later, it was Sigmund who informed the Jews that they were to be permitted to shop only at specified times in specified stores. He also did some of the dickering with the storekeepers in regard to this matter, and with barbers, in regard to the times when Jews could get their hair cut. His position as a representative of the Reichsvereinigung was necessarily known to any Jew whose needs brought him in contact with that organization, and this must have included most of the Jews in Hochburg.

Yet all such knowledge, while it could make Sigmund's exemption from compulsory manual labor both understandable and innocuous, itself contained grounds for resentment and suspicion. Sigmund was "working with the Nazis" and was vulnerable to all the ambiguity in that phrase. Moreover, he was working with them on two different levels. In his day-to-day activities around Hochburg he had to have repeated contacts with officials, most of whom, by 1940, were Nazis. In addition, as a representative of the Reichsvereinigung, he was also participating in an organization that acted as an instrument of Nazi policy. Both levels of Sigmund's cooperation had other aspects, but those mentioned loomed large in the consciousness of people who were so dependent on the administrative whims of Nazism.

Inevitably both trust and suspicion of Sigmund Stein existed in the Hochburg Jewish community in its last years. The trust has, on the whole, been more enduring. But the suspicion was real and in its way realistic. One of the forms it took was resentment of Sigmund's exemption from work in the streets.

In the complexities of fact or memory or the two together, this resentment gets mixed up with the differences in Jewish Orthodoxy between Sigmund and most of the members of the work gang. It was Samuel Gluckmann, one of the most Orthodox members of the crew, who commented audibly one day as Sigmund passed close to the place where the gang was working, "There goes the man who doesn't have to work in the streets."

The irony of this situation lies in the fact that two characteristics of Sigmund which come through time and time again are a lack of snobbishness in regard to manual labor and a certain peasant simplicity, and both of these appear in connection with the work crew itself.

In the time records of the gang's work which survive in a tattered notebook of Johannes Demut, there are several incongruous entries which read, "Mowing at Schmidt's place." This refers to an unofficial, though apparently not illegal, arrangement between Schmidt, who owned a large hayfield in the relatively rural "Sunny Meadows" section of Hochburg, and Demut. The latter, with four or five of his men, would leave the street work at noon, go up to Schmidt's place, mow until late afternoon, and then return to the job in the streets. Demut says that Sigmund knew of the arrangement and had asked to be included as one of the workers.

This explains how it was that Herr Benzheim, who with his wife was close to Sigmund after 1940, was provided with his illustration of how unaffected a person Sigmund was. Benzheim is entirely unaware of the existence of Demut and has only the vaguest notions about the Jewish work crew, but he tells of meeting Sigmund several times on the street, Sigmund dressed in old clothes and more cheerful than was usual in those years. To Benzheim's query he explained that he was going mowing, and Benzheim says —a little obtusely it may be—that you would not find other men of Sigmund's station walking down the street in tattered old clothes, happy to be going mowing.

Sigmund Oppenheimer apparently worked with the gang regularly until October, when he got his job in the Koerner carpentry shop. The normal working day appears to have been eight and a half hours, with five and a half on Saturdays. Extraordinary jobs are noted, such as an emergency main break in the old town, when part of the work was done at night. Several jobs are labeled "Gas mains—*Flachviertel.*" These were jobs along the Flachstrasse, and one of the streets leading off the latter is the Treitschkestrasse, where Sigmund Stein and his family lived after December, 1940. Work around the intersection of the two streets occurred off and on from November, 1940 to February, 1941, so that there were numerous opportunities for Sigmund to pass in the vicinity of the crew.

Henrietta Korbmacher knows about Samuel Gluckmann's reference to "the man who doesn't have to work in the streets" and describes an incident which shows Sigmund's despair at the situation. Sigmund was tormented by the occasional upwellings of resentment toward him. Almost of necessity, these bit deeply into the rationalizations behind which Sigmund normally existed. The protection was sufficient in his routine, day-to-day relationships with his fellow Jews, because they did like him, respect him, and recognize his importance to themselves. But when a man is exhausted from working in a ditch, when the past is filled with a thousand humiliations and the future is a nightmare of anxiety, it is hard to dam the flood of bitterness by tact and understanding. Thus, when Sigmund Stein went by, no shovel in his hands or mud on his feet, and no likely prospect that he would have either, resentment overflowed into bitter words, intended to be overheard.

In one form or another, this kind of thing must have happened often. Sigmund finally reacted. Swinging a scythe in a hayfield on a late summer day is a diversion. But diversion was not the goal on that day in January, 1941, when Sigmund went to Johannes Demut to insist on taking a shovel and getting into the hole with the rest of the men. Demut says that he worked for about four hours, during which it became clear that he could not take it. Probably he did get blisters on his hands, but Henrietta Korbmacher says that both Sigmund and his mother-in-law told her that the reason for stopping was that the police would not let him remain at the job. Sigmund had other things to do. The fact that a poignant and sudden sense of his entrapment in these "things" had driven him to try to identify himself physically with the work gang could not change the cold reality of his entrapment.

Thus, Sigmund went back to doing his duty. The whole incident must have been deeply disturbing. Simon Goldberg and several Goldberg "supporters" were members of the crew. Frau Goldberg was accustomed to bring her husband's lunch to him each day. The incident quickly became common knowledge in the Jewish community. It may have been interpreted in Sigmund's favor; the despair which the act embodied made it more than a gesture. The trouble was that the work crew continued to have cold hands and muddy feet, while Sigmund went back to a dry office, to varied and meaningful—whatever the meanings—activity.

Although the record in Johannes Demut's tattered notebook comes to an end in April, 1941, a statement of Demut's indicates that the work gang continued after that. One reason, he says, why the men liked the work on the street jobs was that they were permitted to remove their jackets and thereby rid themselves of the Jewish Star badge which they hated.

The Jewish Star, "a black-bordered star of yellow material, the size of the palm of a hand, bearing the word 'Jew' in black letters," had to be worn "sewn to the outer garment on the left-hand side at chest level" by all Jews over six years old. Since the decree embodying these rules went into effect in September, 1941, and since Demut spoke of the matter in a way which indicated that the wearing of the star had become customary, it seems likely that the crew continued as a unit until the winter of 1941–1942 and possibly later.

The introduction of the Star badge was not only a return to the Middle Ages. More importantly, it was an ironic admission by the Nazis that a vast amount of their literature about "racial sense" and "race consciousness" was nonsense. Certainly ideas of race and "blood" have a long history in Germany, yet the idea of racial purity is grimly amusing among the conglomeration of physical types which is to be met there. True, there are sections where frequent inbreeding has produced a relatively uniform physical type. Rural Hesse has such sections. Thus, it is not surprising that

Hochburgers sometimes comment on Sigmund's appearance, but it is surprising that they refer to it as "foreign, maybe Turkish" and do not fit it into the Jewish section of the system of stereotypes which exists, since his dark hair and broad face did give him a vaguely eastern Mediterranean appearance—something which could not be said of his brother, David, nor of Meyer Rosenblum, for example, neither of whom would have stood out in the market day crowd in front of the town hall. Sigmund would have. But so would hundreds of other "Aryans."

As far as Sigmund was concerned, the Star was gratuitous in the streets of Hochburg. There he was known as a Jew, not because of his appearance but because of his history, because of the trail of paper he and his family had left behind them. But Sigmund in his "official" capacity had to travel to the towns and villages around Hochburg. These trips were normally made by train—and even if Sigmund had driven a car, as a Jew, he would have had his driver's license taken from him late in 1938. On a train, Sigmund was likely to meet people who did not know him and whose "race consciousness" could not be depended on to recognize him as a Jew. Thus, even for Sigmund the Jewish Star had its dubious use.

Almost all Jews, of course, hated the Star. Since the Star was a pure symbol of their Jewishness, some Jews wanted to wear it with pride and defiance. But no symbol is that pure, and the wearing of the Star meant an extension of the circle of pain. It also meant that the wearer was occasionally confronted with a show of sympathy and solidarity for which, in the absence of the Star, there would have been no reason. At best, this was an ambiguous comfort, and the rarity of the gesture emphasized the wedge which had been driven between the Jews and their fellow Germans. The whole subject of face-to-face meetings between Jews and non-Jews at this time, especially meetings between friends, demonstrates the crushing of substance on the faces of the wedge.

It is reasonable to believe that Sigmund Stein was able to deal with these confrontations for a longer time and with less loss of countenance than his fellow Jews in Hochburg. The respect in which he had been held until 1933 had acquired a momentum of its own which long defied the shift in the ideological wind, and it is indeed part of Sigmund's tragedy that there were people like Landrat Kleinwitz who continued to like Sigmund and to dole out to him a respect which consistency would have forbidden. Sigmund could hardly have remained unaware of the emptiness of such gestures, however much superficial comfort he may have drawn from them.

Most Hochburgers' memories of meeting Sigmund and other Jews stem from the last few years during which Jews could still be met in Hochburg, when such instances of recognition and friendliness took on the rarity which made them memorable. These occurrences became increasingly infrequent from March, 1933, to the end in 1942. The relationship between Sigmund Oppenheimer and Officer Schumann deteriorated from the very beginning. Sigmund Stein's condolences to the Schlossers were already diffident in 1935. But the ill-fated Luftwaffe lieutenant, Karl Heinz Lessing, went out of his way to greet Jeweler Meyer's son in 1937, and similar instances occurred thereafter. The sentimental idea of friendships which endure in the face of great adversity is not meaningless, but if one should be grateful for what truth there is in it, he should also be able to see the way in which it becomes a camouflage for the gradual dissolution of friendships under the pressure of external events.

The greetings of the later years were surrounded by obvious and imminent, if not always compelling, dangers. Although this was reason to remember them, it did not mean that no one saw how the friendships which the greetings symbolized had been robbed of much of their substance by the smaller and larger cowardices of the preceding years. Konrad Muenschner says that in Sigmund's greetings of the last years there was an element almost of scorn toward his good Christian friends who were now so timorous. It would be wrong to make too much of this, but there was certainly a great deal that was furtive and very little that was defiant in such greetings. Sigmund Oppenheimer tells of an acquaintance, a locomotive engineer, who, upon their meeting in a side street, made the sign of the clenched fist and whispered quickly, "Just wait until the change comes, then you'll see something!" But this, too, was done surreptitiously. It was bad enough to be seen greeting a Jew and worth your head to identify yourself as a Communist.

Despite the fact that Muenschner read scorn into Sigmund's attitude, the general impression emphasizes Stein's consideration in these greeting situations. He wanted to avoid putting his friends in an embarrassing or perilous spot. (He was not unique in this; it will be recalled that when Heinrich Meyer saw Karl Heinz Lessing approaching him on the street in 1937, Meyer's initial impulse had been to avoid the meeting.) For a long time, behavior varied in such situations according to circumstances. Elisabeth Kohlhausen from Bachdorf met Sigmund for the last time by chance, on a visit to Hochburg in 1938. They ran into one another on the Bahnhofstrasse bridge over the Felsen, a thoroughly public place, yet nothing she says about the meeting points to any diffidence on Sigmund's part. By the end of 1940, however, this would not have been the case.

Konrad Muenschner has lived on the Hospitallerstrasse for forty years. His apartment is just opposite the point where the Staustrasse ends at the Hospitallerstrasse. Muenschner can see the intersection from his window, and in 1940 and 1941 he used to observe Sigmund, waiting for the mailman near the intersection. By meeting the postman at this point, Sigmund was able to get his mail almost an hour before it would normally be delivered at the Treitschkestrasse address. He was careful to be inconspicuous while waiting, but Muenschner attributes this to discretion rather than to anxiety. Indeed, what anxieties there were at the time seemed more often associated with non-Jewish timidity than with Jewish fear.

Toward the end, in 1941 and 1942, it became more genuinely dangerous to greet one's Jewish friends, and nearly all the accounts of meetings with Sigmund during this period stress his concern that the greeter avoid getting himself in trouble, as well as various expedients which were used to this end. One of these was "the blink," which was just that: a blinking with both eyes, often used in place of the customary, "Good day." Another expedient form of behavior is described by Sigmund's neighbor in the Goering Strasse, the teacher Klingelmann, though the particular incident did not take place until after Sigmund had moved to the Treitschkestrasse apartment.

On German streetcars, smoking is permitted on the front and rear platforms, which are often separated from the interior by glass partitions. Furthermore, it is more customary in Germany than in America for men and young people to give up their seats to women and older people. Men often stand on the platform to smoke, or to avoid the fuss of getting up for courtesy's sake. In any case, it is not and was not unusual to see a man riding on the platform when seats within the car are available. Despite this, in the spring of 1941, Sigmund was probably riding on the platform because he was a Jew, and this is where, on the occasion in question, Klingelmann met him. Klingelmann lit a cigarette after he got aboard, and thereby gave himself an excuse to remain on the platform with his former neighbor. He spoke to Sigmund, and they shook hands. But Sigmund did not say anything in reply, apparently because there was a third man on the platform. When this third man got off at the Heinrichplatz, Sigmund turned to Klingelmann and asked, "Will you go forward and sit down, or will I? It could be dangerous for you to be seen talking to me here." But Klingelmann did not go forward and neither, in the end, did Sigmund. Instead, he got off at the next stop. Klingelmann thinks he was really going to the Bahnhofstrasse and got off before he wanted to in order to avoid embarrassing his companion. It may be; nevertheless, the teacher seems unaware that the next stop after the Heinrichplatz was the appropriate one for the Treitschkestrasse.

Dorothea Schlosser and others also tell of Sigmund's riding on the platform of the trams, and she, too, explains it by his desire to avoid unpleasantness. She adds, however, that the conductor, who walked around collecting fares and usually stood on the platform himself during lulls in this activity, would greet Sigmund in the usual respectful fashion—but out of the corner of his mouth.

From 1938 to 1942, Hochburg must have been a limbo of such ill-defined situations for the Jews. In many ways, every meeting between Jew and non-Jew in the Germany of that era was a mockery. The rules of the game still applied, the more so, perhaps, because they were the only familiar element in the situation. But an undercurrent of the bizarre comes through the accounts as Sigmund's "scorn" for his good Christian friends, or the "wildness" of his insistence, on one occasion, that Frau Huss should not talk to him for fear of what might happen to her. Friends could and did remain friends, but how could you ask a Jew how it was going, or say good day, when you knew full well how it was going, and that the days had ceased to be good?

The Jews were the official pariahs of Hochburg and Germany, and by the early forties their pariah status was complete. Their actual situation would get murderously worse, but sometime between 1940 and 1942 the point of diminishing returns was reached as far as the inflammation of the German people against the Jews was concerned. At no time was this inflammation complete, and popular feeling never ran as sharply and consistently against the Jews in the Nazi era as it had in Western Europe in earlier centuries or in Russia during the first decades of the twentieth century. With the questionable exception of the Kristallnacht there was never any real upsurge of popular feeling against the Jews. There were many isolated instances of unofficial anti-Semitic action, and the semi-official agitation of the Nazi party decked itself out in popular forms. But there were penalties for the person who tried to settle "the Jewish question" with his own hands, and the situation in Hochburg from 1938 on suggests that not many people wanted to do so.

Despite the absence of pogroms, a tenaciously rooted tradition of anti-Semitism existed as a dark background. It had been declining in effectiveness before 1933, but from the very beginning of the Nazi regime the rational arguments against these ancient attitudes were cut to pieces, not so much by the threat of punishment as by the plausibility and rationality of anti-Semitism when the dark background became the officially assumed reality. The red embers of an anti-Jewish tradition which had been slowly dying were brought to a heat which lit the fires of Auschwitz. Yet the murder which spread into the ghettos and concentration camps of the East does not disprove the comparative weakness of popular feeling against the Jews in Germany, and this is part of the tragedy of the German Jewish catastrophe.

Officer Schultheiss assisted the Gestapo. His colleague, Schumann, carried out the duties he found objectionable. The Landrat Kleinwitz believed in the Nazi program. All these men, at one time and another, displayed their modicums of decency and benevolence. Others, like Konrad Muenschner, Frau Huss, the teacher Klingelmann, and Johannes Demut were more fully decent and less involved, yet each, at one time or another, displayed a cowardice hard to measure. None of this was sensed as behavior which would speed up or slow down the descent to the murder of an innocent people. Yet in hindsight all such behavior was a link in the direction of murder, just as the Reichsvereinigung was, or as Sigmund Stein was. The madness of Nazi anti-Semitism had gone so far that good was indelibly stamped with evil—hence, Sigmund Stein's concern for his fellow Jews; while evil was more delibly stamped with good—hence the measures which drove Jews against their will and against all justice to flee.

16

[The annunciations]

In the last years of the Hochburg Jewish community, Sigmund Stein was constantly associated with the departure of Jews from the town. He advised them on emigration and helped with the legal details of achieving it. He took over the care of the property they left behind. If they moved from Hochburg to another location in Germany, Sigmund was responsible for the proper reporting of the fact.

He was also associated with the departure of Jews from Hochburg by another route: death. While here too he was responsible for the proper reporting of the event, in larger part his activities on the occasion of a Jewish death were his own choice. Wilhelm Klagemann had retired from a lifetime of plumbing to his house on the Kreuzheimer Landstrasse, the old road from Hochburg to Kreuzheim and Hugeldorf. Early in 1940, Klagemann agreed to take over the care of the Jewish cemetery which was on the Landstrasse not far from his home. He says that Sigmund Stein was present at every Jewish funeral in the last years—a fact which particularly impressed Klagemann because all Jewish funerals in the period took place at night. He feels that Sigmund looked upon it as a duty and made a special effort to attend the funerals. This fits with descriptions of Sigmund as a "nurse" to the Jewish community in the last years, during which, for instance, he used Sabbath meetings in the Treitschkestrasse as opportunities for counseling and for making announcements to the community as a whole.

Klagemann's recollections, like those of many other people, tend to be immersed in present dissatisfactions. He points out how difficult it was to be caretaker of the Jewish cemetery between 1940 and 1945, how gravestones were broken by rowdies, his tool shed ransacked. He complains of lack of recognition for the trouble he went to—"They don't remember old Wilhelm." He does not recognize that his difficulties are due to the fact that the Jews, a small portion of whose interests he took care of, were stripped of a larger portion and often robbed of life itself.

Sigmund's greatest enmeshment with the departure of Jews from Hochburg, and the one where the net cut sharply into his flesh, was the role he played in connection with the transports for the East, in Hochburg's contribution to the "final solution" of the Jewish problem by the Nazis.

When, on the day after the Japanese attacked Pearl Harbor, the first transport of Jews left Hochburg, the forty individuals left behind them a community of about sixty-five people. There was an ebb and flow of Jewish population in Hochburg from 1930 to 1941. At the earlier date, there were close to 250 people listed as Jews in the town. During the intervening years ninety people came into the community, five boys and three girls by birth. Many came from the surrounding villages, but by far the largest proportion, nearly a third, came for periods of one to four years as boarding pupils at the school in the Helenastrasse. In the same period, 210 Jews left Hochburg; 120 of these emigrated, half going to the United States and the next largest group, twenty, fleeing to countries which would ultimately be occupied by Germany. Ninety left Hochburg to take up or resume residence elsewhere in the Reich.

Fifteen Jewish deaths, two of them suicides, occurred in Hochburg between 1930 and 1941.

There were from the first, of course, many aspects of compulsion about this movement. No one, at the beginning or for a long time thereafter, forced Jewish families to move into Hochburg from the surrounding villages. Life simply became too unpleasant in the isolation and exposure of a small community. A background of friendly relationships between Jewish and non-Jewish villagers could help matters for a time, but eventually the official anti-Semitism from above met the grass-roots anti-Jewish tradition from below to form a wringer in which friendship and sympathy were squeezed out. Strangely, the explicit anti-Semitism of the regime effectively cushioned the impact of later extremes on non-Jews. Picturing the Jews as Germany's misery, invoking a dogma of race purity, and propagating a flood of pseudo-scientific or astutely selected scientific facts as proof, the regime maintained that its Jewish policy was dictated by the necessity of protecting Germany from Jewish malice and subversion.

The claim is not false because of the ultimate slaughter it cloaked, but rather because its premises are wildly untrue. To the degree that these premises were believed—and the grass-roots anti-Jewish tradition created an atmosphere favorable to belief —the harshness which was observed fell into a pattern of "regrettable necessities."

And the harshness was not rampant sadism or an incredible extermination. A few weeks after the Second World War broke out, four young men from Jewish families well known to all Hochburgers were sent to the Spreewald, near Berlin, to help with the harvest. A year later Israel Stern of Dreistadt, long since forced out of his drygoods business, and other Jewish men of the town were to be assigned as harvest helpers to peasants in the vicinity. In Hochburg, the four young men came back promptly after the harvest was in, and the mayor of Dreistadt told Israel Stern that care would be taken to see that the Jews would be sent only to peasants who were "clean" and who would be decent to them—a promise which Israel Stern says was kept.

When in late 1941 the first general transport of German Jews "to the East" for "agricultural labor" was prepared, members of the Nazi League of German Girls had for some years been doing twelve-month stints as agricultural conscriptees. Naturally, there is little comparison between Jewish compulsory labor and compulsory labor in the context of a more or less enthusiastic national movement; nevertheless, the conscription of the girls altered the perspective from which the non-Jewish German viewed the compulsion of the Jews. The participants in the Jewish transport were notified several weeks in advance and were informed that they would be able to take baggage and household goods with them. In Hochburg it was Sigmund Stein who passed around the notifications.

Among those so notified was the widow of Heinrich Wolff (mother of Frau Wolff-Foerster), who went to Sigmund to plead and remonstrate with him. Why, she wanted to know, should her mother in particular have been chosen to go? She reminded Sigmund of the suspicious circumstances surrounding her father's death and bitterly protested this second blow. Frau Wolff-Foerster speaks today with understanding and restraint about Sigmund's position, but her admitted bitterness at the time comes through clearly. She says that Sigmund was terribly upset by her pleas but stood his ground with the defense that there would be little point in sparing her mother at the time, since that would only postpone the day. "We will all be sent away in the end," he said.

In late 1941, several facts must have stood out with terrible clarity to the German Jews. Anti-Semitism had emerged beyond any question as the viciously indispensable policy of the Nazi regime. Deportations were occurring, not to some remote fastness in Germany, not even to the known if brutal order of concentration camps, but to "the East." The East, of course, was what all Germans had been brought up to view as a region of disorder. The German Jews, with a mixture of realistic sympathy for their coreligionists and unrealistic superiority based on their own perspicacity at being German, had looked upon it as the center of popular anti-Semitism which it was. The East had but recently been a battleground and was now a rear area of the front against Russia.

It seems incredible that there could still be illusions, but there were. Both the possibility and the necessity of illusion arose from the way life is lived. Having accepted the responsibilities he had. what was Sigmund to say to the widowed Frau Wolff? Was he to tell her, a sixty-year-old woman, of any suspicions he may have had about the lot which awaited her in the East? Was Sigmund to add to her fright and desperation?

Perhaps he should have. Nevertheless, everything we know about human behavior makes it more likely that Sigmund would try to reassure her, presenting the matter to her as it had been presented to him; she would be living among her own kind; she could take baggage and personal effects with her, the right to do so being embodied in a baggage declaration to be filled out and returned to Sigmund; the emigration was under the direction of a Jewish agency, the Reichsvereinigung. None of this could be disproved by any of the rumors, the second- or third-hand tales, some of which Sigmund undoubtedly had heard. Indeed, illusion was at a premium, and the premium was paid then and later.

None of the forty men, women, and children of the first transport out of Hochburg is known to have survived. This does not mean that death awaited them immediately upon their arrival in Riga, Latvia. It does not mean that they acquired a certainty of their fate at any time before it overtook them. To most of these people before their departure from Hochburg, Sigmund had to say something reassuring, and the only reassurance he had available was a repetition of the official explanations. It is most unlikely that he was skeptical enough to disbelieve all he was saying. At the same time, he was confronted by possibilities which could not be talked away.

Frau Barbara Kastner is a member of Hochburg's intellectual and social elite. She has not always despaired of organized group action as she does today, and during the Nazi era she and her daughter, a physician, were imprisoned for a time because of anti-state activities. Both before and after her imprisonment, Frau Kastner was known to sympathize with the Jews. It was because of this that the three Morgenstern brothers came to her when they learned they were to be included in the second transport to the East. They needed reassurance, and she told them that, at the worst, they were being sent to a forced labor camp. She insists that this was the worst shape of the knowledge which she and her friends had, and she frames her guilt in personal terms, regretting that she encouraged the Morgenstern brothers to accept their lot without protest.

There are people for whom the situation is murkier. Herr Bosch, who in his capacity as deputy Landrat worked with Sigmund in matters pertaining to Jewish persons and property in the villages around Hochburg, says he was aware of rumors about "actions" which had occurred in the wake of the German advance into Russia. Soldiers on leave from SS units would either tell stories to their wives under the seal of domestic confidence, or make obscure allusions to such actions elsewhere. The matter would then get around slowly, as confidences about confidences, allusions to allusions—all this in a situation where the immediacies of war twisted reflections about trust and moral responsibility. Herr Bosch is indignant at the idea of collective guilt because, as he says, if he as a deputy Landrat had only the vaguest inkling of what was going on, how much more unwitting was the peasant or the little man in town? He is especially indignant at the idea that Sigmund Stein might be criticized for his activities. Doctor Stein, he stresses, was in the same position of uneasy ignorance as all of them. Over and above that, he was subject to pressures and demands from which they were free.

For an understanding of the situation in which Sigmund as well as non-Jewish Germans found themselves during the war, it must be remembered that psychological warfare is a fact, and the purposeful spreading of rumor is a fact. People who know the world will be aware of their own side's use of such tactics and can reasonably assume that the other side uses them. Most people have not attained such sophistication, and those who have are usually committed to the state and social structure which have offered them the opportunity to become sophisticated. These people may be written off by the enemy, who proceeds to concentrate his efforts on the unenlightened.

And, with greater refinement, propaganda may be designed to work on whatever groups of enlightened dissidents may exist. For these, genuine torment may be the result. Rumor is always more effective when true, while truth and half-truth buttress the strategic fabrication. As a Jew in Nazi Germany, Sigmund Stein was a dissident. As an educated man, he was aware of psychological warfare. The rumors he heard about what was happening in the East were not always true, but in many instances they understated the horror of events there. Sigmund loved Germany, and his desire not to believe the worst could have arisen out of what he felt was fundamental patriotism. He could reasonably disbelieve much that in the end proved to be true.

Officer Schultheiss tells how Sigmund worked with him in combating rumors in the Jewish community. Sometimes the source of these rumors was unknown. At other times, the source would be a letter or a postcard which one of the Jewish families had received from relatives or friends who had been deported. Sigmund and Schultheiss were not cooperating in the suppression of "hard" news. To have spread information with the indiscretion and vagueness which automatically turn it into rumor was dangerous for both sender and receiver. That subsequent revelation has confirmed the worst of such sporadic disclosures does not alter the fact that at the time a reasonable man had no right to generalize on the basis of them. Sigmund was not only a reasonable man but had been a lawyer, familiar with the vagaries of evidence. Beyond that, he must time and again have seen the damage that rumor, ungrounded hopes as well as ungrounded fears, could inflict on the morale of the Hochburg Jewish community.

At the same time, he was in a position to sense the direction in which the rumors were pointing. There must have been a point at which Sigmund's conviction of possible disaster in the East could no longer be suppressed. Had this conviction been based on positive evidence, he might well have braved danger to himself and others in order to express it. But the trap was too cleverly contrived. It caught the Jews and sometimes enlisted their own help in the process.

Not long after the first transport left Hochburg, the lists for the second were sent to Sigmund from Kassel. One of the most poignant of the several minor mysteries about these lists concerns the amount of leeway Sigmund had in administering them. Some witnesses go so far as to say that he was given a quota and had to supply the particular names himself. This is almost certainly mistaken. Sigmund did receive lists of names, but he does seem to have had some leeway in applying them. Israel Stern, who shortly before the second transport became Sigmund's assistant for the towns and villages around Dreistadt, says that Sigmund was very conscientious in his administration of the lists. In the presence of conscience, however, the existence of any leeway with the lists created one more impossible situation for him to deal with.

What was he to do, after all, when his sister-in-law's name appeared on the list for the second transport?

Rosa was a schoolteacher, a spinster, and a neurotic. It is clear, as Henrietta Korbmacher tells of the turmoil the list caused, that she sympathized with these new neighbors. But it is also clear that she failed to sense the bitterness and conflict of the situation. Frau Mendel, Rosa's mother, demanded that Sigmund remove Rosa's name from the list of those scheduled to be sent away at the end of May, 1942. Sigmund did try to arrange matters so that there would be a "legal" reason for delaying Rosa's deportation; with Esther's assistance, he sought to persuade Rosa to marry a widower many years Rosa's senior. Herr Blankenstein had been a prosperous Hochburg merchant. In early 1942 he was living with one of the families in the Treitschkestrasse and had managed to secure for himself a "place" in the "Jewish Settlement Theresienstadt." This meant—with how much certainty it is impossible to say—that his deportation would coincide with that of the Steins and the older Mendels. For by mid-spring of 1942, Sigmund had learned that he and his family would probably end up in that same "Jewish Settlement." In the terrible pressures of the times such arrangements as the proposed marriage of Rosa to Herr Blankenstein were not uncommon. But there was always much about them that was grotesque, and they did not always work out. They did not work out *this* time, Frau Korbmacher says, because Rosa refused. That Rosa, still a maiden lady, was deported with the second transport is an established fact.

Frau Mendel is supposed to have maintained bitterly that Sigmund could have saved Rosa. Sigmund argued that he would have lost the respect and confidence of the Jewish community if he had shown his sister-in-law special consideration. A matter which may have been decisive in Frau Mendel's bitterness turns up among the things which Frau Hessler of Hof Hessler had to say about Marion Stein.

One day Esther, instead of her daughter, appeared at the farm. Frau Hessler immediately thought that Marion must be sick again, because on the one previous occasion when Marion was ill, her mother had come out to insist on working in place of her daughter and, against Frau Hessler's protests, had worked all three days of Marion's sickness.

This time, however, Marion was not sick. Instead, as her mother told Frau Hessler in great agitation, an order had come that she was to be sent away, "to some out of the way Russian place." As it turned out, this was Riga, and despite the fact that the available records of the first transport suggest that families were usually sent away together, one must conclude that Marion's name had been on the list for the first transport in December, 1941. She had been beside herself at the prospect and threatened suicide if she were separated from her family. The conclusion is inescapable. Sigmund was able to do for his daughter what he later said he could not do for Rosa: get the order quashed or remove her name.

There is of course a great difference between the emotional attachment to a daughter and that to a sister-in-law. Furthermore, in the May, 1942, transport to Lodz in Poland, the deportation of Rosa Mendel separately from her parents was not exceptional. The records reveal other such separations. Yet Rosa Mendel was Frau Mendel's daughter, and Sigmund had been able somehow to get his own daughter exempted from a transport in which Marion had originally been included. Hence, Sigmund's explanation that he would have lost the respect of the Hochburg Jewish community had he made an exception for Rosa must have rung false to Frau Mendel and perhaps even to himself.

Under some circumstances, postponements in deportations were nearly automatic. One of the families deported in May, 1942, was that of Simon Goldberg, Sigmund's sometime rival for leadership of the Hochburg Jewish community. Frau Baker Schmidt remembers with startling accuracy that they were sent away on the morning train at 9:48, May 30. She explains her exact recollection by association, for on the same morning she had received a phone call from her sister in Cologne with the information that the sister had just been bombed out in an air raid. According to Frau Baker Schmidt, the Goldbergs were to have been included in the first transport, but Netti, the daughter, had been sick with scarlet fever. Because this automatically exempted her from the transport, the deportation of the whole family was postponed.

Both Frau Baker Schmidt and the physician who confirmed Netti Goldberg's illness and cared for her speak of Sigmund from the perspective of non-Jewish Hochburg residents who became involved with him through closer relationships with other members of the community, chiefly the Goldbergs. Both manifest a certain detached sympathy for Sigmund based on the assumption that he had been forced to work against his fellow Jews. Both seem to hover benevolently around the truth without ever quite touching it.

Of course Sigmund was forced into his position, and of course there are respects in which he can be said to have worked against his fellow Jews. It is highly probable, too, as Frau Baker Schmidt suggests, that he hoped to "get something out of it." But such phrasings are meaningful only if they are carefully taken apart, and this they are not. Sigmund's freedom had prepared the compulsion. He was not a hapless creature of circumstance. Every choice he made could have been different, had he been willing to pay the price. He made the choices he did because their prices seemed less than those of the alternatives. It was part of his freedom to err in the assessment of the prices, but to the extent that the individual does not understand the consequences of the alternatives before him, or is unaware of them, freedom loses meaning. In Sigmund's case, in the case of the Germans and the German Jews generally, freedom was severely limited by the nearsightedness resulting from the accumulation of everyday experiences called German history.

The belief that Sigmund worked against his people acts as a salve to the consciences of those who express it, since they know that they as Germans were deeply involved in the "work against the Jews," and this involvement can somehow be seen as less if it is shared by the Jews themselves. Sigmund's situation was a part of the human condition, but it was elevated to tragedy by the constellation of events in which he found himself. The consequences of every choice are hidden in the future. Werner Hagen must have lived through several years of satisfaction with his decision to flee to France. He was out of Germany yet still surrounded by the European culture in which he had grown up. For several years he was probably happier and may have been better off than he would have been had he chosen to settle elsewhere. Yet in the end, the Nazis overran France and engulfed Werner Hagen.

In the series of choices which led to Sigmund Stein's activities during the early forties, the better alternatives had seemed obscure, although the worse ones were plainly evident. Toward the end, every alternative had become stamped with ambiguity. In general, war increases the amount of coercion which hard necessity appears to justify. In Germany, tradition and history had combined to make the increase in coercion a great one; they had also provided the soil in which Nazi anti-Semitism could flourish. Thus, the Jews were doubly victims. Any German could count on the *probability* that subversive activity on his part would be revenged on relatives and friends. The Jews could count on the *certainty* of retribution. This *Sippenhaft,* this guilt by familial association, twisted every viable and virtuous personal alternative into a possible and likely evil.

Herr Korbmacher's criticism of Sigmund is a distorted reflection of the actual situation: that it was all right if Sigmund wanted to be a hero, but that he should not have subjected his wife and daughter to danger. If Sigmund had really "wanted to be a hero," if he had refused all cooperation at some point, he would have subjected his wife and daughter to hopeless danger. Moreover, a general refusal to cooperate would have carried with it the inability to refuse his cooperation in particular instances. As it was, his general cooperation with the town authorities established a framework of relationships within which Sigmund's refusal to go along on a particular measure *might* carry weight. The argument is treacherous, and it is a typical rationalization, yet its core of truth need not be denied.

Sigmund was afraid for himself and his family; it is the converse of this fear, the hope to preserve both himself and them, which defines what he may have hoped to "get out" of his position. If this was weakness on Sigmund's part, it is a weakness which must always be reckoned with. Behavior which appears to contradict a commitment to the resistance against the Nazis must be looked at very closely. When this is done, it will be seen that the men and women who so jeopardized their families, friends, and themselves, did so on the often correct, sometimes tragically incorrect, premise that they had a sporting chance to evade detection and arrest.

Sporting chances steadily diminished for the Jews in Nazi Germany. This particular German Jew, Sigmund Stein, had lived himself into a situation where one of the last such chances open to some Jews—suddenly disappearing, becoming a "U-boat," as they were called, to live a life of precarious hiding in the garret or storeroom of some "Aryan" friend—for Sigmund, this last chance was cut off by the fact that he constantly had to appear in the official eye. His absence would have been noticed immediately.

Sigmund was, however, confronted with the possibility that such submersion might be possible for Marion. Herbert Durckheim makes much of Marion's charm and asserts that she could have been saved if only Sigmund had listened to him. His plan was to hide Marion in the attic of his house for an indefinite period, in order to spirit her across the French border when the opportunity arose. He shows the entrance to his attic, pointing out how unobtrusive it is, and expands on the way Marion could have lived quite comfortably up there, coming out at night for surreptitious walks. While it is easy for Durckheim to elaborate a casual suggestion into a plan, especially after the fact, there is little doubt that Marion's submersion was seriously proposed. But the idea was rejected because Sigmund and his family wanted to remain together. It is also possible that Sigmund had doubts about entrusting his young daughter to Herr Durckheim.

Sigmund and his family had not been able to emigrate legally. They could not go underground. By May, 1942, it is all but certain that they knew they were going to be transported with the remnant of the Hochburg Jewish community later that year. Sigmund did not and could not know what their ultimate fate would be, yet he knew enough, and had reason to suspect enough more, to fear deportation.

He had already begun to think of escape. As the pressure grew more intense, as men in Sigmund's position began to suspect more about the true nature of the deportations, the possibility of escape with the tacit connivance of German authorities was apparently dangled in front of such men as a means of securing continued cooperation. Officer Schultheiss insists that sometime in the late spring or early summer of 1942 he was in a position to offer Sigmund and his family the opportunity to leave Germany and that Sigmund turned it down because of his sense of duty to his people. The Benzheims, whose association with Sigmund was rapidly increasing at that period, say that if such an offer had in fact been made it would have been accepted. They maintain that the nearest thing to it was actually a piece of Gestapo devilishness: that Sigmund was given the opportunity to escape, but without his family.

The facts which lie behind these conflicting stories are no longer accessible. In view of the happenings which will engage us in the next chapter, the Benzheims' story may be the more credible.

17

[Destinations]

During the Peasant Revolts of sixteenth-century Europe, the Lake of Constance, forming as it does part of the border between Switzerland and Germany, was a convenient avenue of escape for German refugees. In 1942, the avenue was still there for men and women fleeing from the Nazis. The surpassing beauty of the lake, and its usefulness, are not changed by history.

The Ueberlinger See is an arm of the Lake of Constance which takes its name from the lovely town of Ueberlingen and washes the base of the cliff from which Meersburg castle dominates the town of Meersburg behind it. Frau Elsa Ritter, who lives in Meersburg, manages to bring some order into the many stories about the Stein family's plan to flee to Switzerland in August, 1942. Many of these stories implicitly converge on a point which only one of them explicitly identifies as the *Hospiz Heller Blick*. This is the "Clear View" guest house and rest home which Frau Ritter has run since the death of her husband in the mid-thirties. The guest house is situated high on the southwestern slope of a hill outside Meersburg. From it one can see the Lake of Constance itself to the south, and, on a clear day, look west across the Island of Mainau, across the lake-locked peninsula between the Ueberlinger See and the Untersee almost to the point where the Rhine flows out of the valley after it has spread itself into this entire complex of lakes. Konstanz, the nearest large city, lies almost out of sight on the narrow estuary which connects the Lake of Constance with the Untersee. Konstanz itself is German; its immediate hinterland is Swiss. It is thus well situated to be a center of smuggling and other border-oriented delinquencies.

Much of Frau Ritter's account is unique, but much of it is a confirmation and integration of stories told by people in Hochburg who were closer to Sigmund Stein and his family. Accordingly, it seems desirable to approach Frau Ritter's account through the sometimes poorly marked path of the Hochburg stories.

One of the ways in which Officer Schumann illustrates his general benevolence to Jews and anti-Nazis during the years from 1933 to 1945 is by describing what he had to do with Sigmund Stein's attempt to flee Germany in 1942. The old man's defense is persuasive, despite his almost compulsive dedication to order and discipline which led a few people to detest him and others to dislike the hypocrisies to which his dedication led. It is in part because of this attitude toward order and regulations that his behavior in 1942 is interesting. Sigmund, he says, was a prisoner in the town jail sometime around the middle of August that year. The jailing had something to do with an attempt by Sigmund to arrange for the smuggling of certain securities belonging to the von Schlegel family across the border at Konstanz. Schumann was already aware of a relationship, innocent in his policeman's eyes, between Sigmund and the von Schlegels.

Since the two men had long been acquaintances, Schumann was not surprised when the turnkey brought him a note in which Sigmund asked to see him. Schumann went around to see what Sigmund wanted. Sigmund complained about the food he was getting and apparently said, without making a direct request, how pleasant it would be if he could have some home-cooked food.

"Of my own free will . . . "—since any response to a request would have been against regulations—Schumann took his briefcase, got on the tram, and rode out to the Humboldtallee. It should be noted that he did not go to the Treitschkestrasse which was only a short distance from the jail. For in July, 1942, Sigmund and his family had moved again, and by this move the wheel of Sigmund's life in Hochburg moved full circle. Once again, he was living in the house on the Humboldtallee where he had spent his Gymnasium years as a boarder in what had then been Doctor Jungmann's Boarding Home for Jewish Students.

It is hard not to be impressed by the symbolism of this move, or by the intensity of David Stein's reaction to it. David feels that his own removal from Bachdorf to Hochburg and life in the boarding home was a very disturbing experience and believes that the same could be said of his brother. He pictures the house in the Humboldtallee as a place of grim discipline and thus is less impressed with the formal symbolism of Sigmund's return there than with the reimmersion, after a quarter of a century, in a host of painful memories and associations.

Symbol and old memories were probably not uppermost in Sigmund's thoughts about the transfer to the Humboldtallee in the summer of 1942. For by this time he could definitely recognize the move as a preliminary to the deportation of the Steins and the other remaining Jews in Hochburg. Despair was hovering close, and it was a gesture of despair which led to Sigmund's jailing and Officer Schumann's tram ride to the worried, confused family.

Esther Stein, even in her affliction, was not incapacitated. She hastily got together a good dinner for her husband, which Officer Schumann then packed into his briefcase and took back to Sigmund. This was repeated on each of the unstated number of days Sigmund remained in jail. On the last day, while waiting for Esther to prepare the food, Officer Schumann was sitting at a table; across from him was Esther's father, Herr Mendel, who simply happened to be present—for the Mendels had not made the move to the Humboldtallee with their daughter and son-in-law. After Esther had brought the dinner and while Schumann was packing it into his briefcase, Herr Mendel pushed a well-filled purse across the table, saying that Officer Schumann should take it for his troubles.

Schumann's explanation of his refusal to take the money is a mixture of naiveté and practicality, inasmuch as, on the one hand, he says he refused the money with indignation that anyone might think he was acting other than out of the goodness of his heart, yet on the other hand, in a slightly different context, he admits that he appreciated the offer, but it would have been his head if he had taken it and the gift had been discovered.

In telling his story, Officer Schumann does not bring the von Schlegel daughter-in-law, Frau Kleppmeier-Schlegel, into it except to refer vaguely to her death in Konstanz as having been in some way connected with the jailing. Fräulein Dr. Gottfried, the "mongrel" daughter of Professor Gottfried and his Jewish wife, is an "educated person" and was well acquainted with Frau Kleppmeier-Schlegel. Fräulein Dr. Gottfried knows little or nothing about Sigmund's imprisonment, and nothing about any connection between him and the von Schlegel daughter-in-law. She says that Lotti Kleppmeier-Schlegel had apparently been able to smuggle articles across the border at Konstanz a couple of times, but was too trusting and loved to talk. She finally told the wrong person of her activities, was informed on, and arrested on her next trip to Konstanz, where she committed suicide in a prison cell.

Only Meyer Rosenblum speaks with assurance about attempted flight as the reason for Sigmund's arrest in August, 1942. He claims that Sigmund was in the Hochburg jail eight days and knows that the "daughter of a professor up on the hill" was somehow involved. But his assertion that the Benzheims in Hochburg would know some of the details is true. They know some of the details about many aspects of Sigmund's life in Hochburg in the early forties. It would be unreasonable to expect that anyone would know the whole story. Social ignorance is too pervasive a phenomenon in general not to have become an overriding fact in the particular situation of Nazi Germany, where it was possible for knowledge to be dangerous.

The Benzheims *do* know that Herr Krapf, of the Hochburg trucking firm, was supposed to have taken the Stein family to

Konstanz in one of his vehicles. But Herr Krapf is very vague on what happened. He says that "sometime" in the early forties, Sigmund came to him to inquire about the possibility of his family's being carried in one of Herr Krapf's trucks from Hochburg to Konstanz. Like Officer Schumann, Herr Krapf is ambiguous in his explanations, saying first that it was out of the question because the Wehrmacht had requisitioned all his trucks. Later he returns spontaneously to the point, saying, "After all, it would have been the death penalty if I had been found out." He seems to know nothing about any connection between Sigmund and the unfortunate Lotti Kleppmeier-Schlegel. Frau Wolff-Foerster, on the other hand, has Sigmund and his family actually getting as far as Konstanz with Lotti, only to be caught in the act of trying to get across the border. The Steins, she says, were sent back to Kassel, where they were temporarily imprisoned; their companion was imprisoned in Konstanz and took poison after she was released, probably because she felt she had doomed the Steins. How Sigmund got from Kassel to the Hochburg jail, Frau Wolff-Foerster does not seem to know.

Typically, a combination of circumstances which on the surface appears fortuitous finally led closer to the actual events of August, 1942. The alert octogenarian, Professor Luther, who was Sigmund's teacher at the Gymnasium, knows very little about Sigmund's later life and nothing about any connection between Sigmund and Lotti. But he did know the widow, because his son had been a good friend of the young Professor von Schlegel who committed suicide in Italy, and Professor Luther points out that Karl Gruen and Frau Professor von Schlegel were cousins. He also recommends the Dienstbachs as a couple well acquainted with the affairs of the von Schlegel family from many years of service to it as housekeeper and caretaker.

The Dienstbachs know a great deal about the von Schlegel family, and Frau Dienstbach's bitterness about the treatment meted out to the old Frau Professor von Schlegel has already been noted, as has her knowledge about Sigmund Stein's connection with the family. The Dienstbachs also say that it was Lotti Kleppmeier-Schlegel herself who told them that her trip to Konstanz was to be an attempt to get the Steins across the border.

To pursue the tangle of accounts further: it will be recalled that Karl Grün and his wife took over the apartment in the Goeringstrasse from Sigmund. That there was some relationship between the families is suggested by the fact that Karl Grün, although he did not know at the time about the Steins' involvement in the Konstanz affair, had learned about it shortly after it happened. The brother-in-law from whom he learned about it appears to be the only person who knows the crucial role which Frau Elsa Ritter played.

Frau Ritter had known Lotti Kleppmeier from a time well before Lotti married the young Professor von Schlegel. The women had become widows within a few years of each other and Frau Ritter had opened the Hospiz Heller Blick shortly after her husband's death. Prior to this time, their visits with one another had been in Hochburg or Meersburg, as convenience dictated. After Frau Ritter opened the Hospiz, however, she was not only tied down more than she had been, but the situation was also ideal for having her friend as a frequent guest.

In August, 1942, Lotti Kleppmeier-Schlegel was at the Hospiz on one of her periodic visits. She had been there several days, during which nothing was said about helping anyone to flee Germany, when a "middle-aged Fräulein," a spinster, arrived from Hochburg with the explanation that a Jewish lawyer from that town was planning to flee across the border with his family, that transportation to Konstanz by truck had been arranged, and that she had been sent on ahead in order to arrange the crossing.

Frau Ritter does not remember the name of the Hochburg spinster but does remember enough for her to be identified as Fräulein Lehner, proprietress of a well-known Hochburg delicatessen, about whom more will be said later. Frau Ritter goes on to say that her friend Lotti of course recognized Fräulein Lehner and also seemed to be completely aware of who the lawyer was. Without, apparently, mentioning his name, she vouched for him in every way, telling Frau Ritter that he had been of great help to the whole von Schlegel family and stressing his widely recognized decency and trustworthiness.

Frau Ritter is by no means able to answer all the questions which arise. For instance, she does not know whether there had been previous contact among Sigmund, Fräulein Lehner, and Lotti Kleppmeier-Schlegel. It is clear, however, that there must have been. Frau Ritter describes her friend as having appeared surprised at the arrival of Fräulein Lehner, but also as having immediately urged that she be given every assistance. Lotti also suggested that she accompany Fräulein Lehner on a trip across the lake by ferry to Konstanz in order to make contact with any addresses Frau Ritter could give them. Frau Ritter gave them three, and the two women left for Konstanz on the morning after Fräulein Lehner's arrival. About twelve hours later, Lotti returned alone. They had been unsuccessful, and Fräulein Lehner had left by train for Hochburg directly from Konstanz.

Frau Ritter is not the only person who believes her friend Lotti was an intelligent and resourceful woman. Consequently, she is still baffled by the imprudence Lotti was to show. Yet even at the time she must have had some reservations about her friend's discretion. When Lotti suggested that she and Frau Ritter make another trip, Frau Ritter insisted on a strict condition: *she* would do the talking when it came to the point of any actual negotiations. Lotti agreed, and they set out the following morning.

It seems apparent that the condition as described contained an ambiguity: where do cautious preliminary conversations become actual negotiation? And this ambiguity, in view of the complete trustworthiness which all attribute to Lotti Kleppmeier-Schlegel, seems necessary to account for what happened. The two women went in Konstanz to the inn "Zum Weissen Löwen," which Frau Ritter knew as a possible contact. Frau Ritter, however, says she immediately got a very bad impression of the woman who ran the place, and warned her friend that nothing at all should be said; they would instead spend a little time there to get the lay of the land and then leave for another address. They were sitting at a table on the outdoor terrace. After a time, Lotti got up and went into the inn proper. Frau Ritter thought she was going to the lavatory. When Lotti had been absent an inordinately long time, however, Frau Ritter thought she should investigate, went in, and found her friend talking to the proprietress about the project. Frau Ritter was shocked and indicated that the conversation should be broken off. But Lotti said the woman was prepared to assist them, but only if a sister, who ran a restaurant on the other side of town, would cooperate.

Since now the only thing to do was go ahead, Frau Ritter and Lotti started out on foot for the other restaurant, which was nearer the border and frequented by border guards. On the way, Frau Ritter pleaded with her friend to be more cautious and not to go ahead on her own again. Despite these admonitions, however, Lotti once again took the initiative and spoke directly with the proprietress, going so far as to discuss the money involved. Frau Ritter was appalled and thoroughly frightened; she made an excuse for them to leave at once, but it was too late. The woman apparently informed on them immediately to some border guards who were in the restaurant, and they were arrested almost before they had gotten out of the door.

They were taken to the Konstanz jail, put in adjacent cells, and closely questioned separately for three days. Frau Ritter says that the questioning was severe and threatening, but that she was not mishandled and believes that Lotti was not either. Frau Ritter did overhear the torture of a Polish farm laborer, a prisoner of war who had become the lover of the war widow for whom he was working, and this added to Frau Ritter's agitation and fright.

On the third day of their imprisonment, Frau Ritter was left alone in her cell, but Lotti was taken for questioning early in the morning and was not returned until late in the evening, after Frau Ritter was asleep. The next morning she awoke as she had the preceding days to the sound of the turnkey bringing breakfast, but became aware that something unusual had happened when she heard the man exclaim as he approached the adjacent cell, "Jesus, what has she done!" Frau Ritter was not told of what had happened but was able to gather from the subsequent flurry of activity that Lotti Kleppmeier-Schlegel had committed suicide by hanging herself. After being released two weeks later, Frau Ritter learned more details of what had occurred, and still later she learned that her friend had left behind a letter taking the whole blame upon herself and exonerating Frau Ritter, who thinks that this action represented Lotti's exaggeration of a genuine feeling of responsibility for their having been caught.

Within twenty-four hours of the arrest of the two women in

Konstanz, Sigmund Stein and his family were seized in Hochburg and were sent immediately to the Gestapo prison in Kassel. The details of what happened in this connection are obscure. One reason for this is that Sigmund Stein, with all but four of the remaining Jews in Hochburg, was deported to the East within two weeks of his arrest. Another reason is the great reticence of one of the persons closest to the situation, Fräulein Lehner.

There is, certainly, no guarantee that if Fräulein Lehner were more willing to talk she would be able to clear up the obscurity surrounding the arrest of Sigmund and his family. Yet it seems incredible that she would not have made every effort to find out what was happening in regard to Sigmund as well as Lotti Kleppmeier-Schlegel. Actual ignorance could have been as dangerous to her as the appearance of knowledge. She is by no means completely uncooperative and supplies some information of considerable value, particularly in regard to the Steins' last few days in Hochburg. She admits having made the trip to Konstanz for the family, and she is aware of Lotti Kleppmeier-Schlegel's suicide. It is clear from other information that she was close to the Hochburg Jewish community in general and to Sigmund and his family in particular—indeed, when they asked after "Auntie" on postcards from Theresienstadt to Casimir Dombrowski, it was to Fräulein Lehner they were referring.

A clue to, but no real explanation of, her hesitation appears to lie in the extent to which she became involved in the matter of Jewish possessions which had been given to her for safekeeping. There is no question but that she was friendly and helpful to several Jewish families and at some risk to herself. On the other hand, some of her actions in regard to the objects entrusted to her were open to ambiguous interpretations, and whether or not she did anything for which she feels guilty, she is aware that there are those who think she ought to feel guilty.

Sigmund, Esther, and Marion Stein were arrested and were sent to Kassel for jailing. Officer Schumann's story of Sigmund and the food at the Hochburg jail is supposed to refer to the several days Sigmund was kept in jail following his return from Kassel. Yet the Benzheims and Frau Jesberg, who still lives in the house next to the Jewish property in the Humboldtallee, all say that Sigmund returned from Kassel and was in the Humboldtallee apartment *before* his wife and daughter got back. The Benzheims simply state this as a fact, but Frau Jesberg says that she and her daughter visited him the night of his return in order to get a book which he had borrowed. When she asked him, with a natural if indiscreet curiosity, what had happened in Kassel, he replied deprecatingly that it had been nothing and made no reference to his wife and daughter, who were not there.

It is not possible to resolve entirely the conflict which appears here. What seems most likely is that the short period between the return of Sigmund and his family from Kassel and their deportation two weeks later has caused a compression of time between the imprisonment and the deportation. The effect underlines the fearful isolation in which Jewish families must have lived in the last weeks before their final exile . . . even when, as in Sigmund's case, there were people who continued to associate with them until the end.

18

[The night of farewells]

Sometimes it seems as though half of Hochburg visited the
Stein family in the Humboldtallee on the evening before Sigmund,
Esther, and Marion were finally deported to the East. Closer attention to the pattern of visits suggests that, while not all of them
occurred precisely on the last night, there was nevertheless a remarkable coming and going that evening, which was the climax
of progressively accelerating activity over the few evenings leading up to it.

The motives behind and meanings of these visits encourage a
cynicism which must be held in check. When Jews departed for
the East, they usually left silver and furniture behind in the safekeeping of friends. It was a reality of the time that some of the
visitors came hoping to "inherit" certain of the Steins' possessions.
But even this reality allowed for other, admirable motives.

Two kinds of attitudes seem to characterize this final association with the Steins. Some of the visitors recognized the problem which Sigmund and his family faced in the disposal of their possessions, but there was a reluctance to accept the things, as gifts or for storage, because "there was blood on them." The other attitude is more ambiguous and more common. Both Franz Wilhelm and Frau Huss speak of the people who hovered around the Steins in the last weeks hoping to inherit something. The accusation, in specific cases, may well have been unjust. But the situation itself was something real.

These attitudes and the behavior by which they manifested themselves deserve exploration. It must be understood, however, that they appear in the general and particular framework of saying farewell. The Jews and the people of Hochburg were looking at one another across a precipitously widening chasm of the unknown, and it is hardly surprising if, on both sides, the flesh and blood of emotion were being sublimated in a concern for the material things into which that flesh and blood had extended itself.

The feeling that Jewish possessions "had blood on them" was still figurative in 1942. Frau Huss, for instance, says that Sigmund wanted her to take a valuable rug. Her husband had wanted to accommodate the Steins, but she herself shrank from having the rug in the house because it would be a constant reminder of what had happened to their friends. The rug would not speak of actual and bloody fate, but it would recall the cruel injustice of how the Jews had been harried out of Germany.

Frau Baker Schmidt has already been mentioned in connection with the coal dealer, Herr Solomon, and his kindness to her and to her husband. Before the elder Solomons were sent away with the first transport—their children had been able to emigrate several years earlier—the old lady came to Frau Baker Schmidt with a crystal vase, a gold bracelet, and a costly and beautiful brooch. They were intended as mementos, Frau Schmidt says, adding that Herr Solomon was much upset to find that his wife had failed to surrender these two years earlier when the government, paying minimum compensation, had requisitioned such items from Jewish families. For her part, Frau Schmidt accepted the items and tells of trying to get them to the Solomon children after the war. She never wore the jewelry during the Nazi period, because, she says, the pieces would have brought bad luck.

The Steins tried to press upon Dr. LeMaitre and his wife certain valuable household objects. It was the same as with the Husses: the wife hesitated because of "the blood that was on them." The LeMaitres did accept the objects, however, and returned them to Frau Mendel, the sole survivor of three Steins and three Mendels, after the war.

In most situations of this kind, the motives of the receivers may be questioned. That there was "blood on" the objects left for storage, and that they would "bring bad luck" are perhaps strange statements to be made by people who presumably did not know what really awaited the Jews. Another question turns up in the account of Dorothea Schlosser, daughter of Counselor Schlosser and neighbor of the Steins in the Goeringstrasse. Speaking of how she came to receive part of the Steins' household linens, she insists that Sigmund took the attitude that he was leaving these things for safekeeping and that he looked forward to getting most of them back on his return from the East. She goes so far as to say that Sigmund had made extra purchases of household goods at this time, because he felt that he and his family would come back impoverished and would need the things so purchased. She relates these purchases to her belief that the Steins apparently did not lack money in the spring and summer of 1942. Loans made to Sigmund during this period, for instance, were promptly repaid. She says that Sigmund offered her a large portion of the Stein family silverware, but she felt obliged to refuse because it bore the Steins' monogram, recognition of which would have led to trouble—there were two Nazi enthusiasts in her house before whom she had to exercise caution.

There is every reason to believe that Sigmund felt a real need to dispose of his possessions before deportation and looked upon Dorothea Schlosser's willingness to accept them as a favor. Yet the situation was ill-defined. Sigmund's asserted belief that he and his family would be coming back almost certainly masked moods of desperation and hopelessness. The state of his feelings during the two or three months before deportation was such that it must be studied before one proceeds to the simpler ambiguities of the persons around him.

Sigmund was not a conspiratorial type. Even in 1942, he continued in many ways to give the impression of being a solid German burger. This impression became ever more incongruous, but it was never entirely dispelled. He had, of course, every reason to conspire. He was confronted with malignant and overwhelming odds; his approaching deportation was an unknown which, if it permitted certain hopes, also and by the same token permitted far more tangible fears. Unspeakable and incredible rumors he may have dismissed, but the Nazi malevolence to which these rumors pointed was a clear fact. He touched the edges of conspiracy in his attempt to escape. As much as anything else, however, this particular brush with conspiracy shows why a general relationship to it never developed. Sigmund and all the Jews were too directly threatened; he himself was too conspicuous. There is never a hint of reproach toward him by any of the people who *were* conspirators at the time. The Jews were doing enough merely by being Jews.

Thus, it is especially incongruous that so much of the real content of Sigmund's life during the last few months in Hochburg took place, as the Germans say, in *"Nacht und Nebel,"* under cover of night and the fog. Yet it was literally true. Social visits from friends; visits for harmless, non-social purposes; and even visits from men with whom, during the day, Sigmund had official contacts took place on the characteristically misty Hochburg evenings of summer and early fall, 1942. Sigmund often repaid such visits. The furtive process had been going on for some years, but it accelerated as the end approached. Among the most frequent participants in these visits were the Benzheims, and in Sigmund's relationship with them appears evidence for the emotional peculiarities of a situation where conspiratorial behavior lacked a conspiracy.

The Benzheims had come to Hochburg from Frankfurt-am-Main late in 1940. As a young couple who had been close to many members of the large Frankfurt Jewish community, they had been in trouble with the Nazis from the beginning. While they had escaped the extreme consequences of their insistent flirtation with danger, both of them were familiar with the courts and the jails.

Benzheim was a *Kommerzienrat,* a commercial consultant. Frau Benzheim, a woman of eager intellectual and literary interests, seems never to have found appropriate outlets for these pursuits. Both were "educated" though not "academic" people. So much is clear. A friend of Sigmund's says that the Benzheims came to Hochburg and immediately *affected* to be great anti-Nazis. How this remark is to be interpreted is not clear. The Benzheims were in fact anti-Nazis. If the accusation they had had to face in Frankfurt—that they had signaled enemy bombers from the windows of their apartment—was ridiculous, the attempt of the Nazis to "get something on them" had a real basis in their attitude toward the regime which found expression in association with and assistance to Jewish people.

In the provincialism of Hochburg and amidst the psychological conflicts of many of the "philosophical" opponents of Nazism who lived there, the Benzheims were a disturbing element. They are not easy to understand. Herr Benzheim's scorn of and bitterness toward the Nazis is so apoplectic as to suggest that he may be protesting too much. But he reacts just as violently to anything he is against. Frau Benzheim, a small and pretty woman, who must have been strikingly attractive in 1942, is the antidote to her husband's wrathfulness. Considering this long role, one is not surprised to find her soft-spoken calm touched with nervousness.

One of the traits which increases the difficulty of understanding the Benzheims' attitudes and actions may well have appealed to Sigmund Stein. This is the fact that, except perhaps for Herr Benzheim's personal choler, they have never been radicals. Instead they give the impression of being very German, with many typically German and conservative opinions and viewpoints. Sigmund grew close to both of them, closer, perhaps, to Frau Benzheim—in part because it was she who had the leisure necessary to implement her concern for Jewish friends, in part because of her literary interests, and in part because she was a woman.

Sigmund had aspirations to be a writer. A few people mention "the" novel he was writing. David Stein agrees that Sigmund had literary ambitions, adding a little regretfully that the family had always laughed at such pretensions. Fräulein Mendelsohn also speaks of Sigmund's "novel," and her aging mother once saw the manuscript. Frau Jesberg, the Steins' neighbor in the Humboldt-allee, speaks of Sigmund's having read a new chapter to her and her daughter when they paid him an after-dark visit on his return from the imprisonment in Kassel. The manuscript of the novel and the text of one poem are extant. The autobiographical value of the manuscript fragment is very general but touching.

In contrast to the novelette, the poem is explicitly autobio-graphical and alludes to the catastrophe which was overtaking Sigmund at the time he was writing both. Its text was memorized by Frau Benzheim when Sigmund recited it to her shortly before his deportation.

> *Noch einmal sah ich ins jene Tal*
> *Wo ich geboren bin.*
> *Ist es das letzte Mal?*
> *Kam es mir in den Sinn*
> *Da habe ich den Wald gefragt*
> *Er rief, lebst noch ein gutes Stück,*
> *Sei unversagt.*

> Once more I looked on the
> valley of my birth
> and the thought occurred to
> me, is this the last time?
> I put my question to the wood,
> which answered, your life is
> far from done;
> do not despair.

Frau Benzheim is better able than an outsider to appreciate the conflict between Sigmund and the life which both novelette and poem conceal, for this late sharing of emotion and thought be-tween Sigmund and an attractive, sympathetic woman could not remain neutral. Indeed, it seems clear that Frau Benzheim was significant in his life.

When Werner Hagen's philandering is mentioned, an ex-plicit contrast is often drawn to Sigmund Stein's respectability. In the last few months of his life in Hochburg, Sigmund appears to have maintained his emotional solidity. Yet this can only be a relative statement. He was frightened, harassed, and perplexed. Most of his fright, much of his harassment, and more than enough of his perplexity focused on his family. His parents-in-law, the Mendels, were a direct and vocal entanglement. They, too, were frightened and, unlike Sigmund, were in a position of total dependence and impotence. Sigmund, too, was powerless, yet he constantly had things to do which involved control and mastery of details and may well have contributed to the illusion that he still governed his fate.

Esther and Marion Stein, however, were breaking during the last two months in Hochburg. At different times both threatened suicide, and both clung to one another, offering mutual support in strength as well as in weakness. Sigmund loved them both; from this love arose self-reproach, which reflected back on, and qualified, his love. His wife, daughter, and parents-in-law came somehow to be components of the trap which was closing in around him.

It was natural, in view of her status as an object of events, that Esther Stein had long wanted to leave Germany. It was also natural that her position in life, her role of respectability, and the esteem which before 1933 had been so much a part of things, had failed to give her the toughness demanded by the collapse of the fragile reality which shored up that esteem. Life had given Esther a low breaking point; one feels compelled to admire her for having lived so long beyond that point with no more than a trace of querulousness and a suspicion of hysteria.

In these last few months, Sigmund found his family a source of torment. It is therefore hardly surprising that his relationships with two women outside the circle of anguish should have become more than casual. How far the emotional entanglements went is not clear and perhaps does not matter. It seems certain that Sigmund and Dorothea Schlosser were not much more than good friends. He seems to have meant more to her than she meant to him. Some echo of past hope may come through in her recalling how, in his last months in Hochburg, Sigmund became a lonely man and was getting further and further away from the whole Mendel family. She tells, too, of a walk with Sigmund in the meadows near the town shortly before his deportation. At one point, she says, Sigmund asked her to go on ahead a little bit because, as she saw, he was weeping.

No one suggests that there was an affair between Sigmund and Dorothea Schlosser. There is talk, however, about Sigmund and Frau Benzheim, the whole matter being greatly complicated by the animus other friends of Sigmund hold for the Benzheims. This animus may explain the exaggeration of certain casual, man-to-man comments which Sigmund may have made and the inflation of rumors far beyond the size which their vagueness and the special surreptitiousness of the times would have given them.

At a time when Sigmund's need for support was greatest, his home was one of the places where he could not seek help. Esther, Marion, and the Mendels embodied the looming consequences of the course he had taken and were reminders of his helplessness. He found substitutes in the sympathy of Dorothea Schlosser and in Frau Benzheim's attention to his writing and her concern for him as a man. When one adds to this the fact that meetings had to take place in *"Nacht und Nebel,"* in the diffuse excitement of danger, one current within the swirl of rumor becomes entirely believable —that Esther Stein was jealous and her unhappiness thus compounded.

There may be a trace of coquetry in Frau Benzheim's expression of her fear that Esther Stein was jealous of her. But there is also accurate observation and genuine regret, for she had been a friend of the family. She had, for instance, done the Steins' laundry while they were in the Kassel jail, and she washed Marion's reddish-blonde hair after they returned. There is poignancy in the way both she and Dorothea Schlosser speak of Sigmund—quite independently, since there is no indication that these two women ever had more than their interest in Sigmund Stein in common. Sigmund's ability to leave behind him this evident depth and color of feeling in two women adds a relieving softness to the impression of bourgeois solidity which his figure otherwise makes.

One incident of his relationship with Frau Benzheim was probably the occasion of the poem she remembers so well. At the beginning of August, 1942, she had to make a trip by train on the line which went through Friedenberg, not far from Bachdorf. Sigmund may actually have had to make a trip to Friedenberg at about the same time, or he may have arranged to make one. In any case, they traveled on the same train and, by exercising caution, were able to ride as far as Friedenberg together. This became the last time he was to see his native valley, despite the hope expressed in the poem.

It is possible that Herr Benzheim's jaundiced view of the world ("If you know of anywhere they may be launching a rocket to the moon, get us two one-way tickets!") draws some of its energy from the same source that provided Esther Stein with her jealous unhappiness. Yet this mood is very much a part of the man, and his prosaic yet strong affection toward Sigmund's memory contains too many convincing details to dismiss it as feigned.

Most of the other people who were around Sigmund and his family as August, 1942, slid into September were simpler than the Benzheims, then and now, whatever the complexity of their motives. Sigmund's situation in respect to them paralleled the general situation of the Jews in Germany during the whole period of emigration, dispersion, and deportation. He had possessions, the value or usefulness of which was not decreased by the injustice of what was happening. His collection of Hessian genre paintings by a locally well-known artist was familiar to many Hochburgers and had a particular appeal in the Folkish atmosphere of the time. Much the same was true of his nicely bound edition of Knut Hamsun's writings. The furnishings of the Stein household, executed in what an outsider would probably call "heavy German taste," appealed for that very reason to the people around him.

Beyond such domestic articles lay property in land. Sigmund himself had no real property except, for a time, his share in the family house and land in Bachdorf. Nevertheless, he had a relationship to property, arising out of his position in the Hochburg Jewish community, which could not be overlooked by anyone who might be greedy. It has already been noted that, right as Frau Huss and Franz Wilhelm may have been in their general judgment about people who "hung around" the Steins toward the end in the hope of "inheriting" something, they may well do injustice to specific individuals.

Herbert Durckheim is a good example. Here, surely, was

a man who "hung around" the Steins during their last weeks in Hochburg. Here also was a man who, as an amateur and vaguely professional collector of art objects in the local taste, had an interest in Sigmund's paintings as well as in his books and furniture. Here, too, was a man who owned property adjacent to the Jewish communal property in the Humboldtallee where Sigmund was repeating his occupancy of thirty years earlier. Durckheim was interested in certain abutment rights. He has and had, without doubt, an eye for the main chance. And yet at least until 1942, the main chance in Germany was to play ball with the Nazis, and beyond the immediate necessities of living, Herbert Durckheim did not play ball with them.

Durckheim is a bit of a lady's man, a bit of a fop. Frau Jesberg, who knows of his relationships with the Steins, think that he is touched in the head. He is not. Johannes Korbmacher, an active anti-Fascist during the Nazi years, says without rancor that every time Herbert opens his mouth a lie or an exaggeration pops out. The hyperbole of his statement is misleading. Dorothea Schlosser says that Durckheim has always been an odd one, but that he was a true friend of the Steins. Fräulein Mendelsohn agrees. They are nearly right.

Apparent in everything that Durckheim says is the same flair for self-dramatization which was evident in his account of his 1937 advice to Sigmund to emigrate. He is nothing if not immodest in his estimate of himself as a connoisseur; as a judge of human nature; as a secret agent ("Sigmund should have known better than to let a woman try to arrange his escape. He should have let me do it. I wouldn't have blabbed"); as one who knew the Hochburg scene. The interesting thing is that he never advances himself as a hero, a great anti-Nazi, or as morally admirable for what he did.

It is crystal clear that he had long admired Sigmund's art objects and that the abutment rights on the Humboldtallee were part of the relationship between the two men—it would have been contrary to everything we know about people for such things not to have played a part in the relationship. Durckheim came from a background of material and cultural scarcity; to triumph over it meant a great deal to him. After all, Franz Wilhelm, who is scornful of many of the people gathered around the Steins in the last weeks, himself exploited a different side of Sigmund. Coming from a background of wealth and culture, Wilhelm had no reason to be impressed by Sigmund's possessions. But there had come a point in the summer of 1941 when Wilhelm desperately needed something which Sigmund had—legal acumen—and he was as willing then to take it as Sigmund was to give it.

Wilhelm remembers Sigmund's assistance with gratitude and appreciation. It was possible, he recognizes, only because Sigmund was in the position he was. At bottom, no more and no less can be said of Herbert Durckheim. Sigmund did transfer the abutment rights to Durckheim and he did in the end give to and leave with Durckheim some of the objects which the latter had admired. These acts were certainly conditioned by the trap in which Sigmund found himself, but they were also conditioned by the real help and emotional support which any friendship and human contact gave to Sigmund and his family at this time. Durckheim is indignant that the transfer of abutment rights has been expunged from the register of deeds by the restitution program, and he is even more indignant that the "Jewish House" in the Humboldt-allee has become a motion picture theater. It is wrong, he says, that the scene of so much tribulation should have been turned into a place of laughter and entertainment.

It is unlikely that Sigmund failed to perceive the "ulterior" motives of Herbert Durckheim, but almost as unlikely that they affected him deeply. He seems, in fact, to have been on terms of genuine friendship with this odd and complicated man. Durckheim tells of a distressing incident which suggests that an ingredient of Esther Stein's fear and unhappiness in the last months was a bitter awareness of the "ulterior" motives of the people around her.

On the last night before the deportation of the remnant of the Hochburg Jewish community, Sigmund, Herbert Durckheim, and Dorothea Schlosser were in the living room of the Humboldtallee apartment where they had been drinking wine and discussing the disposition of the Steins' household effects. Sigmund had offered the silverware to Durckheim who, with neither the problems nor the compunctions of Dorothea Schlosser, had expressed his willingness to take it.

At this point, however, Esther Stein, who had been half-listening from another room, came in quickly and said, "Oh, Sigmund, you're not really giving away the silverware?"

This angered Sigmund, and he retorted that, yes, he *was* giving it away. When Esther protested further, he blurted out, "You and your Jewish manners!"

A moment's irritation in a strained and disruptive situation —sometimes the bridges people build from one to the other are forced to carry too great a load. For Sigmund, the center of gravity, Jewish identification, was getting out of its precarious balance. If Esther Stein was the victim this time, what happened between Sigmund and the erstwhile Reichsbanner chief, Theiss, in these last days shows how Sigmund, too, suffered in a similar situation.

Theiss spent the first year of the Nazi regime in prison, its last two years in a concentration camp. He was a die-maker, and die-makers were desperately needed in the German war economy, but in 1942 he had for several years been selling newspapers from a stall in the railroad station. Here Sigmund Stein and other Hochburg Jews, forbidden to subscribe to the paper by this time, used to get their copies of the *Frankfurter Zeitung*. Theiss was forbidden to sell it to them, but this ban was circumvented by a small strategem which also enabled Theiss on occasion to have a quick and cautious exchange of gossip and news with his "black" customers. Thus, Herr Theiss learned of the September deportation several weeks before it was to take place.

One day, shortly after he had learned of the deportation, he asked Sigmund, "Do you have a suit for me, maybe?" Sigmund replied he was sorry, but all his possessions had already been registered. However, he went on, one of the men who was to be deported with him, Herr Rosenblum, the cattle dealer from Gosmarshausen, did have an unlisted suit, a fine English tweed which, Sigmund felt, he would be glad to turn over to Herr Theiss. But suddenly, as Herr Theiss says, one day Sigmund and Meyer Rosenblum and the rest of the Hochburg Jews were gone, and he had no suit. Herr Theiss introduces this tale, after making the usual complimentary remarks about Sigmund, with a change of tone and the words, "I cursed him once, though. In spite of everything, he was still a Jew."

Coming from people who presumably should be more enlightened, this kind of remark never ceases to startle. Herr Theiss is not an anti-Semite, but he proves the tenacity and diffusion of the Jewish caricature and comes close to being blind to the connection between this caricature and what happened to the Jews.

In a moment of irritation, when the unknown was hanging over their heads because they were Jews, Sigmund threw his wife's Jewishness at her. At about the same time, Herr Theiss, victim of Nazism, was throwing Sigmund's Jewishness at him.

Dorothea Schlosser's story of the "last night" parallels Herbert Durckheim's in all important respects. But Dorothea adds something which Durckheim does not mention. She says that Fräulein Lehner, the spinster who made the trip to the Bodensee for the Steins, was present and that Sigmund had also offered the silverware to her. Over and above the definite facts that Fräulein Lehner was close to the Steins in the last weeks and that they left an appreciable portion of their household goods with her, her precise role is lost in the exchanges between pro- and anti-Lehner factions.

Only Casimir Dombrowski, who dislikes her, supplies a clue to the facts from which the opinions diverge. According to him, after the Jews were deported and before the end of the war, Fräulein Lehner disposed of some of the articles which had been left with her by sending them to Strasbourg, where, Dombrowski believes—although he does not know—that they were sold. Dombrowski also believes that Fräulein Lehner realized the Jews would not be coming back, and felt herself incriminated when she was unable to return "all" of the Steins' possessions to Frau Mendel after the war. Yet Fräulein Lehner's defenders can point not only to her behavior toward the Jews long before the deportations but also, quite specifically, to the way she took care of and returned the articles left with her. Fräulein Mendelsohn soberly comments that it was generally hard to get back things which had been left with friends, not only because of the confusions and uncertainties of the war years, but also because of the displacements and disturbances arising from the requisitioning of space for the occupation troops after the war.

As to Fräulein Lehner herself, it would be ridiculous to interpret her reticence as a proof of some kind of guilt, but it is impossible not to see it as strong indication of her failure to reach some equilibrium between self-accusation and self-justification. Until she does, she may well feel that her stance in the face of a society whose judgments are themselves changing has to be a cautious one.

Several people who visited the Steins on the "last night" in Hochburg sought nothing from the family and were hesitant or adamant about taking objects which Sigmund tried to press on them. Others sought to help. Johannes Korbmacher and his wife, avowed anti-Fascists, are the only ones who speak of taking "going away" presents to Sigmund and Esther. Their visit may have taken place on what was in fact the last night because one of the going away gifts was a pound of butter—a treasure in Germany after three years of war. Another gift suggests that Sigmund's literary tastes went well beyond Knut Hamsun, for it was a two-volume edition of Dostoevsky's *The Brothers Karamazov*. For both the Korbmachers and Franz Wilhelm, who accompanied them on this visit, it was the first time they had called on Sigmund since he and his family had moved from the Treitschkestrasse. Both Korbmacher and Wilhelm were at the time under suspicion of being involved in an oppositional movement recently uncovered in Kassel, and they had not wanted to jeopardize either Sigmund or themselves by being observed making contact with him.

For both Officer Schumann and Officer Schultheiss acknowledge that constant surveillance of the comings and goings on the Humboldtallee was considered the most natural thing in the world, as of course it was. Both policemen were direct and indirect participants in the surveillance, during which no one seems to have been molested. Frau Jesberg admits that when the Steins were arrested in connection with the events in Konstanz, she became panicky about the book she had let Sigmund borrow, fearing it would be found in the inevitable search of the Stein premises. So she went to Officer Schultheiss privately and explained the situation to him. In her words, "he jokingly admonished" her, promising he would keep an eye out for the book and forestall embarrassing questions about it. In the end, the police did not find the volume, because, Frau Jesberg says with admiration, Sigmund had hidden it too well.

Frau Dienstbach, housekeeper for the von Schlegels, was another who visited the Steins on the "last night." She says Sigmund wanted to give her a book as a memento, but she was unwilling to take it because the policeman who was "on watch outside the house" would have seen her going away with it and this would have been bad. Nothing she says indicates a concern about the possibility that the policeman would see *her*.

There were others who visited the Steins on this prolonged "last night." Herr Krapf, in one of whose trucks Sigmund had hoped to travel to Konstanz, and in one of whose rooms there now hangs a picture from Sigmund's collection, was there. Sigmund Oppenheimer was there. His visit may well have been on the actual final night, since he helped the Steins pack. His presence may have had something of the grotesque about it, because he was one of the Jews not facing deportation. Frau Professor Mendelsohn and her son were there; it was to them that Sigmund gave the manuscript of his unfinished novelette.

Certain people, whose presence might have been expected, were not among the visitors. Frau Benzheim was inexplicably away, on a trip to Berlin. She was due back on the morning of the deportation and says that in fact her train came in while Sigmund and his fellows were waiting on a remote section of the outgoing platform of the station. She waved, but she believes that he did not see her. Frau Mahler, who had nursed Sigmund and Marion through serious illnesses, had talked too much about six months before the deportation. When the Steins left, she was sitting in jail for having insulted the Fuehrer. The Klingelmanns had visited the Steins in the Humboldtallee, but make no claim of having been there the "last night." Yet their son did take Marion a novelty bracelet as a going away present, delivering it stealthily on "the last night."

Casimir Dombrowski who, like Sigmund Oppenheimer, would be left behind in Hochburg, says nothing about having been at the Humboldtallee in the final hours. He was close to the family during this period and tells of repairing a fur coat of Marion's in anticipation of the departure, but the chances are he felt too insecure to risk a visit. Like Oppenheimer, he was being left behind and he knew it. Unlike Oppenheimer, however, his Jewish identity had always been stronger and he was, on top of that, a Russian citizen.

In the accounts of the people who visited the Steins on that "last night," as well as in the statements of various town officials who were visited by Sigmund in an almost formal gesture of farewell during the last few days before deportation, there is frequent mention of Sigmund's depressed and despairing state of mind. These comments predominate over those which describe him as "cheerful" during this period. But it is probably the fact that some ground existed for both descriptions which indicates he was deeply upset.

The tone of these last few days must have been pitched to the disharmony among the routine preparations for departure, the prosaic leave-takings, the shattering leave-takings, and the frightening imminence of an ominous unknown, for this departure was the climax of a development which had given the unknown its menace. Sigmund had reason to fear and Esther was openly afraid. If, as Dorothea Schlosser says, Sigmund was beginning to walk alone, this is at least partly understandable as a result of the gap which had opened up between his private estimate of the situation and the optimistic front, long genuine, which he still had to show to his family and his people.

The friends who were closest to Sigmund saw his fear and his despair. Franz Wilhelm says he seemed to be a man who had prepared himself for death. Dr. LeMaitre, one of the few who places his last visit a few days before the actual departure, explicitly contrasts Sigmund's mood on this occasion, "downcast, with tears in his eyes as we parted," with the cheerful optimism which had struck him in Sigmund up to this point. It seems clear that this very real crisis in Sigmund's life was accompanied by a psychological crisis within him. Although Casimir Dombrowski did not comment on Sigmund's state of mind in the last few days before the deportation, his completely ungrounded belief that Sigmund eventually committed suicide is a significant index of that state of mind.

Sigmund writes, at the beginning of his novelette: " . . . however, if a man in the prime of life leaves the city to take up a new life in the country, the chances are he will amount to nothing there, whatever his achievements in the city may have been." Where, buried in Sigmund's consciousness, the relationship between this sentence and what lay before him as he wrote it existed, and whether in fact there was such a relationship at all, are questions which cannot be answered. Yet, despite Sigmund's romantic nostalgia for the soil, his life and his achievements had been concentrated in the town of Hochburg. Now he was heading for "the country," for "agricultural labor" at best. The doubts and the rumors about what actually lay ahead could only deform his feelings into a catastrophic uncertainty, from the depths of which he had to pack his bags and keep his wife and daughter in a semblance of self-possession.

19

[Theresienstadt]

Sigmund Stein, his wife Esther, and their daughter Marion
left Hochburg on the 10 A.M. local train from Frankfurt, Saturday,
September 12, 1942. There were thirty-eight other Jews with them,
fourteen men and twenty-four women, including Esther's parents, the
Mendels. They all rode in an extra coach which had been attached
to the train for the deportation. The belongings which they had
been permitted to take with them were in a baggage car at the
very end of the train. When they first got aboard, they were no
more crowded and no more physically uncomfortable than the
passengers in any such German local train. Sigmund and his
family shared a seating section with three Rosenblums from
Gosmarshausen; the Mendels rode in the section opposite them
with people of their own age, who constituted a large proportion
of this transport. There were to be two other stations between
Hochburg and Frankfurt where Jews would be put aboard. At one

of these, Dreistadt, Israel Stern would get on to join the Steins and the Rosenblums in their section.

The notion that the train ride from Hochburg to Frankfurt may have been an interlude of comparatively good spirits for Sigmund is hard to suppress. The basis for any such notion is shaky: Casimir Dombrowski's description of the train trip to Buchenwald after the Kristallnacht makes it seem to have been almost cozy; Meyer Rosenblum asserts that he does not remember the 1942 train ride as a bad experience; and Israel Stern recollects a "comradely" spirit during this part of the trip. This basis is weak. But the actual start of the transport was a definite and, in its way, active event. This, after the uncertainties and torments of the preceding weeks, contained at least the possibility of relief. It would, of course, be a travesty on understanding to think that there was not deep sorrow and real fear, yet there is no dismal tone in the accounts of the trip. A journey between two prisons, through its mobility and novelty, may produce a fleeting illusion of freedom.

They were headed for the unknown. At least, the Hochburg and Dreistadt officials, in filling out the bureaucratic records of the departure, had written, after "Destination," "Unknown." Ignorance was official. In fact, however, Sigmund and Israel and the rest of the Jews on the transport did know where they were going, and this was more than could be said of their fellow Jews who had been deported earlier. They were going to the formally proclaimed Jewish Settlement Theresienstadt, in the Reich Protectorate, Bohemia-Moravia, near the point at which the River Elbe and the smaller River Ohre meet.

The concentration camp, Theresienstadt, was one of the strangest growths on the rotten structure of Nazi ideology. It was a specific product of the anti-Semitic malice in that idelogy, for unlike other concentration camps, it was solely for Jews. Officially, it was not a concentration camp but instead a *Siedlung,* or settlement. Nor was it, like other exclusively Jewish communities such as those within Warsaw, Riga, or Lublin, a ghetto. It involved not the slums of a large city but the entire confines of a small town, a fortress and barracks erected in 1780 by the Hapsburg Emperor, Josef II, and named after his mother, Maria

Theresa, who died shortly after the work on the town started. Zdenek Lederer, who was there, has written: "The environments of Theresienstadt are pleasant. Theresienstadt is situated in a plain broken by slightly undulating hillocks which stretch to the conical peaks of the Middle Bohemian Hills: at sunset they look not unlike a strange swelling of the earth. The green fields and the clusters of trees along the shores of the river Ohre add to the idyllic character of the scene; vegetables, fruits, and vines grow in the peaceful fields. . . ." What gave Theresienstadt its special incongruity was not the falseness of the official descriptions but rather their truth and the manner in which that truth rested on unspoken horrors.

It was indeed a Jewish settlement, with its own administration, its own functioning facilities, its own money, and its own social institutions. It even included a ghetto of sorts . . . for the SS garrison.

There were temporal changes in the place which Theresienstadt occupied in the Nazi scheme of things. At first it was to have been an internment camp, primarily for the Jews of Prague and the smaller communities of Czechoslavakia. By the time Sigmund and his companions started out, however, the Nazi plans for Theresienstadt had acquired a fluidity in which several motives were apparent. It was to be a settlement for Jewish men who had won decorations in the World War. It was to be the bait dangled in front of the functionaries of the Reichsvereinigung. It was to be a source of funds for the Gestapo and the SS: Jews who still held title to properties of various kinds were to yield it to the Reichsvereinigung as the purchase price for "a place in Theresienstadt."

A somewhat later development was the idea of using Theresienstadt as a kind of showplace, where the skeptics of occupied and neutral Europe could be shown that the Nazis knew how to take care of the Jews in "humane" fashion. This motive became mixed with another in the last years of the war: Theresienstadt was to be the place where prominent European Jews could be held as hostages, to be bargained off for the lives or security of prominent Nazis.

The idea of using Theresienstadt as such a hostage center for

Jewish prisoners never really got beyond the confusion which surrounded its origin. Its functioning was contingent on the spread of defeatism, and it demanded clear-cut judgments by the various Nazi leaders about which of the Jews should be bargained off. In the end, Theresienstadt became a painful step on the road to the extermination camps. Death and cruelty lay not only beyond but within its walls.

Sigmund Stein, Israel Stern, and those who were with them on the little train to Frankfurt knew that they were headed for Theresienstadt. As German Jews, Sigmund and Israel were both members of the Reichsvereinigung and both had "worked for" it—Sigmund, in the ways we have seen; Israel Stern, as Sigmund's helper in the Dreistadt area since the spring of 1942. Stern had not been happy about going to work "for" Sigmund. He had been lucky in escaping the first transport; more luck and the collusion of the Dreistadt authorities enabled him to escape the second transport at the end of May.

When Sigmund wrote Isaac a postcard asking him to come to Hochburg for a talk, he was willing. The two men were not close acquaintances, but they had had professional relationships before 1933, and Stern's business as a grain dealer had been closely enough related to the cattle business of Sigmund's father-in-law for him to be acquainted with Jakob Mendel and the latter's daughter, Esther. On the basis of these connections and their common situation as Jews, Stern declared himself ready to take on the task of notifying Jews in the Dreistadt area of their deportation and helping them prepare for it.

"Naturally" he did not like the work. In and of itself it was a thankless, painful task which required that he go around on foot among the villages in the Dreistadt area. In the course of doing this he was exposed to the insults and assaults of small boys who tried to show their devotion to Hitler and Germany by throwing epithets and stones at a Jew. Israel Stern was not without resentment toward Sigmund for getting him into the work. Yet everything he says and the tone in which he says it indicate that the two men felt a comradeship of mutual understanding.

Israel Stern is able to clarify details of "purchasing" places in Theresienstadt. Places, of course, were not really *purchased*.

According to him, in the early spring of 1942 a levy was imposed on the liquid assets of all Jews who still had any. This levy was explicitly described as being for the establishment of a "Jewish Old People's Home" at Theresienstadt. The actual deeding over of property was done through the Reichsvereinigung, and within the distorted context of the time, the procedure was made to appear more or less equitable. It was, however, a thoroughly coercive action. No one was given a receipt or any other indication that he was entitled to a "place" in the "Old People's Home." It was not a contractual arrangement. At most, it had a certain appearance of orderliness.

It is quite possible that, behind this arrangement, deals of one sort or another were concluded with the Gestapo or with other functionaries of the regime. What seems clear, however, is that the very nature of the procedure was such as to encourage illusions among those who were subjected to it. Insecurity, dread, and occasional wild hope were rife among the German Jews in the spring and summer of 1942. The agents of the Reichsvereinigung, men like Sigmund Stein and Israel Stern, were already mediaries in a process which had sent their fellow Jews off into the unknown. By the time of the levy for the "Old People's Home," they were completely subject to the threats and forces under which they were carrying out their functions.

Because of this, the announcement about Theresienstadt was a faint hope which they could seize on. By passing on the official explanation they could lighten their own burdens as harbingers of bad tidings. Thus, it is to be expected that the official explanation was sometimes supported with conviction, sometimes with exaggeration. What a relief it must have been for Sigmund to be able to tell people they were going to a place set up especially for them, with a Jewish administration and a Jewish life of its own. How much better than before, when the destinations were known only vaguely and lay deep in the traditionally scorned disorder of the East. The nature and consequence of this kind of reaction would seem to be enough to account for the stories of men who, upon arriving in Theresienstadt from Germany, asked to be shown the apartments with western exposure and private bath to which they were entitled. Such stories are told with morbid humor by survivors, but the substance is confirmed by competent observers among them.

Illusions and hopes were therefore still possible in the local train to Frankfurt that Saturday morning in September, 1942. The deportees were formally under guard, one policeman getting on with each group. The policeman who got on with the group from Dreistadt was an old "Skat colleague" of Israel Stern. They were still good friends, and there is no trace of sarcasm in Israel Stern's voice when he says that this policeman shook his hand and wished him the best of luck at their parting in Frankfurt. The same kind of farewell took place between Sigmund and the policeman who accompanied the Hochburg group.

The hopes and illusions which may have persisted during the trip were soon destroyed by the Gestapo and the SS in Frankfurt. Sigmund and his companions arrived there in the middle of the afternoon and were taken from the Hauptbahnhof to a large school yard, where they were given a scanty ration of bread and soup and were then left to make their own sleeping arrangements with straw which had been doled out to them. During the course of the afternoon they were joined by other groups of Jews from Frankfurt and its hinterland, so that a throng of nearly three hundred people had to spend the night in the open school yard.

The next morning they were taken into the school to be registered. The behavior of the Gestapo, the SS, and the SA during this process betrayed the shape of the deportees' future. In Israel Stern's account of this episode, the tripping and the blows on the way into the school are reminiscent of the "games" which Casimir Dombrowski describes the SA men as having played with the Jews who were bound for Buchenwald after the Kristallnacht.

At the registration, men and women were separated and relieved of all money, personal effects, and papers, a body search being made in the interests of thoroughness. Like Sigmund, Israel Stern had been decorated with the Iron Cross in the World War, and because of the stories which had gone around about Theresienstadt as a haven for decorated war veterans, Israel had the medal in his pocket. There it was found by the SA man who frisked him. The SA man threw it to the ground with the old taunt, "Where'd you buy that thing?" Israel does not know what happened to Sigmund during the registration, on the completion of which, according to Stern, a significant part of the processing occurred. The adults had to go up one by one to a desk, behind which sat an official of the regional tax office. Here they were handed a printed statement to the effect that all their residual property —by this time it could not have been much—was being requisitioned by the Reich because "the undersigned" was a Communist and subversive. Stern says that old women who did not even know what a Communist was had to sign. Dr. Bauer, Sigmund's mentor at the University of Augsburg many years earlier, went through the same ordeal at about the same time; he does not remember a particular reference to Communists but rather to "enemies of the state," which, as he points out, added up to the same thing.

During the physical and economic denudations of these procedures, Israel Stern and Sigmund Stein were separated, but despite the confusion and the malign attentions of the Gestapo, the SA, and the SS, they found themselves together again in a compartment on the train from Frankfurt to Bohuvice, the railroad station nearest Theresienstadt. This was a special train, filled with Jews destined for the "Old People's Home" and manned by the SS in full military dress. The trip was painful, because no food or water was given out during it, and slow, because additional cars were attached in each of the major towns along the way. The treatment in Frankfurt had destroyed whatever consolation there had been in the knowledge that Theresienstadt was the ultimate destination. How many of the passengers knew that the car with their baggage had been left behind in Frankfurt is not mentioned by Israel Stern, but many Jews, including the Gosmarshausen Rosenblums, had had their hand baggage ransacked in Frankfurt. Many passengers had been mistreated themselves, and all had seen the blows meted out. Aside from the withholding of food and water—a large aside on a long trip—no other mistreatment on the train itself is reported by Herr Stern or by a few others who were there and have survived.

Frankfurt must have been a searing experience for Sigmund Stein. For all his sentimental attachment to Germany, Sigmund was no fool, and by September, 1942, he was fully aware of the cruel refinements, if not the extremes, of Nazi anti-Semitism. Nevertheless, Frankfurt was his first intimately personal experience of blows, kicks, and humiliations. He had not been sent to Buchenwald in 1938, and his recent experience in the Gestapo prison in Kassel, while harsh and unpleasant, had had too specific an occasion and was too individualized to constitute a recognizable foretaste of what was ahead. After Frankfurt, remorse, fear for self and family, and bleak despair were his closest traveling companions on the road to Theresienstadt.

The tide of catastrophe rises in waves, and the recession of one of these says little about the final destructive flood. For the deportees, the arrival in and accommodation to Theresienstadt would appear to have been such a transitory recession of misery and despair. To many of the Hochburg Jews, the now evident absurdity of having a room brought deeper despair. But many others, torn from the relative security of their homes, abased and abused during the journey, and plunged into the depths by this treatment, must have drawn a breath on their arrival in Theresienstadt: "It isn't as bad as it might be."

Sigmund and his companions may well have been especially susceptible to such alternation of feeling. It is true that the Hochburgers were frightened and depressed people when they got on the local train to Frankfurt. But Hochburg was a comparatively small town, with a Jewish community which even at the end had not been concentrated in a ghetto pattern. Fifteen people in the last transport looked upon the Humboldtallee as their last address in Hochburg, but the twenty-six others came from eight different addresses, widely scattered through the town. What this means is that the Hochburg Jews had not lost touch with their non-Jewish environment. Every little cluster of Jews in Hochburg was surrounded by non-Jews. However abrasive this situation may have been under the Nazis, there were humanly meaningful compensations—acts of decency and friendship, made the more touching by their very inadequacy and surreptitiousness, and the more dramatic by the risk which, if not always as great as Hochburgers sometimes maintain, was real enough.

Thus, the Jews from Hochburg were able to set out on their journey with memories of something other than total rejection by their fellow Germans. Facts made the Hochburg Jews outcasts, but the memory of belonging survived, so that hope could feed itself on illusions during the brief trip to Frankfurt. The harsh treatment in the schoolhouse and yard was therefore all the more foreboding.

Whatever impressions Sigmund and his fellow Jews had of Theresienstadt during the first few hours there, the succeeding days were a confusion out of which each individual's adjustment emerged as conditioned less by his anticipations than by the grim and fantastic reality of the place itself. People who arrived with the same transport were separately swallowed up in the over-crowded streets and barracks. Meyer Rosenblum and Sigmund Stein had been good friends in Hochburg, and Israel Stern had worked with Sigmund; yet both men saw him and his family in-frequently and only by chance during the months they were to-gether in the settlement. Others, like Dr. Bauer, who renewed his university friendship with Sigmund there, or like Rabbi Stein-berg, who had never met Sigmund before 1942, saw more of him than his former associates did.

Sigmund was to remain in Theresienstadt for two years. He is reported to have worked at four jobs in that time. Frau Mendel, Sigmund's mother-in-law, is a very old woman. She speaks un-willingly of things she should not have to remember. She describes Sigmund's work as the collecting of wastepaper and other rubbish with a pushcart. This was an occupation in the course of which he was able to find old bread, which he shared with her and with her husband until the latter's death from causes as natural as they could be in the environment of the settlement. Frau Mendel also refers vaguely to some sort of work that Sigmund had in connection with incoming packages.

Frau Anna Hermann says nothing about Sigmund's collecting trash, but she does add a few details concerning Frau Mendel's hazy reference to the work with incoming packages. Frau Her-mann may be the only survivor of Theresienstadt who has re-turned to the home she left in the vicinity of Hochburg. It is in the village of Kirchdorf, not far away, yet deep in rural Hesse. She is very old and very much the Hessian peasant woman, even though that is not her calling. Once again she manages the little hardware business her husband left her on his death in the late thirties. One reads in her eyes a sadness which her apparent stoicism does not betray. The wife of the peasant family with whom Frau Hermann lives is an understanding person, and there seems to be a genuine companionship between the two women. But when Frau Hermann takes a visitor to her room to talk of Sigmund Stein and to show the comb he gave her, she speaks from another world. She says that Sigmund had access to packages, because he worked in the Theresienstadt post office and was able to obtain some food from packages which had been sent to people already transported *away* from the settlement.

Meyer Rosenblum and his wife go into somewhat more detail about Sigmund's work, but the job they describe bears only a slight—if real—relationship to those spoken of by Frau Mendel and Frau Hermann. It did have to do with trash, and it did result in Sigmund's being able to share small amounts of foodstuffs with the Rosenblums. According to them, Sigmund, along with a couple of other "citizens" of Theresienstadt, was given the job of clearing out the bunker or cellar that had been used to store the odds and ends discarded by, or taken from, new arrivals. He used a paper-baler in this work. Dr. Bauer, who knows that this bunker was called "the department store" and that the discarded items were those declared contraband by the Theresienstadt administration, to be collected, sorted, and stored prior to baling for shipment to the Reich, does not know about Sigmund's connection with it. But he does know about the pushcart and collection of trash.

One day, at a time when Dr. Bauer had no idea that Sigmund was a "fellow citizen," he saw two shabbily dressed men pulling a hand-wagon filled with wastepaper. Something seemed familiar about one of the men, but it took a few moments for Dr. Bauer to recognize Sigmund under the outer covering. With recognition, however, their old friendship was renewed, and Sigmund told Dr. Bauer something of his work. He related how, on his own initiative, he had gone before the Jewish administration of the camp with the request that he be given authority over the trash baskets of the entire community. This plan was approved, and after working by himself for a time, he was even given a helper. Dr. Bauer says that Sigmund expressed satisfaction with the work, that he looked upon himself as an entrepreneur who sometimes profited by the fact that food was thrown away.

Dr. Bauer explains the paradox of discarded food in the endemic hunger of Theresienstadt by telling about the sardines from Denmark. A large shipment of these had been sent in by the Danish Red Cross and were at first a welcome addition to the inadequate diet. But the shipment was very large, and hunger at the time was less than it had been and would be. Eventually, people got fed up with sardines and began throwing away unopened cans of what had previously been a delicacy. Not many did this. But "not many" is relative, and if a hundred out of thirty or forty thousand people threw away cans of sardines, the person who was in a position to collect those cans was thereby supplied with a little cache which, then or in the foreseen future, could be shared with relatives and friends or bartered.

Another advantage of Sigmund's work, according to Dr. Bauer, was the fact that it took him all over the settlement and therefore allowed him to see his wife and daughter more frequently than would otherwise have been possible. Marion and Esther both worked, and if Frau Anna Hermann's assertion that Esther had supervision over "something" is correct, it suggests an interesting improvement in Esther's grip on herself and the world. Marion Stein is said to have done secretarial work at one time and to have participated in taking care of the settlement's children at other times.

It is obvious that Esther and Marion, like Sigmund, could have held several different jobs in the course of their two years in the settlement. Israel Stern's belief that Sigmund did office work must be interpreted in this light. Nevertheless, a repeated note in the comments of other people who have been mentioned has an interesting relevance here. Frau Mendel, Dr. Bauer, and the Rosenblums all speak of an explicit rejection of office work by Sigmund, and the Rosenblums and Frau Mendel go so far as to say that this rejection was in response to a definite offer of such work. This apparent selectivity on Sigmund's part is significant.

The illusion of self-determination which the Germans, for

their own reasons, wanted to foster in Theresienstadt led to the development of an ugly caricature of social life. Like any caricature, this showed genuine resemblances to the original, some of which were deep and instructive. All the men and women lived within and subject to a system of forces over which they had no control as individuals. If the dynamics of the system dictated hunger, they starved; if plenty, they ate. The externals of settlement society also resembled conventional forms. There was a ruler, an administration, a police force. But always, the main purpose of the external trappings was to conceal the underlying impotence of the inhabitants.

Any man with the training and experience of Sigmund Stein had a better than average chance of installing himself in the system. And in this particular context, Sigmund was not just any man, for he had a friend in the administration. This was Peter Oppenheimer, who had been born, like Sigmund, in a village not far from Hochburg, who had studied law at Hochburg University with Sigmund, and who was a cousin of Sigmund Oppenheimer. In the early thirties, Peter Oppenheimer had settled in Berlin. In the course of his practice there, he had defended with great success a man who was to become an important figure in the SS. Oppenheimer's client was grateful and later remembered the Jewish lawyer's services by providing him with a degree of protection which got Oppenheimer his "place" in Theresienstadt and gave him an assured non-deportable status.

Dr. Bauer, who supplies most of the foregoing details—though several people are aware in a general way of the connection between Sigmund Stein and Peter Oppenheimer—is in no sense critical of Oppenheimer. Bauer himself went through the mill and is aware that in periods of great social pressure the bridge of personal relationship with an influential antagonist will always be walked to save self or the people one loves.

Through Oppenheimer, as well as through his own undoubted qualifications, Sigmund could have had a job in the administration of the settlement. It is all but certain that he never had such a job. He seems to have been one of a group of people whose adjustment to life in Theresienstadt was determined by a hard-headed recognition of reality and by a more subtle awareness of the penalties of responsibility in such a situation—penalties he had every reason to know as a result of the position he had occupied in Hochburg. Rabbi Steinberg, whose impression it is that Sigmund worked on the roads, says that the lawyer wanted to regain the respect and social standing he had once enjoyed in Hochburg. Yet Sigmund had the sense to steer clear of the poisonously tinseled variety available in Theresienstadt. (In the end Oppenheimer *was* deported and killed.) All of the jobs with which Sigmund is said to have been connected offered him the chance of supplementing food rations for himself, his family, and his friends. None of his jobs involved the higher responsibility for his fellow Jews which he had come to know so well in Hochburg.

This avoidance of a burdensome responsibility may account for the fact that Frau Anna Hermann speaks of Sigmund as "cheerful and happy" in Theresienstadt, or for these lines in a letter written by a woman who knew the Steins in the settlement as well as in Hochburg: "By chance one day in Theresienstadt I met Dr. and Frau Stein on the street. They spoke to me, were very friendly, and looked well. They were contented and in a good frame of mind."

These two women were not blind to the conditions of life in the settlement. Their words were implicitly qualified by the assumption of common knowledge about the crazy and deadly framework on which the fabric of Jewish life was stretched and explicitly by their descriptions in other contexts of the hunger, uncertainty, and inhumanity which were a constant undertone of life in the settlement and often rose to a cruel crescendo.

Rabbi Steinberg feels that Sigmund continued to be optimistic in Theresienstadt, though "certainly not as optimistic as he had been earlier." Meyer Rosenblum says that Sigmund seemed to find his work congenial but thinks his optimism had vanished. These are more considered judgments than the women's, yet they mirror contacts with Sigmund on a different social and emotional level.

Dr. Bauer also speaks of Sigmund's satisfaction with his work. For himself, he describes as something pleasant and positive the opportunities he had for interesting and probing discussions with the six other physicians who shared his quarters. Yet

Dr. Bauer was expressly aware of the hunger, misery, and disease around him, of the continual transports to the East, of the way people would disappear into Theresienstadt's "little fortress," a part of the settlement where death and the SS held sway. He was aware of the urns of human ashes. No purposeful mass exterminations took place in Theresienstadt, but hunger and typhus were at times effective substitutes. The bodies were cremated and the ashes long kept in urns, to be scattered in adjacent fields, finally, in order that a visiting international commission would not discover them.

In Theresienstadt the violent contradictions of life were compressed into one small, close-packed town. It was like all towns, because it existed in a social order and was subjected to the rules and pressures applied by that social order. It was unlike other towns, because the external order was visibly present in the form of the SS, and because one of the rules of the external order was an all but unequivocal rejection of the town's inhabitants. These inhabitants were normal in their desire to escape awareness of the forces which enveloped them. The forms which the escape took were often normal, too. But the people of the settlement were ultimately abnormal because, despite the visible presence of the SS, they were so often successful in blocking it out. The differences between Theresienstadt and other human communities were differences in degree, but the degree was so extreme that the settlement became a different kind of community: it became a concentration camp.

Here Sigmund and his family spent two years. During this time there were continual transports to the East. In some periods these occurred at regular intervals; at other times, they were sporadic. But the transports were always there, as both reality and possibility. Nominally they were labor transports; deportees in several of them actually did forced labor under abominable conditions in Poland, the Baltic States, German-occupied Russia, and elsewhere. Those who survived the ordeal were gassed. Most people so transported were killed shortly after their arrival in Auschwitz, Belsen, or Treblinka, the three death camps which were the most frequent destinations of the transports. A few went through the purgatory of the Polish camps and the hell of evacuation in front of the advancing Russians; a small proportion of these survived.

The "citizens" of Theresienstadt were effectively deceived about the destination of the transports and the fate of those transported. The woman who writes of the pleasant meeting she had with the Steins survived the ceaseless transports of September and October, 1944. She was later included in the "Swiss Transport" of January, 1945, which confounded the skeptics in the settlement by actually going to Switzerland. This woman also writes, " . . . but we knew nothing of the gassing, for we had neither newspapers nor sources of news in Theresienstadt, and it wasn't until after I arrived in Switzerland that I heard of what was going on in Auschwitz." Marta Dannenberg, a younger woman, was less naive or perhaps had more access to the settlement's grapevine. She says she and some others knew that Auschwitz was the worst but did not know what went on there. She was to find out, however. She was sent to Auschwitz on the first of October, 1944, one day after Sigmund was separated from his family and sent to the same destination in a transport of 1,500 persons.

According to his mother-in-law, Frau Mendel, Sigmund was transported because Peter Oppenheimer lost his position in the change of administration which occurred shortly before the September-October transports began. Oppenheimer himself having been transported, Sigmund, according to Frau Mendel, was without his protector and became a candidate for Auschwitz. It is clear from many reports that deportation could be forestalled or perhaps escaped altogether if one had the right protector. But it is even clearer that such protection was no guarantee. The September and October transports of 1944 were massive and, with but few exceptions, left only the old and infirm in Theresienstadt. Even if Oppenheimer had remained in the administration, the likelihood that Sigmund would have been spared was almost nil.

Nearly three weeks after Sigmund was transported, Esther and Marion followed him. Marta Dannenberg saw and spoke with them in Auschwitz during the short period between their arrival and their deaths. There is a veil between the gentle and intelligent personality of Marta Dannenberg today and the inferno which she survived, but there may be a relationship between her ability to forgive the person who disturbs that veil and her ability to see through it into the past. She says that Marion was at first "selected" to be spared, at least temporarily. Esther Stein was not. But Marion insisted on remaining with her mother and was unexpectedly allowed to do so—with what mixture of cynicism, indifference, cruelty, or even compassion on the SS's part it is impossible to say. Because she had been allowed to stay with her mother, Marion was somewhat less wretched than Esther, and it is clear from Marta Dannenberg's words and tones that the depth of the mother's wretchedness can only be suggested. Esther Stein, she says, had no desire to live. She of the "Jewish manners" was now unkempt, haggard, and emaciated. And so was Marion. Before the two women disappeared forever, they told Marta that they had seen Sigmund "through the wire" when they first arrived.

This was an excruciatingly pathetic finale. For it was impossible that they should have seen Sigmund.

From the records in its possession, the Czechoslovakian Red Cross is able to provide the serial and transport numbers under which Sigmund and his family arrived in Theresienstadt and, two years later, in Auschwitz. They are unable to provide any details *after* the arrivals in Auschwitz. The International Tracing Service in Arolsen, Germany, has nothing in its records about Marion and Esther Stein, but it does furnish the information that three days after Sigmund arrived in Auschwitz he was again transported, this time to one of the outlying labor camps in the Auschwitz complex, Golleschau. When, therefore, Esther and Marion Stein arrived in Auschwitz nearly three weeks after Sigmund, he was thirty miles away.

Golleschau was a satellite camp of Auschwitz. It consisted of a cement factory, the limestone quarries which supplied the raw materials for this factory, and the barracks which housed the forced laborers for both factory and quarries. Opinions vary about conditions in Golleschau, and this variation reflects the usual differences in the experiences of the survivors. Such variation does not disguise the murderous inhumanity of Golleschau at its worst; it does not brighten the average level of life there beyond its grey callousness and hunger.

It is the fact that Golleschau was sometimes murder and death in the limestone quarries, sometimes the kindness and self-sacrifice of a Jewish prisoner-physician, sometimes the arbitrary cruelty of the SS, and sometimes the erratic decency of a particular SS man that throws a cloud of obscurity around the ultimate fate of Sigmund Stein. Death was less certain in Golleschau than in Auschwitz itself.

Yet Sigmund was assuredly dead. He had entered Golleschau when conditions were only to get worse. In January, 1945, this worsening suddenly dissolved into a horror of frozen marches and transports in open railroad cars as the SS fled with their charges before the oncoming Red Army.

In the wild flight back to Germany to escape the advancing Russians, the SS men and their remaining prisoners entered a ghastly realm where death could no longer be meticulously recorded. During the disorders of these last days in Golleschau itself or on the ways over which the SS hurried from the East, Sigmund Stein vanishes. The bookkeeping had broken down at last.

The survivors of the flight from Golleschau and other eastern camps poured into the concentration camp, Sachsenhausen, in the early weeks of 1945, arousing horror, pity, and despair among the still relatively well-off inmates. These survivors of the East were the "Musselmänner," living skeletons waiting to be beaten off the edge of a life to which they clung tenaciously. How many there were and their individual fates are as unknown as their identities.

And so the story of Sigmund Stein ends in an obscurity from which it has never really escaped.

[A note on sources]

I used four kinds of sources to establish the life of Sigmund Stein and its interaction with the culture in which it was embedded. In order of the extent to which I drew upon them, they are: conversations, letters and personal documents, archival material, and published literature.

I spent approximately 250 hours talking with people during two stays in Germany and in the intervening period in the United States. In all, I talked with 172 persons. Ninety-two per cent of these conversations took place in Germany, a large proportion of them in Hochburg and within a thirty-mile radius of the town. Twelve per cent of those with whom I talked were Jewish and 2 per cent part Jewish.

I got in touch with almost all of these people through what might be called a "spreading network." Whenever possible, I obtained the addresses of people mentioned in the course of conversation; occasionally I found names in newspapers and court records, or in letters. No one refused to talk with me. There were some instances of reluctance which may have indicated a sense of guilt, but more likely they arose from a fear of adding further to knowledge about behavior that had been condemned.

I took notes during each conversation and tried to write them up at length within four hours afterward. Accuracy and objectivity are of course always problems with such a procedure. I doubt that a tape recorder would have added greatly to the faithfulness of the transcription—and might well have increased the problem of rapport. As for objectivity, I believe my approach to those with whom I talked minimized the urge to lie. I explained my purpose and methods clearly, emphasizing that I was piecing together information to establish what had actually happened, that I did not expect all truthful descriptions of a particular event to jibe.

Infrequently I was suspected of being an intelligence agent or detective, but several factors militated against such an attitude: I was obviously operating on a shoestring; persons could (and occasionally did) check on me through their network of friends, for I lived entirely within such networks, seldom left the town, and had minimal contact with other Americans; my inquiries were relaxed and non-directive for the most part; and, finally, confidence in my work increased as people found they were in no way disadvantaged as a consequence of talking with me.

Conscious dishonesty was not my chief worry. More important was the matter of unconscious dishonesty, rationalization, or earlier lies which had become subjective truth. Cross-checking could be of some help in determining truth, but I could not rely on it completely because many distortions were products of common pressures on people in a common situation. A quite consistent response, for example, was that no one had mistreated the Jews with malice aforethought. I could interpret such an answer in different ways:

(1) Some of these people certainly did treat the Jews with conscious malice.

(2) Some were aware that they had, at the time, borne malice toward the Jews, but they were unaware of the manner in which this feeling had been energized by long-held traditional attitudes.

(3) Malice was offset by rationalizations which the regime offered ("Jews are Germany's misery," etc.), so some did not see themselves as "malicious people."

(4) They now recall that status of being "non-malicious."

(5) Regardless of this explanation, the responsibility of these people was clear, and the system revealed by their rationalizations was clearly capable of telling me most of what had actually happened.

Another common point of distortion centered on the question of loyalty to the regime. Almost every German who shared most of the Nazis' goals nevertheless had his moment of opposition. This could arise from career frustration, personal feud, local ideological disagreement, or friendship with a victim of the state's workings. With the end of the war and the subsequent premium placed upon opposition, it was an easy psychological maneuver for such people to inflate, in memory, their moment of opposition. It became for them something very like principled ideological rejection.

Finally, I believe minimally self-serving failures of memory must be granted. In the dramatic and often threatening immediacies of the war years, what was happening to the Jews in one's environment was often but a tiny segment of everything that was happening.

Despite the enormous amount of information gathered from all the conversations, it was necessarily inadequate for a full biography of Sigmund Stein, for a history of Hochburg during the Nazi era, or for a complete picture of the people with whom I talked. Virtue and vice in the character and style of the book come largely from my effort to reconcile uncertainty with readability.

Some eighty-odd letters addressed to me bear directly on the life and death of Sigmund Stein. Well over half of these are from people with whom I could not arrange a personal meeting. The other letters supplement my conversations in various ways. They are superior to conversations in terms of accuracy, but inferior in most other respects. The letters come predominantly from Jews who emigrated before or survived the "final solution" *and* who were acquainted with Sigmund.

Archival material included newspapers, pamphlets, articles, and the novella fragment by Sigmund Stein; censuses of Jews from the nineteenth and twentieth centuries; transcriptions of letters and postcards belonging to others; lists of Jewish businesses in Hochburg; the mayor's reports; school records; denazification court records; addresses, and so forth.

The nature of this material and the nature of the book combined to minimize problems of authenticity. A newspaper report of the burning of the Hochburg synagogue, for example, becomes less important for its accuracy than for the style of the report. A census of Jews in Bachdorf in 1840 or in Hochburg in 1939 is used largely for general information, not to locate particular people or make population studies.

Among published literature, generally I found those works of most value which were either dated or clearly slanted. Such sources have a legitimate function as indicators of mood and opinion, but they may also be valuable because their tendentious nature is clear and can be "drawn into the reckoning," as the Germans say.

The problem of knowledge is not solved by even the most diligent concern for the sources. How much less, then, the problem of wisdom.

[Key to names in the text]

*In the left-hand column appear the fictitious names used in the text for real people—
out of consideration for family situations when this book was first published. In the
right-hand column are the actual names, now published for the first time.*

FICTITIOUS, i.e., ASSIGNED NAMES   ACTUAL NAMES

FICTITIOUS, i.e., ASSIGNED NAMES	ACTUAL NAMES
Adler, Frau	Frau Geilfuss
Altman	Blumenfeld
Altman, David	Frank Blumenfeld
Bacharach	Rosenberg
Bauer	Dr. Allschoff
Baumeister, Dr.	Eckel
Bernstein, Heinz	Meier Wolf
Bernstein, Moses	— Wolf
Blankenstein, Herr	Herr Katz
Blau, Bruno	Bruno Blau
Bosch	Seufner (Seufert)

Meyer, Karl	Sigmund Freund
Michael, Friedrich	Otto Grimm
Michelheim, Studienrat	Studienrat Stier
Morgenstern Family	Moses Family
Mühlenbach	Koch
Müller	Schmidt
Münschner, Konrad	Herman Bauer
Oppenheimer	Hermann Plaut
Oppenheimer, Peter	Leo Plaut
Preusser, Heinrich	Phillip Grösser
Rabenstein	Pfifferling
Reidt, Sophie	?
Rembrandt	Brand
Remsbach	Mueller
Ritter, Frau Else	Frau Käthe Jung
Rosenblum, Meier	Rauisch-Holzhaus Mendel
Rosenblum, Meyer	Julius (?) Stern
Roth	Peretz
Schäfer, Hugo	Hagenbach
Schlosser	Bachmeister
Schlosser, Dorothea	Erika B.
Schmidt, Frau	Frau Müller
Schmidt, Lieschen	Luise Koch
Schmidt, Robert	L. Sälzer
Schnitzler, Bertram	Hentrich
Schönbaum, Willy	Sally Haas
Schreiber, Thomas	Ernst Schröder
Schuhhaus, Goldmann	Spinat
Schultheiss	Herrmann
Schumann	Heyer
Siebert	Weber
Siegfried, Hans	Harry Bauer
Solomon	Julius Goldschmidt
Sorge, Frau	Frau Bäumer
St. Ursula	St. Elisabeth
Stadtmaier, Hermione	Frau Prof. von Behring
Stadtmaier, Prof. Dr.	von Behring
Stärke	Schwebel
Stein Family	Reis Family
Stein, Benedict	David Reis
Stein, David	Julius Reis

Stein, Dela	Berthe Reis
Stein, Emma	Settchen Reis
Stein, Esther	Selma Reis
Stein, Isaac	Moses Reis
Stein, Marion	Marion Reis
Stein, Meta	Erna Reis
Stein, Sara	Karolina Reis
Stein, Sigmund	Hermann Reis
Steinberg	Neuhaus
Stern	Bachenheimer
Stern, Israel	Josef Abraham
Tannenbaum	Walter R. Rothschild
Tannenbaum, Maria (?)	Frau Rothschild
Tellermann, Dr. Edu.	Dr. D. Schlossberg
Theiss	Boltzel
Vogtmann, Ludwig	"H.R." Klee
von Schlegel	Flottmann-Hensel
Wagenrecht	Ritter
Werkmeister	Hanneman
Wiegand	Mütze
Wilhelm, Franz	Herr Siebecke
Winkelrod	Müller-Eigner
Wolff, Heinrich	Ludwig Beck
Wolff-Förster, Frau	Frau Beck-Müller
(Anon)	Schweinsberger
Bachdorf/Frieden	Allendorf/Eder
Hochburg/Fesen	Marburg/Lahn
Dreistadt	Treysa
Felsen River	Lahn River
Frieden River	Eder River

[Index]

A NOTE ON THE AUTHOR

John K. Dickinson first became interested in Sigmund Stein in 1951, when he was in Germany helping Milton Mayer with research for *They Thought They Were Free.* He returned twice more to Germany before completing this unique biography. Most of the facts for his re-creation of Sigmund Stein's life come from his interviews with almost two hundred persons who had some contact with Stein while he lived. Mr. Dickinson for many years taught sociology at Springfield College in Massachusetts, and now lives in Cambridge, Massachusetts, with his wife.

IVAN R. DEE PAPERBACKS

European and World History
John Charmley, *Chamberlain and the Lost Peace*
John K. Dickinson, *German and Jew*
Lee Feigon, *China Rising*
Lee Feigon, *Demystifying Tibet*
Mark Frankland, *The Patriots' Revolution*
Lloyd C. Gardner, *Spheres of Influence*
David Gilmour, *Cities of Spain*
Raul Hilberg, et al., eds., *The Warsaw Diary of Adam Czerniakow*
Gertrude Himmelfarb, *Darwin and the Darwinian Revolution*
Gertrude Himmelfarb, *Marriage and Morals Among the Victorians*
Gertrude Himmelfarb, *Victorian Minds*
Thomas A. Idinopulos, *Jerusalem*
Thomas A. Idinopulos, *Weathered by Miracles*
Allan Janik and Stephen Toulmin, *Wittgenstein's Vienna*
Hilton Kramer and Roger Kimball, eds., *The Betrayal of Liberalism*
Ronnie S. Landau, *The Nazi Holocaust*
Filip Müller, *Eyewitness Auschwitz*
Clive Ponting, *1940: Myth and Reality*
A.L. Rowse, *The Elizabethan Renaissance: The Life of the Society*
A.L. Rowse, *The Elizabethan Renaissance: The Cultural Achievement*
Scott Shane, *Dismantling Utopia*
Alexis de Tocqueville, *Memoir on Pauperism*
Paul Webster, *Petain's Crime*
John Weiss, *Ideology of Death*

American History and American Studies
Stephen Vincent Benét, *John Brown's Body*
Henry W. Berger, ed., *A William Appleman Williams Reader*
Andrew Bergman, *We're in the Money*
Paul Boyer, ed., *Reagan as President*
William Brashler, *Josh Gibson*
Robert V. Bruce, *1877: Year of Violence*
Douglas Bukowski, *Navy Pier*
Philip Callow, *From Noon to Starry Night*
Laurie Winn Carlson, *A Fever in Salem*
Kendrick A. Clements, *Woodrow Wilson*
Richard E. Cohen, *Rostenkowski*
David Cowan and John Kuenster, *To Sleep with the Angels*
George Dangerfield, *The Era of Good Feelings*
Clarence Darrow, *Verdicts Out of Court*
Allen F. Davis, *American Heroine*
Floyd Dell, *Intellectual Vagabondage*
Elisha P. Douglass, *Rebels and Democrats*
Theodore Draper, *The Roots of American Communism*
Edward Jay Epstein, *News from Nowhere*
Joseph Epstein, *Ambition*
Peter G. Filene, *In the Arms of Others*
Richard Fried, ed., Bruce Barton's *The Man Nobody Knows*
Lloyd C. Gardner, *Pay Any Price*
Lloyd C. Gardner, *Spheres of Influence*
Paul W. Glad, *McKinley, Bryan, and the People*
Eric F. Goldman, *Rendezvous with Destiny*
Sarah H. Gordon, *Passage to Union*
Daniel Horowitz, *The Morality of Spending*
Kenneth T. Jackson, *The Ku Klux Klan in the City, 1915–1930*
Edward Chase Kirkland, *Dream and Thought in the Business
    Community, 1860–1900*
Herbert S Klein, *Slavery in the Americas*
Aileen S. Kraditor, *Means and Ends in American Abolitionism*
Hilton Kramer, *The Twilight of the Intellectuals*
Hilton Kramer and Roger Kimball, eds., *The Betrayal of Liberalism*
Irving Kristol, *Neoconservatism*
Leonard W. Levy, *Jefferson and Civil Liberties: The Darker Side*
Leonard W. Levy, *Original Intent and the Framers' Constitution*
Leonard W. Levy, *Origins of the Fifth Amendment*

Leonard W. Levy, *The Palladium of Justice*
Heather Mac Donald, *The Burden of Bad Ideas*
Myron Magnet, ed., *The Millennial City*
Myron Magnet, ed., *Modern Sex*
Seymour J. Mandelbaum, *Boss Tweed's New York*
Thomas J. McCormick, *China Market*
John Harmon McElroy, *American Beliefs*
Gerald W. McFarland, *A Scattered People*
Walter Millis, *The Martial Spirit*
Nicolaus Mills, ed., *Culture in an Age of Money*
Nicolaus Mills, *Like a Holy Crusade*
Roderick Nash, *The Nervous Generation*
Keith Newlin, ed., *American Plays of the New Woman*
William L. O'Neill, ed., *Echoes of Revolt: The Masses, 1911–1917*
Gilbert Osofsky, *Harlem: The Making of a Ghetto*
Edward Pessen, *Losing Our Souls*
Glenn Porter and Harold C. Livesay, *Merchants and Manufacturers*
John Prados, *The Hidden History of the Vietnam War*
John Prados, *Presidents' Secret Wars*
Patrick Renshaw, *The Wobblies*
Edward Reynolds, *Stand the Storm*
Louis Rosen, *The South Side*
Richard Schickel, *The Disney Version*
Richard Schickel, *Intimate Strangers*
Richard Schickel, *Matinee Idylls*
Richard Schickel, *The Men Who Made the Movies*
Edward A. Shils, *The Torment of Secrecy*
Geoffrey S. Smith, *To Save a Nation*
Robert W. Snyder, *The Voice of the City*
Bernard Sternsher, ed., *Hitting Home: The Great Depression in Town
    and Country*
Bernard Sternsher, ed., *Hope Restored: How the New Deal Worked
    in Town and Country*
Bernard Sternsher and Judith Sealander, eds., *Women of Valor*
Athan Theoharis, *From the Secret Files of J. Edgar Hoover*
Nicholas von Hoffman, *We Are the People Our Parents Warned Us Against*
Norman Ware, *The Industrial Worker, 1840–1860*
Mark J. White, ed., *The Kennedys and Cuba*
Tom Wicker, *JFK and LBJ: The Influence of Personality upon Politics*
Robert H. Wiebe, *Businessmen and Reform*
T. Harry Williams, *McClellan, Sherman and Grant*
Miles Wolff, *Lunch at the 5 & 10*
Randall B. Woods and Howard Jones, *Dawning of the Cold War*
American Ways Series:
    John A. Andrew III, *Lyndon Johnson and the Great Society*
    Roger Daniels, *Not Like Us*
    J. Matthew Gallman, *The North Fights the Civil War: The Home Front*
    Lewis L. Gould, *1968: The Election That Changed America*
    John Earl Haynes, *Red Scare or Red Menace?*
    D. Clayton James and Anne Sharp Wells, *From Pearl Harbor to V-J Day*
    John W. Jeffries, *Wartime America*
    Curtis D. Johnson, *Redeeming America*
    Maury Klein, *The Flowering of the Third America*
    Larry M. Logue, *To Appomattox and Beyond*
    Jean V. Matthews, *Women's Struggle for Equality*
    Iwan W. Morgan, *Deficit Government*
    Robert Muccigrosso, *Celebrating the New World*
    Daniel Nelson, *Shifting Fortunes*
    Thomas R. Pegram, *Battling Demon Rum*
    Burton W. Peretti, *Jazz in American Culture*
    Hal K. Rothman, *Saving the Planet*
    John A. Salmond, *"My Mind Set on Freedom"*
    William Earl Weeks, *Building the Continental Empire*
    Kevin White, *Sexual Liberation or Sexual License?*
    Mark J. White, *Missiles in Cuba*